verseas, 1714

E A N

AY

SWEDEN

St. Petersburg · Yakutsk · Okhotsk
Moscow · Yeniseisk
Yenisei   Lena
S i b e r i a
RUSSIAN EMPIRE
Irtysh   Ob
Volga

THE POLAND
ust. Hung.
EMPIRE;

Constantinople
OTTOMAN EMPIRE
rca,
13–83
TUNIS

TRIPOLI

Cairo

Arabia

EGYPT

Nile

r a

ABYSSINIA

Congo

ZANZIBAR

PERSIA

AFGHAN-
ISTAN

Delhi

MOGUL EMPIRE

1539, *Diu*
1558, *Daman*
1661, *Bombay*

1565, *Goa*
1565, *Mangalore*
1661, *Quilon*
1656, *Colombo*
Ceylon

XINJIANG

TIBET

MONGOLIA

MANCHU EMPIRE
(CHINA)

Hwang-ho

Beijing

KOREA   JAPAN

Yedo

Deshima (Nagasaki), 1641

Macao · Yangtze-kiang
1555

Calcutta, 1698
Serampore
1616
BURMA
Masulipatam

1605 to Neth.
1611 to Eng.

Formosa
1683 to China

TONGKING
ANNAM
SIAM   COCHIN
CINNA

Philippine Is.
1570

Sakhalin

Mariana Is.,
1668

Caroline, 1696

PACIFIC

1649, *Atjeh*
Sumatra
1685, *Batang Kapas*
1684, *Benkulen*
1685, *Silebar*
1610, *Batavia*
Java
Kapang, 1633

Malacca, 1641
Singapore, 1526
Borneo
Makassar

Halmahera
1653/84

Celebes
Ceram
Timor, 1610/75

OCEAN

INDIAN

OCEAN

Madagascar
(Sao Lourenço)

PORT. EAST AFRICA

anda · S. Salvador
1501
ANGOLA
Cacanda
1685

Defagoa Bay
1544

Bourbon
(Reunion)
1642

Mauritius (I. de France)
1598–1710 to Neth.
1715 to Fr.

New Holland

e Town
652

Van Diemen's Land

New Zealand
(Statenland)

N

EUROPE AND THE WORLD, 1650–1830

'This is an accomplished text, written by a leading scholar of the early modern period . . . The style of the work is clear, forceful and unfussy.' *Professor Michael Biddiss, University of Reading*

'This book confidently and cogently conveys a brilliant grasp of communities and change, of broad developments and local complexities. Here is a powerful historical mind, utterly on top of his materials.' *Professor Roy Porter, Wellcome Trust Centre*

Europe and the World, 1650–1830 is an important, thematic study of the first age of globalization. It surveys the interaction of Europe, Europe's growing colonies and other major global powers, such as the Ottoman Empire, China, India and Japan. Focusing on Europe's impact on the world, Jeremy Black analyses European attitudes, exploration, trade and acquisition of knowledge.

Stressing imperial defeats as well as victories, *Europe and the World, 1650–1830* shows the vitality of non-European powers, and how relations during this period frequently involved cooperation between Europeans and non-Europeans, as well as war between them. With an original approach that takes full notice of recent research, this book explores the differences between specific areas of European impact and also seeks to discern common themes. In particular, European attitudes are considered in terms of racism, anthropology, cultural responses, and the impact of the outer world on the European imagination.

Jeremy Black is Professor of History at the University of Exeter. He has published over forty books, including *European Warfare, 1660–1815* (1994) and edited many, including *War in the Early Modern World, 1450–1815* (1999). He is series editor of the Routledge Warfare and History series.

EUROPE AND THE WORLD, 1650–1830

Jeremy Black

London and New York

First published 2002
by Routledge
11 New Fetter Lane, London EC4P 4EE

Simultaneously published in the USA and Canada
by Routledge
29 West 35th Street, New York, NY 10001

Routledge is an imprint of the Taylor & Francis Group

© 2002 Jeremy Black

Typeset in Goudy by Keystroke, Jacaranda Lodge, Wolverhampton
Printed and bound in Great Britain by St Edmundsbury Press, Bury St Edmunds,
Suffolk

British Library Cataloguing in Publication Data
A catalogue record for this book is available from the British Library

Library of Congress Cataloging in Publication Data
Black, Jeremy.
Europe and the world, 1650–1830 / Jeremy Black.
p. cm.
Includes bibliographical references and index.
ISBN 0–415–25568–6 (hbk) – ISBN 0–415–25569–4 (pbk)
1. Europe–History–17th century. 2. Europe–History–18th century.
3. Europe–History–1789–1815. 4. Europe–Colonies. 5. Europe–History, Military.
6. Europe–Territorial expansion. I. Title
D258 .B53 2001
940.2′5–dc21   2001034979

ISBN 0–415–25568–6 (hbk)
ISBN 0–415–25569–4 (pbk)

FOR PAUL FILLERY

CONTENTS

PREFACE

This short study of the interaction between Europe and the world prior to the period when Western imperialism reached its height is thematic rather than chronological in approach. Although the book will concentrate on the European impact on the world, attention will also be devoted to the impact on Europe of the rest of the world. In a short study, it will not be possible to attempt comprehensive coverage, but by focusing on the years between two major periods of European expansion this study seeks to draw attention to an era that deserves re-examination. I have covered some aspects of this subject in other books that have appeared with this publisher: lengthier coverage of some topics is available in my *European Warfare, 1660–1815* (1994), *Britain as a Military Power, 1688–1815* (1999) and *From Louis XIV to Napoleon: The Fate of a Great Power* (1999). I would like to thank two anonymous readers for commenting on an earlier version, and Nigel Aston, Bill Gibson, Ken Morgan, David Sturdy and Trevor Burrard for their advice on particular sections. I would also like to thank Vicky Peters and Philip Parr for seeing this book into production in an exemplary fashion.

There are numerous images of European expansion that vie for attention. Many are military, although there are also the epic voyages of explorers such as Captain James Cook. I began writing this book soon after visiting a site that offers another image. The Mission San Miguel Archangel, just off Route 101 between Los Angeles and San Francisco, was the sixteenth of the Californian missions. Founded by the Franciscans in 1797, the mission was badly damaged by fire in 1806. In 1816 the foundations were laid for the church which survives today. In 1821, Esteban Munras arrived to supervise the interior decorations for which the church is now noted. Produced with Native American help, they offer a syncretic interpretation of Christianity that reminds us of the complex and multifaceted character of the relationship between Europe and the wider world.

Note: The word 'Native' is capitalized when it is used to refer to indigenous inhabitants and set lower case when it refers to white settlers and their descendants born in the area.

1

INTRODUCTION

This book surveys the interaction of the European continent, Europe's growing colonies and the other major global powers: the Ottoman (Turkish) empire, China, the Mughals and Marathas in India, Japan and so on. These interactions are approached from a variety of different angles: military conflict, trade, settlement, slavery, exploration and knowledge, attitudes and power-struggles, both within Europe and between the European and non-European powers. Certain themes emerge clearly. Instead of thinking about relations between Europe and the world in terms of some irresistible and inevitable colonial/imperial drive and triumph, it is necessary to stress the ebb and flow of events and power, imperial defeats as well as victories, partial successes and setbacks, and the gradualism of European encroachment, above all in Africa, but also in many parts of Asia. It is important to emphasize the continued vitality of non-European powers and peoples, such as the Ottoman empire, and the extent to which peoples and tribes were not principally concerned with their links to European endeavours, but were mainly preoccupied with relations (military, territorial, commercial) among themselves. Above all, the power struggles involved co-operation between European and (certain) non-European nations, as well as struggles and war between them. There were always natives who collaborated with European goals, and natives who sought to utilize the Europeans to further their own political, military and commercial ends.

The study of Europe's relationship with the rest of the world over the last half-millennium has focused on European expansion. It is not surprising that this has been the meta-narrative because, indeed, European power helped mould activities across much of the world. However, this focus has a number of unfortunate consequences. First, it can lead to a situation in which the responses elsewhere to European expansion and activity are underrated, as is the extent to which this expansion and activity were in part moulded by these responses. Second, there is an underrating of the degree to which non-European societies had an independent existence. Third, there is a chronological problem. Concentration on European expansion leads to a focus on two periods: first, 1490–1650; and second, 1830 onwards. The first of these comprises two distinct periods: the establishment of the Portuguese presence in the Indian Ocean and the creation of the Iberian empires in Central and South America; and, subsequent to 1590, the creation of the Dutch, English and French colonial empires and the Russian advance to the Pacific. The post-1830 period was when Africa and much of South and Southeast Asia were brought under the control of European powers, while European influence was extended into states that were not brought under direct control: Siam, Persia, China and Japan. In between these two phases there is a long and important period that has received insufficient attention, and is the subject of this book.

This study seeks a balance between the analysis of specifics and the production of broader generalizations, and a thematic approach has been taken. Readers are encouraged to approach the book in the order of the chapters. However, these have been written so that it is possible to read individual chapters independently. In particular, it is not necessary to tackle war and conquest before (or after) the consideration of other factors. More generally, the relatively conventional topics of trade, migration, war and politics receive their due in the sequence running through Chapters 5 to 9. Hopefully, those subjects will be better understood because of the chapters that have gone before: on exploration, knowledge and attitudes. They are not only fundamental to the later argument and to the overall 'roundness' of the volume, but are also rewarding for their presentation of historical issues that are not reducible simply to the political or economic categories.

Historiographical pointer

Much of the literature on the subject has been affected by Edward Said's *Orientalism* (1978), which offers a critique of the way in which Western societies interpreted Asia as at once exotic and stagnant, its attractive decadence evidence and cause of a failure to match the values, or equal the achievements, of the West. This perception was an aspect of power: it contributed to it and flowed from it. This approach has been much pursued, but has inherent disadvantages, not least a tendency to run together a wide range of perceptions and to devote less than adequate attention to the situation prior to the late eighteenth century. This emphasis reflected both Said's focus – on Western attitudes to the Middle East in the last two centuries – and widespread interest in the culture of the European imperialism of the Victorian period. Irrespective of the chronological emphasis, the Said approach put a stress on power and conflict in relations and failed to give due weight to cultural interaction and its impact. The latter has received greater weight in recent studies. For example:

> primary accounts also reveal a possibility of cultural understandings that cannot be reduced to the mere imposition upon an alien world of a set of European prejudices . . . people from different cultures were to a large extent able to meet and learn about each other.[1]

> the role of Indians in shaping the notions of Europeans about India is becoming more and more apparent. Thus the representations produced

in the name of Europeans, be they translations, interpretative essays, paintings or transcriptions of music, are being seen less as European orientalist constructions than as the product of both European and Indian influences.[2]

Controversy over European or Western perceptions and impact is scarcely restricted to orientalism. Both the Pacific[3] and slavery have been particular topics of contention, with, in the former case, critiques of a heroic approach to European exploration and, in the latter, attempts to ascribe all, or much of, the blame to the European-dominated global economy.[4] A measure of caution is helpful, not least before stressing the ability of Europeans to dictate to African rulers in this period.

The European world in 1650

In 1650 the European world was still hard-pressed in Europe itself. The Reconquista of the Iberian peninsula, which had culminated with the capture of Granada in 1492, had not been reversed, but nor had the Turkish advance into the Balkans and Hungary in the fourteenth, fifteenth and sixteenth centuries. The latest major struggles between the Turks and their Christian neighbours – war with the Austrian Habsburgs in 1593–1606 and with Poland in the 1620s – had not led to any significant shift in territorial frontiers. Instead, Turkish control over Hungary and hegemony over the Danubian Principalities – Moldavia and Wallachia – as well as over Transylvania had been confirmed. In the Mediterranean, war between Turkey and Venice, recently begun, was to lead, in 1669, to the Turkish conquest of Crete. Further east, the fate of the Ukraine was also unclear in mid-century, with Russia, Poland and the Turks all seeking to gain it. Since 1556, the Russians had been established at Astrakhan, but they had not been able to expand their foothold on the shores of the Caspian. The Russian expansion to the Pacific had seen Yatutsk founded in 1632 and Okhotsk in 1648, but the Russian presence in much of Siberia was sparse.

Nevertheless, the Russians were pressing south. Towards China, they had occupied the Amur region to the north of the Amur River in 1644; and, in 1652, were to found Irkutsk near the southern end of Lake Baikal. Further south in Asia, there was an important European coastal presence in India, Sri Lanka, the East Indies (modern Indonesia), the Philippines and Taiwan, and there were European trading bases in China and Japan. The coasts of parts of Australia and New Zealand had been followed by the Dutch Abel Tasman in 1642–4, but there was no European base on the continent.

In Africa there were European bases in West Africa and on the Barbary Coast of Northwest Africa, but there was no substantial inland presence, other than in the Portuguese colonies of Angola and Mozambique. The European presence was far more established in islands off Africa, not Madagascar, but Bourbon (Réunion) and Mauritius in the Indian Ocean, and Fernando Po, Príncipe, São Tomé, the Cape Verde Islands the Canary Islands, and Madeira in the Atlantic.

Further into the Atlantic, the Portuguese controlled the Azores, and the English St Helena. Most of the Atlantic islands off the Americas were also under European control, although not yet the Falklands. On the mainland of South America, the Dutch and Portuguese were competing for control of the coastal fringe of Brazil that the Portuguese colony amounted to, while the Spaniards were well established in the valley of the Plate, as well as along the Pacific coast as far south as central Chile and in the lands of the Andes. They also dominated Central America from Mexico, although their presence in some areas, such as the Yucatán, was slight. In North America, there were Spanish settlements in Florida, French in the St Lawrence valley, and English, Dutch and Swedish on the coast from near Pemaquid (modern Maine) to the Chesapeake, but not yet further south.

This is more than a list, and a record of much effort; it also provides guidance to what was to follow. The next chapter looks at a very different engagement with the wider world: exploration.

2

EXPLORATION

Introduction

After discussion of Columbus and da Gama, exploration does not generally play a central role in the history of European expansion. It has a separate literature that is very distant from that of conquest, migration and trade. This is unfortunate, because exploration was important in a number of lights, including that of reconfiguring understanding of the world and of Europe's part in it. Exploration, *not* discovery, is the key term: the peoples visited by Europeans did not need to be discovered.

At the outset, methodological problems require explicit consideration, and serve as a warning about similar issues throughout this book. The standard interpretation of exploration offered in English-language works very much focuses on British explorers, such as James Cook and Mungo Park, with the addition, if a significant US readership is anticipated, of American explorers, particularly the Lewis and Clark expedition. This underrates or elides other categories of exploration. Three, in particular, stand out. First, exploration by other Western European countries, not only France and Spain, but also less prominent states: the United Provinces (Dutch), Denmark and Portugal. Second, exploration by Russians tends to be underrated, both maritime exploration and, more seriously, overland journeys from Russia. Third, there is a focus, in discussion of exploration, on official missions, and a top-down approach to exploration. This may be particularly appropriate for long-range voyages, but is less so for overland expeditions and, in particular, for the process of incremental gains in knowledge that was especially pronounced on the edges of the European world, especially in the Americas.

A vivid account of the difficulty of assessing exploration is provided by the *Atlas Istorii Geograficheskikh Otkrytii i Issledovanii* (*Historical Atlas of Geographical Discoveries of Russia*) (Moscow, 1959), which offers much information on Russian explorers whose journeys are ignored in Western historical atlases. This is particularly so with Russian exploration in Asia, northern Siberia and the northern Pacific in the seventeenth to nineteenth century, all of which are covered extensively.[1] Indeed, the Great Northern Expedition of 1733–42 along the Arctic coast of Siberia was an epic feat, as was Semyon Dezhnev's earlier voyage along the eastern section of the north coast and round the Chukchi peninsula in 1648, through what was later to be called the Bering Strait. The latter, however, had scant impact on contemporaries, both within Russia and more widely, and thus confusion about the relationship between Siberia, North America and the Pacific continued.

The brief survey that follows is offered in the knowledge that description by inclusion (and omission) has serious deficiencies. Voyages are placed before overland journeys, a choice that reflects their impact on contemporaries, and also the greater ease of travel on water. This was true not only of oceanic travel but also of that within continents, as it was possible to move men and supplies faster by river and lake than on land. Thus, the St Lawrence and the Mississippi were important axes for activity in North America, while exploration from the British colonies was delayed by the Appalachian Mountains, and that north from Spanish Mexico by desert and mountain. There is also a particular emphasis on Pacific exploration, because this engaged the imaginative attention of the eighteenth century in a way that the search for the source of the White Nile grasped that of the late nineteenth century.

A chapter on exploration can appear indigestible. The densely fact-packed character of the discussion (so many names of explorers, dates, places explored in quick succession) can make it a hard slog. Yet, in one sense, a catalogue of voyages, expeditions and exploration is important, as it helps provide a chronology and conspectus of activity. Furthermore, the increase in the pace of exploration in the second half of the period was a central aspect of the impact and significance of exploration; namely, like imperialism in the late nineteenth century, it encouraged more. Other aspects of the impact are harder to probe but, none the less, important. Chapters 3 and 4, on knowledge and attitudes, discuss how expectations of the outside world changed. It was in part in response to exploration, and what was seen as discovery, that attitudes changed in Europe. Exploration, charting and cartography also link to the theme of power, as they were means to assert claims to territory.[2]

The oceans in the seventeenth century

The second half of the seventeenth century was not an age of major maritime 'discoveries'. In 1642–3 Abel Janszoon Tasman, a Dutch navigator, had searched for Terra Australis (southern land), the vast continent in southern latitudes that was generally believed to lie to the south of Magellan's westward route across the Pacific in 1520–1. Indeed, such a continent was marked on Ortelius's map of the Pacific in 1589. The investigation of reports of a large southern continent, believed, on the authority of ancient writers, to extend north of the Tropic of Capricorn in the southern Pacific, and assumed to be necessary to balance the land masses of the northern hemisphere, acted as a spur for exploration, because there was a powerful drive within the Western world for new lands to exploit.[3] The Dutch, in particular, hoped to discover a land of riches comparable to Latin America with its bullion. Terra Australis also focused utopian and other aspirations about different ways to organize society, thus fulfilling a role also taken by the 'New World'. Utopian ideas in turn conditioned responses to reports of Pacific exploration.[4] This was part of the interplay of fiction and fact involved in exploration which, necessarily, focused on the search for the unknown and on reports of novelty. Belief in disinformation by rivals, particularly Spain, as well as undoubted efforts to conceal information, made it difficult to benefit from the experience of others.

Dutch ships, bound for the East Indies, were blown ashore on the west coast of New Holland (Australia). The Dutch reached the Cape York peninsula of Australia in 1605, landed on the west coast in 1618, and the south coast in 1622, 1623 and 1627, and explored the Gulf of Carpentaria in 1623. Tasman also found land, touching on Tasmania, New Zealand, Tonga, Fiji and New Guinea, but his voyage did not end reports of a great southern continent. Indeed, as he only touched the west coast of New Zealand, he did not ascertain that it was an island group, rather than the edge of a vast continent. Terra Australis continued to appear on some maps and in 1681 the Vatican created a Prefecture Apostolic for it.

However, Tasman did not find riches; and his voyage along the north coast of Australia in 1644 was no more successful. His disappointment, a growing lack of dynamism in Dutch maritime enterprise, and the problems of navigation in the South Pacific ensured that the voyage was not followed up. The general route to the Orient remained that via the Indian Ocean, a route that did not encourage much exploration of the Pacific. The only regular alternative, the Spanish-controlled route between Acapulco in Mexico and Manila in the Philippines, both Spanish ports, did not lead ships far into the South Pacific.

English explorers showed enterprise at the close of the century. William Dampier, a buccaneer who in 1679 pillaged the Pacific coast of Spanish America, in 1688 sailed to the west coast of New Holland in the *Cygnet*. Government interest led to Dampier being sent out in command of an expedition in 1699, intended to bring more knowledge about the continent. In 1699–1700, in the *Roebuck*, Dampier sailed along parts of the coast of Australia and New Guinea, and discovered that New Britain was an island. Like the Dutch, Dampier found nothing of apparent value. He did not fulfil his plan to sail along the east coast. Indeed, to approach Australasia from the east was not easy, because the prevailing westerly winds combined with what was to be called the Humboldt Current to push ships north as they rounded South America and entered the South Pacific. Dampier published a very successful *New Voyage Round the World* (1697), *A Discourse of Winds* (1699) and a *Voyage to New Holland in the Year 1699* (2 parts, 1703, 1709).

In the same period, the astronomer Edmund Halley explored the South Atlantic in the *Paramore*. Both these voyages were important for providing information and increasing interest in long-range journeys. Halley produced his chart of trade winds in 1689, the first scientific astronomical tables in 1693, and his 'General Chart' of compass variations in 1701, all important tools for navigators. His interest in the transit of Venus looked towards Cook's first voyage to the Pacific. Contemporary interest in distant seas was seen in the fictional Gulliver's voyage to Lilliput, which was located in the South Pacific, and in Defoe's *Robinson Crusoe*, which was based on the marooning of the privateer Alexander Selkirk on Juan Férnandez in 1704–9. Narratives such as that by Dampier, Lionel Wafer's *A New Voyage and Description of the Isthmus of Panama* (1699), William Funnell's *A Voyage Round the World* (1707), Edward Cooke's *A Voyage to the South Sea and Round the World* (1712) and Woodes Rogers's *A Cruising Voyage Round the World* (1712) helped create a sense of the Pacific as an ocean open to profitable British penetration, and one that could be seized from the real and imagined grasp of Spain.[5]

At the same time, it is important to contextualize what might otherwise seem advances in a 'heroic' interpretation of exploration in terms of increased knowledge. For example, in 1687 the buccaneer Edward Davis allegedly discovered 'Davis's Land' in the Southeast Pacific between the Galapagos Islands and South America. The printed account of the expedition spread the news, Davis's Land was recorded on maps, and it was suggested that it was the outlier of Terra Australis. Later explorers searched for 'Davis's Land', which was probably the small island of Sala-y-Gómez and a cloud bank to the west suggesting land.[6]

1700–50

As with so much else, exploration in the early eighteenth century can be seen rather as a continuation of the previous half-century than as a unit also encompassing the second half of the eighteenth. The first half of the eighteenth century did not see important new explorations in the South Pacific, although in 1721–2 the Dutch explorer Jacob Roggeveen (1659–1729) 'discovered' Easter Island, the Society Islands and some of the Samoan islands in a voyage intended to find Terra Australis. By sailing further south on his westward route from Cape Horn than earlier navigators, Roggeveen sighted large icebergs that convinced him of the existence of the continent.[7]

In 1738 the French East India Company sent Jean-Baptiste-Charles Bouvet de Lozier and two ships to make discoveries in the southern hemisphere: his discoveries, however, were limited to the South Atlantic. The Spaniards sought to keep other Europeans out of the Pacific, or, more particularly, to thwart attempts to enter the ocean from around South America. In 1749 they objected to British plans for an expedition to the Pacific and the establishment of a base on the Falkland Islands that would support further voyages in southern latitudes.[8]

In the North Pacific the impulse to Russian territorial expansion and scientific development provided by Peter the Great bore fruit. In 1724 he ordered the Dane Vitus Bering to discover a serviceable sea route from Siberia to North America. Sailing from Okhotsk in 1728, Bering navigated the strait separating Asia from America that now bears his name, although he failed to sight Alaska due to the fog. In 1733 Bering was told to follow a different route, sailing across the North

Pacific. He did so with Aleksey Chirikov in 1741. The two were separated at sea. They explored the Alaskan coast and the Aleutians, but storms, scurvy and an inability to work out his location led Bering's ship to winter in the Komandorskis where Bering died. In 1738–9 Martin Spanberg and William Walton, both in Russian service, sailed from Kamchatka down the Kurile Islands to Japan, 'filling in' the geography of the region. Spanberg produced the first map of the Kuriles. M.S. Gvozdev and I. Fyodorov explored what would later be termed the Bering Strait in 1732.[9]

The British were also interested in discovering a navigable Northwest Passage to the Pacific, and made several efforts from Hudson Bay. James Knight failed in 1719, but in 1741 the Admiralty sent the *Discovery* and *Furnace* to Hudson Bay under Christopher Middleton. The following year he sailed further north along the west coast of the bay than any previous European explorer, but could not find the entrance to a passage. The naming of Repulse Bay testified to Middleton's frustration. In 1746–7 William Moor, who was sent by the Northwest Committee organised by Arthur Dobbs, a critic of the Hudson Bay Company, also failed. One consequence was a scattering of the names of British ministers along the coast of Hudson Bay: for example, Chesterfield Inlet and Wager Bay.[10]

The Pacific, 1750–1830

The exploration of the Pacific by European powers did not gather pace until after the Seven Years War (1756–63) ended.[11] This conflict was important for two reasons. First, British naval success during the war made it difficult for French or Spanish warships to risk voyages. Second, the capture of Manila in 1762 increased British interest in the Pacific. Exploration owed something to scientific interest, but was also driven by the widespread sense that the British maritime dominance recognized by the Peace of Paris of 1763 would be challenged in the future, and that any such war would focus even more on colonial and maritime rivalry than the Seven Years War had done.[12] At the popular level there was also widespread interest in Pacific exploration, and this encouraged, and was sustained by, publications such as Alexander Dalrymple's *Account of the Discoveries Made in the South Pacifick Ocean* (1767) and, more successfully, his *Historical Collection of the Several Voyages in the South Pacific Ocean* (1770–1). A copy of the first was taken on Cook's first voyage.

In 1767, on a voyage organized by the Admiralty, Samuel Wallis, a British naval officer, entered the Pacific through the Straits of Magellan on HMS *Dolphin*. He then sailed on a course different to that of his predecessors, who had followed the route established by the Spaniards. Wallis was able to 'discover' many Pacific islands, including Tahiti, which he called King George the Third's Island, before going on to complete a circumnavigation of the world. After their ships had passed through the Straits of Magellan, Wallis was separated from Lieutenant Philip Carteret and the *Swallow*. Carteret crossed the Pacific further south than any other explorer and 'discovered' a large number of islands, including Pitcairn.

Wallis and Carteret did not repeat their voyages and their reputation was soon to be overshadowed, but they were important, not least in demonstrating anew that circumnavigations could be successful and lead to discoveries. Furthermore, the pace of competition heated up in the late 1760s as Louis Antoine de Bougainville, whose background was in the French army, circumnavigated the globe in 1767–9.[13] The account of his visit to Tahiti helped establish the South Seas in a romantic and ambrosian light in the European consciousness. He also reached the New Hebrides in 1768, showing that they were not part of Terra Australis as the Spaniard Quiros had thought in 1608. However, the outliers of the Great Barrier Reef prevented Bougainville from seeing the east coast of Australia. His *Voyage autour du Monde* (1771) attracted a large readership,[14] and appeared in an English edition in 1772.

In 1769 Captain James Cook was sent to Tahiti in the *Endeavour* to observe Venus's transit across the sun, as part of a collaborative international observation which involved 151 observers from the world of European science. Cook's secret orders – to search for the southern continent – helped lead him even further afield. He conducted the first circuit and charting of New Zealand and the charting of the east coast of Australia. Here, in 1770, Cook landed in Botany Bay, the first European to land on the east coast, and claimed the territory for George III. Then, after having run aground on the Great Barrier Reef and then repaired the *Endeavour*, Cook sailed through the Torres Strait, showing that New Guinea and Australia were separate islands, before reaching the Dutch base of Batavia.

On his second voyage, in 1772–5, Cook's repeated efforts to find the southern continent, efforts which included the first passage of the Antarctic Circle, failed. He had sailed to 71°10′S, farther than any known voyage hitherto, when he encountered the ice outlier of Antarctica, and reported that it was not a hidden world of balmy fertility. The first sighting of the Antarctic continent was not until 1820 when Fabian Bellingshausen, the leader of a Russian expedition that was circumnavigating the ice, mapped part of Princess Martha Coast. However, New Caledonia was 'discovered' by Cook in 1774, while knowledge of the Southern Pacific and Southern Atlantic was increased, and his energetic determination to keep his men healthy ensured that, as in the other two voyages, no hands were lost to scurvy.[15] On his third voyage (1776–9) Cook 'discovered' Christmas Island and Hawaii, while, in 1778, he sailed to a new farthest north – 70°44′N at Icy Cape, Alaska, and proved that pack ice blocked any possible Northwest Passage from the Atlantic to the Pacific to the north of North America.[16] These voyages owed much to technical developments, particularly John Harrison's invention of an accurate chronometer to measure longitude, to an ability to keep crews and ships at sea for long periods, and to governmental support.

The voyages of Cook and others provided much information about what was not and what was. Cook discredited the belief in Terra Australis. Later voyagers benefited from Cook's accumulation of information (Arthur Phillip used Cook's chart when he sailed into Botany Bay in 1788).[17] However, the voyages tended to provide an outline of coastlines, rather than an exact charting. For example,

Cook's mapping of New Zealand incorrectly had Stewart Island as part of the mainland and, conversely, treated the Banks peninsula inaccurately. The Royal Navy's Hydrographic Office, founded in 1795, was responsible for co-ordinating much subsequent surveying. Stewart Island itself was charted by William Stewart, first officer of HMS *Pegasus*, in 1809. It is still named after him, rather than going by the native name of Rakiura. Aside from hydrography, there was also oceanographic research on topics such as tidal ranges and water temperatures.[18]

Cook's voyages had a major impact on European opinion, and also encouraged French and Spanish responses, although these are often overshadowed. Jean François de Surville explored the coast of New Zealand and clarified the position of the Solomon Islands, while Marc-Joseph Marion du Fresne fell victim to the Maoris in 1772. The fate of him and his crew helped undermine the benign portrayal of Pacific islanders. Yves-Joseph de Kerguélen-Tremerec discovered Kerguélen Island in the southern Indian Ocean in 1772.[19]

French activity was cut short by entry in 1778 into the War of American Independence, but, after peace was negotiated in 1783, the pace of French activity resumed and the French navy charted the coast of Asia from Suez to Korea. In 1784–9 France sent ten naval expeditions into the Indian and Pacific oceans. The most famous was that of Jean-François Galoup Lapérouse in 1785–8. This was reported to the British government as intended to establish a convict base in New Zealand. In fact, Lapérouse, having reached the Pacific, sailed via Easter Island to Alaska, followed the American coast south to Monterey, seeking a river that might lead to Hudson Bay, before crossing to Macao, en route being the first European to discover what he named Necker Island in the Hawaiian group. In 1787 he explored the northwestern Pacific, following the coast of Korea, Sakhalin, Hokkaido and Kamchatka. By sailing through the Gulf of Tartary, waters uncharted by Cook, he established that Sakhalin was an island. Lapérouse also sailed along the Kurile chain. Only then did he sail via Samoa to Australasia, reaching Botany Bay in Australia on 24 January 1788, six days after the British had arrived to found a penal colony there. Lapérouse's expedition acquired particular renown because it never returned, being shipwrecked in the New Hebrides, although that was not to be known for a long time.[20] Like Cook, Lapérouse took with him civilian scientists.

An expedition under Bruny d'Entrecasteaux set off in 1791 to find Lapérouse, which it failed to do. The expedition circumnavigated Australia, named the Kermadecs, 'discovered' the D'Entrecasteaux Islands, and explored the Solomons, but the energy that had characterized French activity in the mid-1780s was not maintained, and this activity was cut short by the French Revolutionary Wars which broke out in 1792.

So also was Spanish exploration in the Pacific, which had revived in the late eighteenth century after over a century of limited extent. The Spaniards were worried about British and Russian activity on the northwest coast of North America. The earlier Spanish policy of attempting to restrict information could no longer suffice. Spanish activity also reflected the determination of Charles III

(1759–88) to develop his empire. The surveying voyage of Bruno de Hezeta in 1775 led to the sighting of the estuary of the Columbia River, although the currents were too swift for his scurvy-weakened crew to enter the river. Earlier, seven of the crew had been killed by Natives when they put ashore for water. Francisco de la Bodega y Quadra, who had sailed on when Hezeta turned back, reached 58°30'N, despite scurvy affecting most of the crew.[21] His surveying voyages led to a far better map of the coast from there to 17°N. The Viceroy of New Spain, Antonio María de Bucareli, speculated that the Columbia might be the outflow of the inland sea marked on maps, and in 1793 Revilla Gigedo, his successor, suggested that the river might cross the continent. This led to an unsuccessful attempt to establish a settlement at the mouth of the Columbia and to penetrate up river: it was thwarted by the difficulty of the river channel and the hostile attitude of the Natives.[22]

Meanwhile, the Spaniards made efforts further north to discover a Northwest Passage. In 1788 Estéban José Martínez explored what is now the Pacific coast of Canada, and in 1790 Salvador Fidalgo followed, exploring Prince William Sound and Cook Inlet, while Manuel Quimper explored the Strait of Juan de Fuca. Other Spanish expeditions in 1791, 1792 and 1793 showed that there was no navigable Northwest Passage and no river giving access to an inland sea.

The more wide-ranging voyages of Alejandro Malaspina in 1790–3 reflected the energy of Spanish exploration that was cut short by the French Revolutionary Wars. He had already circumnavigated the globe in 1782–4. Given command of two frigates in 1789 and sent on a scientific expedition to the Pacific, Malaspina sailed along the Pacific coast of North America to 60°N, searching for the Northwest Passage and surveying the coast, before crossing Micronesia to the Philippines, and then Melanesia en route to New Zealand and Sydney, before returning via Tonga. In 1792 Dionisio Alcala Galiano and Cayetano Valdes surveyed the last unmapped portion of the Pacific coast of North America, part of California. The following year Spain went to war with France, beginning a conflict that ruined her empire and cut short the drive for exploration. Malaspina died in 1810, his expedition forgotten.[23]

However, it was British activity that came to dominate the Pacific, and this reflected British maritime predominance and the relative situation of the leading naval powers. In the waters of the Southwest Pacific the British added to their empire Lord Howe Island (1788), the Chatham Islands (1791) and Pitt Island (1791). Captain William Bligh made intelligible charts of Fiji, the Banks group and Aitutaki in the Cooks, Captain Lever 'discovered' the Kermadecs and Penrhyn Island, and Captains Gilbert and Marshall the islands that bear their names. In 1789 Lieutenant John Shortland coasted the shores of Guadalcanal and San Cristobal. Commander George Vancouver, who had been on Cook's second and third voyages, was sent to the Pacific in 1791 in order to carry out survey work and to secure Britain's possession of the Nootka Sound coastline on what is now Vancouver Island. He explored part of the coast of New Zealand, 'discovered' the Chathams and charted the Snares, as well as thoroughly surveying the Pacific coastline of modern Canada and Alaska in 1792–4.[24] This was designed to strengthen the British presence on a coast in which Britain and Spain were in competition, and also showed that there was no water passage between the Atlantic and the Pacific south of the Arctic. Vancouver's expedition also accumulated much information about the areas visited. It was accompanied by a naturalist, Archibald Menzies, who had already visited the Pacific. He brought back a large number of plants, as well as descriptions of new animals and an account of mountains in Hawaii. The expedition also collected items of Native American life.

The contrast between oceanic exploration by Britain and other powers became even more marked after Britain and France went to war in 1793. The French overseas empire was destroyed and exploration was dominated by the British. George Bass and Matthew Flinders circumnavigated Tasmania in 1798–9, establishing that it was an island, and thus that ships sailing to Sydney from around the Cape of Good Hope did not need to round Tasmania, but, instead, could go through Bass Strait. This was an example of the value of exploration for navigators. Having returned to England, Flinders was appointed to carry out an accurate survey of Australia's coast. He explored the southern coast in 1801–2, and was responsible for the first complete circumnavigation of the continent in 1802–3. Britain and France were briefly at peace in 1802–3, and this enabled Nicolas-Thomas Baudin, the commander of a French scientific expedition, to take on supplies in Port Jackson (Sydney) before exploring all but the north coast. Flinders and Baudin exchanged charts.[25] Allied for much of the period, British mariners also helped guide Russian interest in the South Pacific.[26]

British ships charted large portions of the world during the wars that continued with few breaks until 1815. Although naval operations were concentrated in European waters, the far-flung nature of British attacks, including on French bases in the Caribbean and Indian Ocean, and Dutch possessions in Surinam, South Africa and the East Indies, encouraged an intensification of naval experience. The naval presence was not restricted to wartime. For example, in 1764–81 George Gauld charted the waters of the Gulf of Mexico in response to instructions from the British Admiralty which wished to consolidate the recent acquisition of Florida. Similarly, a British coastal survey of 1822–4 brought much information about East Africa.

It is possible to present British maritime activity as the product of a consistent government policy, but at ministerial levels it is more appropriate to focus on episodic interest. The Pacific was not consistently at the centre of government concern. Indeed, naval issues focused on capability in 'known waters', principally in Europe, although also in the Caribbean and off India. As a consequence, the role of individuals in supporting particular initiatives elsewhere was very important.

As with Spanish exploration on the northwest coast of North America in the early 1790s, reiterated voyages that probed every inlet and charted each mile of the shore were as important as the more dramatic 'voyages of discovery' that brought initial knowledge. Thus, for example, in 1794 Vancouver discovered that the body of water in southern Alaska named 'Cook's River' by Cook in 1778 was in fact an inlet. These reiterated voyages contributed to the extent to which European explorers did make genuine discoveries about the Pacific, rather than simply replicating the long voyages of native peoples. One counterpart of charting coastlines was the erection of lighthouses on coasts that were controlled. This was a clear example of knowledge being institutionalized and provided on a regular basis for the purposes of profit. The value of experience brought by repeated voyages was also seen with Vancouver's ability to build upon Cook's programme of maintaining sanitation and good diet in order to fight scurvy and other diseases.

Pacific voyages benefited from the growth in the number of bigger ships and from improvements in navigation, hull design and rigging. For example, eighteenth-century changes in sail plan made ships easier to handle, improved their performance and required less manpower,[27] a crucial consideration on long journeys. Such changes are a reminder of the importance of incremental developments within a given technology, as opposed to the more spectacular paradigm shifts to new technologies, an instance of which was to occur with steam power in the nineteenth century. To return to less sweeping, but still important, developments, the late eighteenth century also saw the copper sheathing of ships' bottoms in order to resist burrowing worms, the *teredo navalis*. This improved both durability and speed.

Arctic exploration

The extent of British maritime power and the range of her territorial presence was such that, after peace returned in 1815, Britain continued to dominate oceanic exploration. Indeed, it helped provide employment for the remaining naval officers. John Franklin of the Royal Navy was sent to descend the Coppermine River and then explore the Arctic coast of North America from the west, and in 1821 explored nearly 1,000 kilometres of coastline, leaving a legacy of placenames including Banks Peninsula, Bathurst Inlet and Warrender Bay. In 1818 John Ross explored openings to the west from Baffin Bay, and in 1819–20 William Parry unsuccessfully attempted to find a Northwest Passage through McClure Strait.[28] In 1827 he tried to reach the North Pole from Svalbard (Spitsbergen), but his sledge-mounted boats did not cover more than a fraction of the distance.

The British were not alone at sea. The Russians explored the coast of Alaska and made unsuccessful attempts to discover a Northwest Passage from the west in 1815–18 and 1820–1.[29] Knowledge of the Arctic Ocean north of Siberia was expanded in 1820–4 by Baron Ferdinand von Wrangel. Further west, the New Siberian Islands had been 'discovered' by the hunters Ivan Lyakhov and Ivan Sannikov, between 1770 and 1806. As so often with exploration, however, it was the subsequent systematic exploration and mapping that was as important, as it fitted these discoveries into the matrices of European knowledge and thus, in their terms, 'validated' them. Matvey Gedenshtrom did so for the New Siberian Islands in 1809–10, and the survey was completed by P. Pshenitsin in 1811. In 1820–4 Pyotr Anzhu, a naval officer, expanded and improved their surveys, part of the process by which knowledge was upgraded and verified. The Russians were also responsible for a major atlas, Admiral Adam John von Krusentern's *Atlas de l'océan Pacifique* (St Petersburg, 1823–6), which recorded the extent of Pacific discovery.

Overland exploration

To turn back to overland exploration is to be reminded of the variety of environments, both natural and human, that faced Western explorers. Again, there is the mixture of major journeys that attracted much attention, such as James Bruce's 'discovery' of the source of the Blue Nile in 1770, Alexander Mackenzie's overland crossing of North America from the Atlantic to the Pacific in 1792–3, and Mungo Park's 'discovery' of the direction of the Niger in 1796, and the mass of less dramatic journeys that offered a more incremental process of exploration. The latter were relatively more important than at sea for two reasons. First, it was easier to organize an expedition on land than at sea, and, second, as a consequence, there were more explorers (and other travellers outside existing areas of Western knowledge) on land and, therefore, a greater tendency in subsequent work to concentrate on an atypical group of great names.

Even allowing for the great names approach, the general list has been somewhat selective. For example, alongside Bruce, Park or Lewis and Clark, it is appropriate to recall Johann Burckhardt (1784–1817), who in 1812 entered Petra and, in 1814, Mecca.

South America

Missionary explorers are generally underrated, but they were important, particularly in South America and Tibet. In South America Franciscans and Jesuits were especially active in exploring the interior. Manuel de Biedma explored northeastern Peru, including the Valley of the Ucayali, between 1658 and 1686, while Antonio de Monteverde explored the valley of the Orinoco in 1663. Based on information from missionaries, the Jesuit Samuel Fritz was able to compile a map of the Amazon published in 1707.

From the late eighteenth century, however, secular explorers became more important, not least because the Jesuits were expelled from Brazil in 1759 and from all Spanish colonies in 1767. Scientific investigation and accumulation became major motives for exploration. In 1735 the French scientist Charles-Marie de La Condamine led an expedition to Quito to test the sphericity of the earth by calculating the length of a degree along the world's surface at the Equator. In 1783 the Spanish crown sponsored a botanical expedition to South America. The Prussian explorer Alexander von Humboldt (1769–1850) produced hitherto unprecedented data on the geography, geology, meteorology and natural history of the Orinoco rainforests and the Andean chain which he explored in 1799–1803.

In 1802 he climbed Mount Chimborazo in the Andes to 19,280 feet, correctly ascribing altitude sickness to lack of oxygen. In 1826–34 the French palaeontologist Alcide d'Orbigny studied the continent's fossil-bearing strata.

Africa

Exploration in Africa was limited in the late seventeenth and early eighteenth centuries. This reflected the limited nature of interest in exploring the interior, as well as the difficulties of so doing. The French Jesuit linguist Claude Sincara (1677–1726) mapped Egypt in 1717, as a result of a visit to gather material about antiquities in which he travelled to Aswan and identified the location of Thebes.[30] Benoît de Maillet, French Consul in Cairo from 1692 to 1708, followed in 1735 with his *Description de l'Egypt*. However, such activity was very much a probing of the Mediterranean world, rather than an attempt to engage with Africa.

European knowledge of the interior of Africa only increased considerably from the 1770s. James Bruce's tour of Ethiopia in 1768–1773 helped to increase interest in the interior of the continent. A landowner, Bruce was fired by intellectual curiosity, rather than hope for economic advantage. He had already shown great interest in the non-European world, including consideration of a career in India, studying Arabic, acting as Consul at Algiers, and travelling in North Africa, Syria and Egypt. He wanted to gain fame by discovering the source of the Nile and journeyed to Ethiopia via the Red Sea. Plunged into the complex and violent world of Ethiopian politics, he was able to reach the springs of the Blue Nile in 1770: 'It is easier to guess than to describe the situation of my mind at that moment – standing on that spot which had baffled the genius, industry, and inquiry of both ancients and moderns for the course of near three thousand years.' Leaving the capital, Gondar, in December 1771, Bruce reached the Egyptian frontier in November 1772 and Marseilles the following March.

Bruce had not 'discovered' the source of the Nile, but rather rediscovered that of its largest tributary, the Blue Nile, which had already been reached by the Jesuit Pedro Paez in 1618, a fact Bruce challenged without due cause. Bruce's *Travels* did not appear until 1790 and he met both then and earlier a mixed reception, in part because his account of life in Ethiopia was doubted. Nevertheless, the very process of controversy helped to increase interest in African exploration. This was directly so with William George Browne (1768–1813), another traveller with independent means, who was encouraged by reading Bruce and the first report of the African Association to visit Egypt where he studied Arabic, and, being thwarted in his goal of visiting Ethiopia, to travel to Darfur in modern southwest Sudan, becoming in 1793 the first European to do so. Like others intending to impress contemporaries and posterity, Browne published his travel account, and these *Travels in Africa, Egypt, and Syria* (1800) were unusual because he compared the customs of the people he visited favourably with those of Europe, a verdict that was not fashionable for this area and period. In 1813 Browne was murdered en route from Tabriz to Teheran.

In 1788 Sir Joseph Banks, President of the Royal Society, played a major role in founding the Association for Promoting the Discovery of the Interior Parts of Africa, or African Association, a society of British scientists and scholars that sponsored exploration.[31] The Association began by seeking to use the trans-Saharan trade routes to send explorers into the African interior. After two unsuccessful attempts by others, Friedrich Hornemann, who posed as a merchant, set off in 1798, becoming in 1800 the first European to cross the Sahara to Bornu near Lake Chad. The Association was also interested in trying to penetrate the interior from the River Gambia. Daniel Houghton, an ex-army officer, who had served at Gorée on the Gambian coast, went further beyond the Senegal into the interior than previous European travellers, but his efforts to open a trade route were unsuccessful, and he was robbed and died in 1791, well short of his goal, Timbuktu.

In 1795–7, the Association supported Mungo Park's first journey to West Africa, in which he investigated the River Gambia and reached the Niger at Segu, showing that it flowed eastward. His *Travels in the Interior Districts of Africa*, published in 1799, was a great success, and went through three editions that year. This was not a matter only of fame in Britain. Editions also appeared in French and German in 1800. On his second trip, in 1805–6, in which he set out to find Timbuktu and the mouth of the Niger, Park reached the city and travelled a long way down the Niger, only to die negotiating rapids on the river at Bussa, possibly as the result of a skirmish. Like other explorers, Park had native assistants, who tend to be forgotten, in his case in 1795 six Africans. Government assistance was of some importance: from 1802 the government took over the sponsorship of the major expeditions from the African Association, and the following year the Secretary of State for the Colonies had invited Park on a second expedition. In 1804 the government paid for him to study Arabic, and he was given the brevet commission of a captain in Africa, as well as £5,000 and the power to enlist forty-five soldiers on the expedition.[32]

The 1820s saw a great increase in the exploration of the interior of North and West Africa. In 1821–5 Hugh Clapperton, Dixon Denham and Walter Oudney travelled from Tripoli across the Sahara to Lake Chad. Denham proved that the Niger did not link with Lake Chad. In 1827–8 the French explorer René Caillié travelled in the opposite direction, going from Freetown to Timbuktu and then crossing the Sahara to Morocco. Caillié won the prize of 10,000 francs offered by the Société Géographique for being the first European to return from Timbuktu.

North America

A division between land and sea is useful in discussing, for example, the Pacific, but has less value in some other parts of the world. This was true, for instance, of René-Robert Cavalier, Sieur de La Salle's attempts to extend French power in North America. In the 1670s and early 1680s, La Salle founded a series of trading posts on the Illinois River, and in 1682 canoed down the Mississippi to its mouth, planting the cross, raising the arms of France, and claiming the river, its tributaries and the lands they watered for Louis XIV. The king initially criticized the discoveries as worthless, for the Mississippi had led to the Gulf of Mexico, not the hoped-for Pacific, but his opinion was changed by clerics eager to extend the sway of the Catholic Church. In 1684 La Salle was sent to the Gulf of Mexico with four ships and 300 settlers, and orders to establish a colony at the mouth of the Mississippi, but, missing the Mississippi delta, he landed in early 1685 400 miles west at Matagorda Bay, where he founded Fort St Louis. From there, La Salle fell victim to the barrenness of the coast, divisions in the expedition (which cost La Salle his life in March 1687), and the hostility of the Karankawa, who wiped out the surviving colonists at the close of 1688.[33]

This is a reminder of the fate of many explorers. Conflict with local people was a problem for marine explorers, such as Cook, killed in Hawaii in 1779; one of his boat-crews had been killed in 1773. Tasman had skirmished with Maoris at Murderers Bay in New Zealand in 1642. Death in conflict was even more of a risk for their land counterparts. In the Carolinas John Lawson was killed in 1711 and Thomas Nairne in 1715. Ulrich Seetzen was murdered at Taiz, and Alexander King at Timbuktu in 1826. Disease, however, was more of a threat. Among the many it claimed was Hornemann north of the Niger in 1801, Burckhardt at Cairo in 1817 and Clapperton in Sokoto in 1827, all of dysentery. Oudney died in the Sudan in 1824.

Again on land, there is the problem of an Anglocentric account that devotes far too little weight to other European explorers, such as those of France, Spain and Russia. Yet, each of these countries produced important explorers, as, to a lesser extent, did other states.

In North America the frontier of European knowledge was pushed back throughout the period. The late seventeenth century saw not only the explorations of Charles Allouez, Charles Albanel, Louis Jolliet, Jacques Marquette, La Salle and Louis Hennepin on behalf of the French, but also expeditions by two Dutch travellers: Arnout Viele journeyed from Albany to the Ohio valley in 1682–4; and Johannes Roseboom travelled from Albany to Lake Michigan in 1685 and 1687 in search of new fur trade routes, but was captured by the French on the second trip.

Exploration was closely linked to a wish to locate and exploit resources and routes. The search for fur took French and British travellers well beyond their bases on the Great Lakes and Hudson Bay. The most far-flung in the late seventeenth century was that of Henry Kelsey, a member of the Hudson Bay Company base at Fort York, who in 1690 joined a group of Crees on their return from trading at the bay, and, by his return in 1692, had crossed the Saskatchewan River and become the first white man to reach the great grasslands of western Canada. Like other overland journeys, Kelsey's was dependent on native support and knowledge.

Further south, from the 1700s, French explorers were sent up the Missouri to find copper mines and along the Red River to find silver and gold deposits or benefit from the Spanish ones in New Mexico, but hopes that Louisiana would be a mineral colony or would serve as a base for trade with the Pacific or, at any rate, with New Mexico proved abortive.

In 1738 Pierre Gaultier de La Vérendrye travelled from New France (Canada) to find the 'great river' reported to run west to the Pacific from near the headwaters of the Missouri. The expedition set off from Fort La Reine on the Assiniboine River and reached the Missouri near modern Bismarck in North Dakota. In 1742–3, he sent two of his sons on a further search for the Pacific. They crossed much of Dakota before turning back short of the River Platte because their native companions feared attack. Further south, Bénard de La Harpe had travelled in 1719 from the French colony of Louisiana as far as modern Oklahoma in his search for native trade and a new route to New Mexico, while in 1729 Pierre Mallet had crossed Kansas en route from the Missouri to Santa Fe.

It is also too easy to forget Spanish explorers, such as Father Francisco Garcés, who in 1775–6 explored what is now Arizona and Colorado and was the first European to enter the Great Basin (between the Sierra Nevada and central Utah) and was thus able to refute the belief that there was a large inland sea there. In 1776 Fathers Silvestre de Vélez de Escalanto and Francisco Atanasio Domínguez travelled further north in what is now Colorado and Utah. The pace of Spanish exploration north from Mexico had slackened considerably in the seventeenth century, after a major burst in the sixteenth, but in the eighteenth it revived, in large part in response to real and threatened moves by other European powers.

Furthermore, overland exploration was necessary in order to support maritime activity. Thus, the establishment of missions on the coast of Lower California led to the search for a land route from Mexico around the head of the gulf in the 1690s and 1700s. Father Eusebio Kino, a Jesuit missionary, who in 1687 founded the mission of Nuestra Señora de los Doloros, was responsible for a large number of expeditions for both proselytizing and geographical ends.[34] Later, the creation of settlements on the Upper Californian coast was followed by a more ambitious search for overland routes.

It is even more easy to overlook Portuguese travellers, although they were important in both Brazil and Africa. In 1798 Francisco Lacerda e Almeida, Governor of Sena on the Zambezi, who was concerned about the recent British conquest of Cape Colony from the Dutch, decided that the Portuguese needed to link their colonies of Mozambique and Angola. He reached Lake Mweru in central Africa, but died of disease there; and this was the end of the attempt, although in 1806–11 two Portuguese half-caste slave traders, Pedro Baptista and Antonio Nogueira da Rocha, crossed Africa from Cassange in Angola to Sena.

The pace of exploration in the interior of North America resumed, and its focus altered, after the War of American Independence (1775–83). Alongside explorers expanding the bounds of British North America – most prominently Samuel Hearne, who descended the Coppermine River in 1771 and saw the Arctic, and Alexander Mackenzie, who travelled from Fort Chipewyan to the Arctic in 1789 – exploration was now part of the effort by newly independent Americans to understand and assert their new geographical identity, a process that was accentuated after the Louisiana Purchase of 1803 greatly expanded the country: the French sold a massive territory, much of which was unknown to seller and purchaser. In 1805–7 Meriwether Lewis and William Clark explored these new lands and reached the Pacific coast at the mouth of the Columbia River.[35] Its largely overlooked counterpart, the Red River Expedition of 1806, provided valuable knowledge, including a map of the river, that was to help subsequent American expansion.[36] Zebulon Pike followed up by exploring the Southern Great Plains, while in 1819–20 Stephen Long expanded knowledge of the Great Plains. Long's expedition included artists whose paintings helped to create an image of the region and thus a new picture of America, one to which Europe had not directly contributed.

Hardship and knowledge

At the same time, other lightly populated arid lands were being explored. This was true not only of the Sahara and sub-Saharan Sahel in Africa, but also of the interior of Australia. Moving inland from Sydney, a route was found across the Blue Mountains in 1813, while, at the close of the 1820s, Charles Sturt explored much of southeastern Australia, paving the way for the foundation of the colony of South Australia in 1836.

The transition from religious to secular explorers seen in North and South America can also be glimpsed in Asia. In 1661 the first Europeans reached Lhasa. They were Jesuits, Grueber and d'Orville, and were followed in the early eighteenth century by other Jesuits who unsuccessfully sought to establish missions similar to those already founded in China. In 1759–60 two Portuguese Jesuits surveyed Chinese conquests in Zungaria and Turkestan for the emperor, part of the process by which Jesuit cartography contributed to Chinese knowledge and power.[37]

By the late eighteenth century, in contrast, the European contacts in Tibet were British, and aspects of the military–commercial presence of the East India Company. George Bogle and Alexander Hamilton were sent in 1774 in an attempt to establish relations, with Samuel Turner following in 1783. William Kirkpatrick led an embassy to Kathmandu in 1798, and the following year Michael Symes led another to Ava in Burma. As with the Jesuits, many explorers and other travellers made a determined effort to engage with at least some aspects of native culture. For example, the Swiss-born Johann Burckhardt (1784–1817), who was chosen in 1809 by the Association for Promoting the Discovery of the Interior Parts of Africa to undertake a mission across the Sahara, learned Arabic and spent some time studying Islam in Syria as preliminary steps. This was particularly necessary as, for reasons of safety, he, like many other travellers to Islamic lands, wished to pass himself off as a native.

Behind the mention of so much travel is the reality of much individual hardship. Conditions were often dangerous and difficult. Bougainville's crew was reduced to eating rats, which, ironically, helped against scurvy as rats can synthesize vitamin C. While the determination shown is obviously impressive, at the same time it is necessary to stress that the consequences of much exploration was disruption, and its ends power and profit, as well as understanding and knowledge. Journeys such as those of Burckhardt and Garcés are reminders of what it is all too easy to forget, but, rather than listing others, it is more helpful to turn to consider the knowledge such exploration brought of the wider world and the exploitation it was designed to facilitate.

3

KNOWLEDGE

Exploration helped bring knowledge, but the character and impact of that knowledge have been matters of controversy. In particular, in recent decades it has been argued that knowledge is a form of power, both used by the powerful and employed to enhance their power. Knowledge has been presented as a struggle, as having its own politics, and as a means by which states and ideologies colonized territories and terrains. This chapter will look at this proposition, focusing on two levels: first, the way in which knowledge contributed to the Western representation of the globe; and, second, the extent to which the knowledge of particular areas was important to the advance of European powers.

Projections putting Europe on top

The globe was understood by Europeans in this period as a product of their voyages of discovery and their cartographic conceptualization. This understanding helped focus a sense of Europe as central to the world. In the case of globes Europe held a prominent position, most particularly because north, not south, was placed at the top. This emphasis on Europe was enhanced by the process of mapping which necessarily involved distortion: a projection is a flat (two-dimensional) representation of the globe, which is three-dimensional. Thus, there can be no 'correct shape' on a map projection. Rectangular maps deprive the world of its circularity: they make each parallel and meridian appear straight, instead of circular, and give the globe the misleading visual character of right-angle corners and clear edges. Europeans sought a map projection that made most sense in terms of the employment of the compass, and of maritime directions and links, especially in the mid-latitudes. Needing to sail great distances, if they were to fulfil the commercial logic of distant possessions and trading opportunities, Europeans could not consider map-making a matter of abstract intellectualism.[1]

In 1569 the Fleming Gerhardus Kramer, Latinized as 'Mercator' (1512–94), utilized trigonometry to produce a projection that treated the world as a cylinder, so that the meridians were parallel, rather than converging on the poles. The poles, instead, were expanded to the same circumference as the Equator, greatly magnifying temperate land masses at the expense of tropical ones. Taking into account the curvature of the Earth's surface, Mercator's projection kept angles, and thus bearings, accurate in every part of the map, so that a straight line of constant bearing could be charted across the plane surface of the map, a goal that was crucial for navigation. To do so, the scale was varied, and thus size was distorted. This was not a problem for European rulers and merchants keen to explore the possibilities provided by exploration and conquest in the middle latitudes to the west (America) and to the east (South Asia).

Nevertheless, there was considerable conservatism in map production, and many navigators continued to use hand-drawn charts of coastlines that were reliant on magnetic compass bearings. These practices, however, were to fall victim to the standardization that was important to the European presentation and use of knowledge, a standardization expressed in the reliance on printed ways to convey information, such as maps. Standardization was not, of course, the same as accuracy. Map engravers preferred the easy option of reusing old plates, rather than incorporating new knowledge.

Unlike medieval Christian maps, the Mercator world was not centred on Jerusalem. Instead, he placed Europe, which seemed most important and could be mapped most readily, at the top centre of his map; and gave the northern hemisphere primacy over the southern, both by treating the north as the top and by giving the south less than half the map. Mercator's is sometimes treated as the archetypal European projection, which is misleading as there was some variety in the projections discussed and employed, which extended to the description of an equal-area projection by Johann Heinrich Lambert in 1772. However, the notion of Europe as central, and the northern hemisphere as on top, was preserved. Mercator was influential, and concern with maritime routes and familiarity with projections of the Mercator type encouraged an essential conservatism in presentation.

Maps

These projections provided a basis for deploying knowledge, literally a map that could be filled in, but one that could be done without challenging a Eurocentric world view. Indeed, the capacity of explorers to provide such information helped enhance a sense that the European world view was correct and should shape the world.

It proved easier to give detailed shape to this view along the coastlines of the world than in the interiors of continents. The context was a search for precision. There had been considerable stylization in the depiction of physical features – for example, islands and coastlines – in medieval and early Renaissance maps, as the map-makers were primarily concerned with recording their existence, rather than their accurate shape. In their *Portolani* and *Isolarii* the Italians simply presented coastlines in a schematic form. In part this was a matter of contemporary conceptual standards, but the nature of the information available to map-makers was also important.

However, from the fifteenth century there was a growing emphasis on the need for precision in the portrayal of the crucial physical outlines: coastlines and rivers. There was also much more information available, and this led to a sense of progress and superiority. Comparisons of ancient and contemporary were common in early modern European culture, and now very much played to the advantage of the latter. In his *New Set of Maps Both of Antient and Present Geography* (Oxford, 1700) Edward Wells, an Oxford academic, revealed contemporary knowledge as far more extensive: the New World was presented as 'unknown' to the ancients, unless it was their Atlantis. Even so, they could not map it, whereas the moderns could.

Modern European maps offered relatively little for the interiors of other continents. This reflected the navigational rationale and source of much mapping. For example, Etienne de Flacourt's map of Madagascar (1666) was accurate largely for the southeast of the island, where the French had established Fort Dauphin in 1642, and not for other parts. The map of India in Joan Blaeu's *Atlas Major* (French edition, 1667) contained much error for the interior, including very inaccurate alignments of the Ganges and the Indus, the movement of the Western Ghats far inland, and a failure to mark in the Himalayan range. Nicolas Visscher's *Atlas Contractus* (1671) was more detailed on the Atlantic coast of North America than on the interior. The Venetian Vincenzo Coronelli's *Route maritime de Brest à Siam et de Siam à Brest* (Brest, 1687) was essentially a map of coastal regions. Louis Hennepin's *Carte d'un tres grand Pais nouvellement découvert dans L'Amerique Septentrionale* (1697) showed the Mississippi and its tributaries, but, due to the difficulty of relating the course of the river to the Gulf of Mexico, put its mouth too far west. In Jean Baptiste Bourguignon d'Anville's *Carte de l'Inde* of 1752 most of east-central India was labelled '*Grand espace de pays dont on n'a point de connoissance particulière*'. This itself was an important sign of the attempt to avoid fictitious topography, and thus to distinguish between areas that were known and what was left blank. D'Anville also mapped the continents bar Australasia and Antarctica. Louis Charles Desnos's map *L'Asie* (Paris, 1789) included all of Asia, but the mapping of Tibet was very vague.

There was also much error in maps. A large inland sea in the northwest of North America, possibly connected to the Pacific, was widely believed in, and it appeared in maps such as that of Joseph-Nicholas Delisle in 1752. The fictitious Mountains of the Moon remained on maps of Africa, including Rennell's of 1799, and this helped to account for the inaccurate belief that the Niger was linked with the Nile. The interior of Australia was believed to contain great inland lakes or seas and major rivers similar to those in other continents. These provided not only a goal for exploration and commercial exploitation, but also a subject for mapping, as in the 1827 map of the 'Coasts of Australia and the supposed entrance of the Great River' drawn for the *Friend of Australia*. This river, the 'Desired Blessing', was shown as flowing from a lake in the centre of the continent to the northwest coast. Another major lake, of Chamay, was long shown in the north of Burma, again as the source of major rivers.

Even coastal regions were often poorly mapped. Joan Blaeu's *Atlas Major* (1662) showed Australia, New Guinea and the Asian coast north of Korea only sketchily. Wells showed California as an island and, more generally, knew little of the northern Pacific. John Senec's map of Asia (1711) depicted a large island, Yedso, to the north of Japan, where Hokkaido is, but far larger, and another, Compagnia, close to the east of Yedso. The latter could have been a misrepresentation of part of North America, but the map was made more confusing by the juxtaposition of these fictions with indications that elsewhere there was a lack of knowledge: to the north of Compagnia was the legend 'these parts remain as yet undiscovered', while, along the inaccurately portrayed eastern coast of Siberia appeared the legend 'It is not known where this chain of mountains ends or whether they are not joined to some other continent'. The islands mapped were based on the voyage of Maartin Fries in 1643, but a mixture of his own misjudgements and the misleading interpretations of later map-makers had led to an inaccurate account of the northern Pacific that was not clarified until the eighteenth century with the voyages of Bering, later Russian explorers and Lapérouse, although even then there was controversy about reports of 'discoveries'.[2] In Robert's map of the *Archipel des Indes Orientales* (1750), a caption '*Le fond de ce Golphe n'est pas bien connu*' appears for the coastline of the Teluk Tomini in the Celebes (Sulawesi). The *Carte plate qui comprend l'Isle de Ceylon* (1775) includes the captions '*Isles Laquedives don't le détail n'est pas exactement connu*' and '*on ne connoit, ni le nombre, ni la grandeur, ni la situation respective des Isles Maldives*'.

Until the eighteenth century there were no clocks accurate enough to give a ship's meridianal position, and longitudinal mapping faced problems. Many islands were placed too far to the west or the east; combined with the failure of captains to know where their ships were, this caused shipwrecks. In 1741 Anson nearly ran aground on Tierra del Fuego; dead reckoning had put his position more than 300 miles out to sea. Coronelli's map already referred to was based on the Jesuit mission sent to Siam (Thailand) by Louis XIV in 1685, and carried a note saying that it employed two sorts of longitudinal markings, those generally agreed and those based on information from the Jesuits. Major differences were revealed by a comparative French map of 1739, *Carte de l'Océan Oriéntale ou Mers des Indes dressée au dépost des cartes plans et journaux de la marine comparée avec la carte hollandoise de Ptietergoos et la carte angloise de Thornton*. In addition to problems with the available information, there was deliberate secrecy about coastlines on which monopoly trading rights were claimed.

With the aid of declination tables, the sun and stars could be used to calculate latitude, although the instruments in general use had limitations.[3] However, longitude could not be checked by observation while at sea at the beginning of the period. The discovery of a method for determining longitude at sea and the establishment of accurate values for longitude can be presented as a heroic achievement of the eighteenth century. It is worth noting that, although Parliament established a Board of Longitude in 1714 and offered a substantial reward for the discovery, and the French followed suit in 1715, the whole process took a long time. William Hogarth, in his series *A Rake's Progress* (1735), presented a madman trying to solve the problems of longitude on the madhouse wall. The accurate calculation of longitude depended on the precise measurement of local time in relation to the time at the Greenwich meridian. It was not until 1761–2 that John Harrison devised a chronometer that erred by only eighteen miles in measurement of the distance of a return journey to Jamaica, although word of the discovery had little initial impact on Hogarth as he republished his engraving in 1763.

Navigators were therefore able to calculate their positions far more precisely. Harrison's chronometer was used by Cook on his second and third voyages. In calculating longitudes, a process that caused him difficulties, Vancouver employed dead reckoning, lunar observation and chronometers, and carried out experiments with the last.[4] There were also improvements in the methods for finding latitude more precisely.

Progress on land, where triangulation had been used to construct maps since the sixteenth century, was swifter, and was extended from Europe to the wider world. Supported by the government, the French played a major role. In 1679–83 the French Académie worked out the longitudinal position of France. In 1708–17 the Jesuit Jean-Baptiste Régis supervised the first maps of the Chinese empire to be based on astronomical observation and triangulation.

As a result of such developments it became possible to locate most places accurately, and the development of accurate and standard means of measuring distances made it easier for map-makers to understand, assess and reconcile the work of their predecessors. Maps also became more predictable as mapping conventions developed. In the eighteenth century north became more commonly placed at the top of maps. Map knowledge of the rest of the world grew and became more readily available.[5] Maps of the West Indies and North America came to play a greater role in atlases published in the first half of the eighteenth century – for example, those produced in London by Moll, Senex and Bowen – and this markedly gathered pace with the Seven Years War and then the War of American Independence. Thus, Thomas Jefferys published a number of atlases including *A General Topography of North America and the West Indies* (1768) and *The American Atlas or, a Geographical Description of the Whole Continent of America* (1776).

Atlases spread news of exploration, making it appear a process of discovery, and consciously emphasized the novelty of the knowledge they conveyed: with the world outside Europe, knowledge, to be valid and valuable, had to be up to date. Thus Antonio Zatta's *Atlante novissimo, illustrato ed accresciuto sulle osservazioni, e scoperte dei piu' prima volat si produce* (4 vols, Venice, 1779–85) prided itself on its account of recent explorations, and provided the first appearance in an Italian atlas of the new islands explored by Cook.[6] The *New Map of South America*, published in 1794 by Robert Wilkinson of London, continued in its title *Drawn from the Latest Discoveries*.

Outside Europe mapping very much reflected the interests of European powers. These helped to dictate what was mapped and how it was mapped. A recent study of Dutch mapping has established that a synergy existed between overseas expansion, navigation and the accumulation of cartographic information. New procedures influenced chart-making. Pilots began to keep logbooks and to produce reconnaissance charts, employing sheets of paper with pre-drawn compass lines. The Dutch trading companies ensured that institutionalized map-making was important. Company ships were provided with navigation instruments, and an East India Company map-making agency was created in Amsterdam from 1616. From 1619, the East India Company directors sought to keep information secret. The company also regarded surveys with information on crops and town plans as essential for management and planning. A wealth of information was accumulated. Topographic maps were made of Dutch colonies in the New World. Thus, a map of Surinam was printed in 1671 and a new survey of all plantations there begun in 1684. More generally, 'it is especially the combination of absolute power, colonial exploitation and the concept of just government which surveyors and military engineers together with the Governors were required to implement with the help of maps'.[7]

Frontiers

Maps were also produced as a result of the border delimitation that was necessary to settle competing territorial claims. The Austrian and Turkish commissioners who sought to clarify their new frontier after the Peace of Carlowitz of 1699 faced the ambiguous and contradictory wording of the peace treaty on such matters as the 'straight' line of one portion of the frontier, the 'ancient frontiers' of Transylvania and the future status of islands where the frontier followed rivers.[8] Following the Austro-Turkish war of 1737–9, and the subsequent Treaty of Belgrade, there were lengthy negotiations to settle the new border, and a satisfactory settlement was not negotiated until 1744.

Natural boundaries were the obvious topic of maps that sought to show the land frontier between Europe and Asia because they were the obvious bases for the frontier. There was no jurisdictional definition of territory reflecting long-established political interests that might act as an alternative to natural boundaries. Instead, force operated with scant reference to historical claims. The exact course of the frontier between Europe and Asia was most important in areas of settlement and along trade routes and, as these were often riverine, it was rivers that provided the necessary definition, although, by their very nature, rivers are fluid and river courses could vary. For much of the eighteenth century the frontier between Russia and central Asia – in so far as one can write of one – east of the Caspian followed the Ural and Irtysh rivers. The Terek and the Kuban defined much of Russia's frontier in the Caucasus in the late eighteenth century. Further west, the Dnieper, Bug, Dniester and Pruth marked successive stages of Russia's advance across transpontine Europe and towards the Balkans. Similarly, the Oltul, Muresul, Tisza, Danube and Sava played an important role in defining the Austro-Turkish border between 1699 and 1878.

Power and pragmatism divorced from the feudal legacy of jurisdictional issues and non-linear frontiers were dominant on the Euro-Asian frontier. This was certainly the case with the Russian impact in the Balkans, the Caucasus and further east.[9] Elsewhere on the Euro-Asian frontier the relationship between the coastal enclaves of European trading companies or states in southern Asia and the locally dominant Asiatic powers posed questions of sovereignty and jurisdictional relationship, but the situation was far from uniform. Aside from differences between the imperial organizations and pretensions of different European societies, it was also the case that some Asiatic polities, such as the Indian Mughal and Persian Safavid empires (but not China or Japan), provided only loose hegemonies, in which it was possible for European interests to establish semi-independent territorial presences, akin to those of some Asiatic regimes. This had consequences in terms of mappability, and the situation was not to change until the British imposed and defined their sovereign power in India.

Power and pragmatism without the feudal legacy of jurisdictional issues and non-linear frontiers was also the case in North America. Natural features were cited as boundaries in treaties between the British North American colonies and native tribes, such as that of 1765 with the Lower Creeks. Maps played a role in locating and representing territorial disagreements between imperial powers in North America. This encouraged the mapping of areas where there was no European presence. Maps were employed in Anglo-French differences in the 1680s over the frontier between Canada and the territories of the Hudson Bay Company.[10] In 1670 this company had been granted by Charles II exclusive trading privileges in the lands drained by rivers flowing into Hudson Bay, but, at that time, there had been no idea about the extent of the area, and, as it expanded the scope of its acitvities, the company needed more maps, although it was not until 1778 that it hired its first surveyor/map-maker.[11]

Differing maps played a role in the failure to settle Anglo-French disputes in North America in 1755. Later, the newly independent USA was involved in frontier disputes with Britain and Spain. In South America, Portugal and Spain sought to locate the border between their colonies, a process that led to much surveying in the second half of the eighteenth century. There was also mapping of the frontiers between colonies within individual imperial systems, a process that thickened the knowledge grid and made mapping and European control increasingly normative. Thus, a survey of 1728 which established the boundary between Virginia and North Carolina greatly increased knowledge of the back country. The Pennsylvania–Maryland boundary was surveyed in 1763–7.

Maps and power

Not only frontiers were mapped: territory was also mapped in order to control and profit from it. The large-scale map of the Danish-ruled Caribbean island of St Croix (1754), the first broadsheet map of any of the Danish islands in the region to be published, was not simply a record of settlement but also an important device for land speculators: 'topographic information and bureaucratic access to land, rather than the availability of capital, were the keys to wealth on St Croix'.[12] When the French mapped Martinique and Guadeloupe after the Seven Years War, their maps recorded the plantation system and were also designed to provide information in the event of future hostilities with Britain. On the maps the names of owners were marked on plantations; not those of workers.[13]

Napoleon's invasion of Egypt in 1798 led to its first accurate map, the French army carrying out the survey. This can be presented as part of a quest for knowledge, but, like other aspects of Napoleon's activities in Egypt, also reflected a wish to use the French presence to ennoble Napoleon in enlightened opinion, while simultaneously enabling Egypt to serve as a base from which the British position in India could be challenged. In the same period John Barrow, private secretary to Lord Macartney, Governor of Cape Colony, which the British had conquered from the Dutch in 1795, was instructed by the governor to gather topographic knowledge so that he could draw up a map, which he did in 1801. Later, as Second Secretary in the Admiralty, Barrow was a keen supporter of polar exploration.

In Australia, once a way had been found across the Blue Mountains in 1813 Governor Macquarie commissioned the surveying and building of a road to the Bathurst Plains, where he established a government settlement in 1815. An active process of land grants helped encourage expansion, and the government sought to control this by organizing surveys, under John Oxley and Thomas Mitchell. This served as the basis for an expansion of government structures. Nineteen counties were declared in New South Wales in 1826. The same process was seen in Tasmania.

In India mapping also served to make Britain understand its conquests, while in addition helping to legitimate the British presence:

> mapmaking was integral to British imperialism in India, not just as a
> highly effective informational weapon wielded strategically and tactically
> by directors, governors, military commanders, and field officials, but also
> as a significant component of the 'structures of feeling' which legitimated,
> justified, and defined that imperialism.[14]

Systematic British surveying and mapping of India followed the appointment of James Rennell in 1767 as the first Surveyor-General of the Bengal Presidency, a post he held until 1777, after which he returned to London. He produced his *Bengal Atlas*, a work based on a series of survey journeys, and followed this, in 1783, with the more general *Memoir of a Map of Hindoostan; or the Mogul's Empire*. Formal trigonometrical surveys followed, with army officers, especially Colin Mackenzie, who became First Surveyor-General of India in 1819, and William Lambton, playing prominent roles. In 1800 Lambton began the triangulation of India. His successor, George Everest, who became Superintendent of the Trigonometrical Survey in 1823, and Surveyor-General in 1830, employed a grid covering the entire subcontinent; Lambton had laid down the 'Great Arc', the central north–south axis for the grid. Also in 1823, and based on the Trigonometrical Survey, the *Indian Atlas* of J. and C. Walker was commissioned by the East India Company. Produced at a scale of four miles to one inch, this topographic map series offered an impressive range of detail, although it was not finished until the twentieth century.

Mapping supported the mental world of empire. In India the Trigonometrical Survey helped present British rule as scientific, rational and thus liberal, in stark contrast to Asian rule, which the British stereotyped as mystical, irrational and despotic. By providing accurate guidance to space, the Trigonometrical Survey also offered a more accurate basis for taxation.

The process of surveying for the Trigonometrical Survey also showed the dominance of European power. Whereas Mackenzie used locally produced compasses and Mughal land records, and had appreciated his Indian informants, now the British carried out most of the surveying, and provided the precision measuring devices, with Indians largely employed as labourers, guards and bearers. Underlying the unreasonably low opinion held by the British of the Indians' worth as surveyors were some basic assumptions about their alleged inability to conceive of space and distance in European terms. The native cartographic tradition was indeed very different and there was no comparable emphasis on fixed scales: instead, the tradition focused on routes, not areas. The British came to discard information from Indian sources.[15]

Yet, more generally, such information could be very important to the process by which Europeans acquired knowledge. This was particularly so given the limited direct knowledge available of the interiors of continents. However, native information had to be understood, and the concepts underlying native cartography had to be interpreted. Such 'assimilation' can be presented in terms both of a failure of comprehension and of distortions arising from European power and goals. With particular reference to North America, Barbara Belyea has argued that

> Eighteenth-century European cartographers tried, and failed, to absorb native data into their own maps. Either the native map signs were simply juxtaposed to their own surveys, or they were radically reconfigured to appear like the signs of surveyed regions, with all the risks of misunderstanding attendant on this transformation.[16]

Yet, while this may be true of the European grid of knowledge reproduction, it is less appropriate as a suggestion of the extent to which the detailed process of knowledge acquisition on the ground, like 'discovery' and exploration more generally, depended on co-operation and can be described in terms of syncreticism. From the same volume as the passage just cited comes

> The importance of Indian informants to the activities of French explorers in the interior remained a constant of French policy as the Louisiana

colony was founded and settled. Readers of Iberville's accounts of his early visits to Southeastern North America will be well aware of his constant attention to the information of Indian informants.[17]

In 1829–33, John Ross's search for the Northwest Passage was helped by native cartographic and navigational knowledge.

Naming

Mapping was linked to the process of naming, an issue that has attracted interest over the last two decades. In both practical and symbolic terms maps served as assertions and communicators of proprietorial and territorial rights, and, conversely, had 'silences' – peoples who were ignored or marginalized. The sense and naming of place of those who suffered from imperialism were appropriated, and their understanding of territory and boundaries was neglected.[18] This owed much to the process by which colonies (and states) were creations, or essays in the structuring of space by power.[19]

There are problems with this approach. The modern theory of knowledge construction offers only limited guidance to the processes and problems of map creation, not least the exigencies and compromises that characterize the collection of data and the decision of what can be mapped. In politicizing these processes of choice and compromise scholars have simplified a complex situation.

Allowing for this, the cartographic process was at the centre of a construction and representation of knowledge that was very important to the extension of European power. In European eyes non-European territories could appear empty, and non-European societies unsophisticated. These lands were appropriated to the European cartographic consciousness either by mapping them as empty, bar a European presence, or by treating them as similar to Europe. Thus Guillaume Delisle's *Carte d'Afrique* (Amsterdam, c.1722) misleadingly divided the whole of Africa into kingdoms with clear frontiers.

The process of naming is readily apparent from modern maps, especially in areas where decolonization has not reversed the process. Dampier's voyage in 1700 led to the naming of islands, such as New Britain, New Ireland, New Hanover and Rooke Island, and of features such as Cape St George, Cape Orford, Cape King William, Cape Anne, St George's Channel and Montagu Harbour. The explorer himself was not forgotten: Cape Dampier, Dampier Strait and Dampier Island are testimony to that. Sailing across the Pacific in 1767, Philip Carteret 'discovered' Osnaburg, Duke of Gloucester and Queen Charlotte islands, each named after a member of the British royal family because Frederick, Prince-Bishop of Osnabrück was also Duke of York, as well as Gower's, Simpson's, Carteret's, Hardy's, Wallis's, Leigh's islands and those of Sandwich, Byron, New Hanover, the Duke of Portland and the Admiralty. Cook's additions included the Hervey Islands and Palmerston Atoll.

The British were far from alone in this process. Easter Island was named because that was the day on which Roggeveen sighted it. In 1821 Bellingshausen discovered and named Peter I and Alexander islands in Antarctica. Similarly, transfers of control led to renaming: in the eighteenth century British annexations from France led to Acadia becoming Nova Scotia, and Île Royale being renamed Cape Breton Island. At another level, those who were enslaved lost their names, and thus had their identities challenged.

Profiting from knowledge

If such naming could make possession seem normative, the general process of acquiring knowledge also had more specific ends. When the French hoped that waterways, and thus trade routes, would lead from Lake Superior to Hudson Bay and the Gulfs of Mexico and California, they were seeking routes for profit as well as prosleytism. Travelling into Wisconsin in 1669, Father Claude Jean Allouez heard of the Mississippi. Two years later, at a ceremonial meeting of Native Americans at Sault-Ste-Marie, French officials laid claim to North America as far as the 'South Sea'. In 1673 a seven-strong mission led by Louis Jolliet, a fur trader, and Father Jacques Marquette set off to find the Mississippi and to travel to its outlet. They travelled as far as the confluence with the Arkansas River. Marquette reported that a route from the Great Lakes to the Gulf of Mexico had been discovered. Naming and map-drawing were parts of this process of extending French knowledge and thus power.

This process could have direct military consequences. In 1736 and 1739 the French launched attacks from New France on the Chickasaws in modern Arkansas. This showed that they could use the Ohio valley to move forces to the Mississippi. They followed the route along the Allegheny and Upper Ohio surveyed in 1729 by Chaussegros de Léry, Chief Engineer of New France.

Similarly, having established bases at San Diego in 1769, Monterey in 1770 and San Francisco in 1776, the Spaniards sought to discover an overland route from Mexico, because boats sailing north along the Pacific coast could be delayed by headwinds. In 1774 and 1775–6 successful overland expeditions were mounted. These, like earlier surveys of the northern frontier of Mexico in the 1720s and 1760s, led to more accurate mapping.

Knowledge served the cause of empire. William Moorcroft, who travelled widely into central Asia in the 1810s and 1820s, crossing the Himalayas in 1812 and reaching Bukhara in 1825, did so, at least officially, in order to find horses for the army of the East India Company, and also to find out about the wool of the Shawl goat.[20] Oceanic voyages identified resources that could be exploited. Thus, Cook reported on the availability of flax, seals, sea-otters, timber and whales. Whalers and fur traders followed.

The process of acquiring and spreading knowledge repeatedly led to change. Thus, following the exploration of the Alaskan coast by Bering and Chirikov in 1741, a Russian company was formed that established fur-trading stations. This led to the near-extermination of the sea-otter and of Steller's sea-cows. As the sea-otter became scarcer, the Russians moved south along the west coast of North

America. Elsewhere, European expansion had a devastating impact on wildlife. The dodo, a bird found on Mauritius and Réunion, became extinct in 1681 as a result of being killed for food and the eating of its eggs by pigs introduced by the Europeans. When the English arrived in the Chesapeake earlier that century, there were numerous buffalo, cougars, elk and wolves, but all were wiped out.

Changes in wildlife could harm Europeans. Cutting down forests in order to provide space for plantations reduced the number of birds and thus allowed the mosquito population to increase. Mosquitoes carried the yellow fever virus. This was an example of the limits of knowledge, for there was little understanding of mortality in the tropics, and, instead, a tendency to understand disease within conventional medical and moral frameworks. Knowledge was designed to be useful, but could only comprehend and accomplish so much.

Nevertheless, knowledge focused on utility: channels to navigate, harbours to use as ports, lands to cultivate and so on. This can be seen not only in official reports, but also in the public discussion of the wider world. Thus, the *St James's Chronicle* of 24 July 1766 printed a letter dated Mobile 21 February that was from Thomas Miller, who was trying to develop a plantation, to John Ellis, King's Agent for West Florida. Having stressed the quantity of wood available, he continued:

> Those swamps appear to me to be good lands, capable of producing either rice, hemp, flax, indigo, or cotton; indeed, indigo and cotton I have seen succeed in them very well. The whole face of the country is covered with grass of so good a kind, that cattle fat to good beef on it . . . the woods abound with deer, turkeys, quails, rabbits, etc. . . . I never saw a place so full of fine fish as this Bay of Mobile.

By 1767 Miller had developed a rice plantation.

The relationship between empire and knowledge was shown at a number of levels. Aside from that of the discourse (or language) in which the two were discussed, it is also appropriate to note the essentials of the infrastructure of acquiring knowledge. Many of those involved were directly in the service of the state, frequently as army officers. They often travelled to distant seas on warships. William Paterson (1755–1810), a British army officer with a strong interest in botany, travelled extensively in southern Africa in 1777–9, reaching the Orange River. His *Narrative of Four Journeys into the Country of the Hottentots and Caffravia* (1789) was dedicated to Sir Joseph Banks and also appeared in a French translation in 1790. Paterson went on to serve in India and Australia, where he ascended the rapids on the Hawkesbury River, and eventually became Lieutenant-Governor. A keen collector of botanical specimens, he left his name on a river, a mountain and a creek in Australia. While not the most forceful of military men, let alone a proconsul of empire, Paterson's career indicated the value of the imperial role for the expansion of European knowledge.

The value of information about distant areas helped to encourage governments to restrict its availability. In particular, the Spanish government tried to keep other

Europeans out of the Pacific and to restrict information about the ocean. In 1680 a band of English buccaneers under Bartholomew Sharp crossed the Isthmus of Darien from the Atlantic to the Pacific. Using a Spanish vessel they had seized off Panama, they then attacked Spanish shipping, before navigating the waters south of Cape Horn from west to east (the first English expedition to do so) and returning to England in 1682. The band included Basil Ringrose, who both wrote a journal of the expedition that was published in an altered form in 1685 (in the second volume of the 1684 London edition of Exquemelin's *Bucaniers of America*) and compiled a substantial 'waggoner' – a description in the form of sailing directions – to much of the coast he sailed along as well as to some parts he never visited. This stemmed from the *derrotero* or set of official manuscript sailing directions, illustrated by a large number of coastal charts, that Sharp seized from a captured Spanish ship in 1681 and that he presented to Charles II of England in order to win royal favour. Such atlases had been regarded by the Spaniards as too confidential to go into print.[21]

More generally, competition was indicated by the different standard meridians used by the maritime powers. For the British, it passed through Greenwich, for the French Paris, the Dutch Amsterdam, the Spaniards Tenerife, and the Portuguese Cape St Vincent. In 1850 the American Congress decided that the National Observatory should be the official prime meridian for the USA. Consistency was not established for a long time, and then only as a grudging acknowledgement of the need for uniformity and of Britain's maritime dominance. An international meeting of 1884 chose the Greenwich meridian as the zero meridian for time-keeping and for the determination of longitude, but the French did not abandon the Paris meridian until 1911 and the American Act of 1850 was not repealed until 1912.[22]

Not all of the process by which knowledge was acquired directly served European imperial states.[23] For example, in 1737–8, Christian VI of Denmark financed an expedition to explore the interior of Egypt, while in 1762 a team of Scandinavian and German experts took part in the first scientific expedition to the Arabian peninsula. Sailing down the Red Sea, this Danish mission visited Yemen, recording its flora and fauna and studying its peoples in 1763–4. Carsten Niebuhr (1733–1815), a German-born surveyor who worked in Denmark and was the sole surviving member of the expedition, published a *Description of Arabia* and *Travels through Arabia* (1772, 1774), accounts that included several detailed maps. However, they did not encourage European imperial expansion in the region, and the expedition itself had only visited a part of Yemen.

Alexander von Humboldt published thirty volumes of data and commentary after his travels in South America in 1799–1804. Much of this was his own work, but he also passed on the material that local scholars had showed him. In combination this was an enormous quantity of material on geological (Humboldt's particular interest), mineralogical, biological, meteorological and other matters. Humboldt was influential in the development of geology as a subject and as an early environmental and ecological (holistic) thinker.

Travellers' accounts

Travel and publication spread knowledge of different environments. North America, for example, had different flora and fauna to that of Europe, as was shown in publications such as Mark Catesby's *The Natural History of Carolina, Florida, and the Bahama Islands* (1731), which was based on his travels in 1712–25. Stephen Long took with him across the Great Plains in 1819 a botanist, a zoologist, a geologist, an assistant naturalist, a landscape painter and two assistant topographers. Edwin James, who replaced the botanist and the geologist in 1820, became the first botanist to reach the alpine flora on Pike's Peak, and left much detail on fauna, geology and Natives in his account published in 1822–3.[24]

The wealth of information discovered about the flora and fauna of other continents posed problems for European classifiers. This was especially true of the very different animals and plants found in Australasia. An artist accompanied Dampier's voyage of 1699–1700 and his drawings were published in Dampier's *Voyage to New Holland*. Far more information came back as a result of Cook's voyages, which returned with sketches, dried specimens and skins, for example of a kangaroo. Banks took two artists with him on Cook's first voyage.[25] Baudin's expedition of 1801–3 to Australasia returned not only with accurate charts, but also with about 200,000 specimens, as well as good descriptions of the Aborigines, resulting in improved knowledge in botany, geology, zoology and anthropology.[26] As exploration brought knowledge of hitherto unknown species, it was harder to credit the biblical account of them all coming from Noah's Ark and Mount Ararat where the Ark supposedly came to rest.[27]

At the same time, knowledge of different animals and plants was seen as valuable, and not only for imperial powers but for Europe as a whole. For example, in 1748–51 the Swedish naturalist Peter Kalm went to North America as a representative of the Swedish Academy of Sciences in order to obtain useful dyestuffs, seeds and plants. As with many travellers, the information was published, his journals being printed in Swedish and also translated into several languages. These, like Niebuhr's books, were examples of the growing volume of available material about the outside world that was increasingly available. Travel literature offered vivid accounts and became an established part of the world of print. Thus, for example, François Bernier's *Voyages*, describing his stay in India in 1656–68, was published in 1709–10. Individual works were given further prominence by being republished in collected works, such as Thomas Astley's *New General Collection of Voyages and Travels* (1745). Interest in travel also led to the publication of translated accounts. Jonathan Carver, who left Michilimackinac in 1766 and spent the winter with Dakota Sioux, published his *Travels to the Interior Parts of North America* in 1778. Fresh editions appeared in 1779, 1784 and 1796, and a French translation in 1784, and the *Travels* appeared in British (1785) and German (1831) collections. In 1826 Humboldt's *Personal Narrative of Travels to the Equinoctial Regions of the New Continent* appeared in London. In addition, material increasingly was rapidly published. Thus, for example, in 1826 Dixon

Denham's *Narrative of Travels and Discoveries in Northern and Central Africa* appeared. It was based on his crossing of the Sahara in 1822–3. Many writers drew heavily on earlier accounts,[28] but the desire for new information and the growing authority of the most recent in European culture in the eighteenth century led to a stress on the authenticity of the latest account.

Travellers' narratives publicized different issues across the full range of human activity and thought, including questions about the causes of human diversity, of God's providential plan, and of the progress and condition of civilization. Such questions were not located in a neutral intellectual world without pronounced values. Instead, as with discussion of place within Europe,[29] changing intellectual and cultural suppositions remoulded assumptions about place and, more generally, about national, ethnic and geographical hierarchies. When travellers wrote about their journeys to the European frontiers they simultaneously contributed to a Eurocentric thesis about the scientific and historical classification of human kinds, and also used that thesis to guide their descriptions. Thus, there was an interdependence of the images of the frontier that travellers constructed and the theories that made sense of life and, more specifically, of the frontier. The debate over what role the environment played in shaping the physical and social identity of those at the frontier was further relevant to understanding the historical identity of Europeans.[30]

Furthermore, the notion of a frontier for European culture served to suggest that it was possible to Europeanize and, therefore, that those who had failed to do so were flawed. The clearest example was Russia under Peter the Great. Emphasizing the role of an individual, and ignoring both his limited success and the activities of his predecessors, Western European commentators, such as Voltaire, presented Peter as bringing Russia into the modern age, and securing its Europeanness, the two being equivalent. *The Oracle: or, Bristol Weekly Miscellany* claimed in 1742, 'since the glorious reformation of Peter the Great, the Russians, from being a lazy, sottish, ignorant, brutish people, are become learned, polite, ingenious, brave and industrious, and as capable of conducting all affairs of government as any of their neighbours'.

As with maps, it is appropriate to note not only bias but also error in the information brought by travellers. There was also straightforward fraud, as in the hoax perpetrated in 1703 by George Psalmanaazar, who arrived in London claiming to be a native of Formosa (Taiwan). He published *An Historical and Geographical Description of Formosa* (1704), with a second edition in 1705, in which he wrote of commonplace cannibalism, a practice that fascinated Europeans, and also provided them with apparently self-evident proof of their superiority. Psalmanaazar, who had also invented a Formosan language, which he was asked to teach to missionaries, was discredited in 1708,[31] but his career is an apt reminder of the need to understand that knowledge had a problematic character in a number of respects.[32]

The grid of control?

Mapping was also important to the local progress of European control and exploitation. It was crucial to the allocation of land, and thus to the way in which terrain was understood and organized for the benefit of Europeans. In addition, towns, including sometimes native areas, were laid out on European-imposed grid plans; although European knowledge of the native quarter was always more limited than that of the European quarter, and this created questions about whether and how best to influence developments in these quarters. Furthermore, there are suggestions that the influence of non-Europeans on settlement patterns has been underrated. This can be seen in discussion of Pondicherry, the leading French base in India. A French base was established in 1673, although the grid system of perpendicular streets was not designed by the French from the outset, but was implemented between 1725 and 1754. However, it has been argued that this represented an extension of earlier local patterns of town layout, and that a relative lack of knowledge of their role in urban morphology reflects a process of Eurocentric selection. Even so, it is clear that in Pondicherry the development of the grid was controlled by the French. For example, the establishment of two main streets, rue de Madras and rue de Valdaour, now Gandhi and Nehru streets, involved evicting people and rebuilding several houses, mostly Indian owned. In the Indian areas brick and tile constructions, not the traditional straw and clay, were imposed.[33]

Mapping and surveying were particularly significant to the process of fortification that was so important in anchoring the European presence around the world. For example, in Pondicherry, a rampart with bastions on the side facing the land was constructed in 1724–35, a rampart on the coast in 1745, and a new Palais du Gouvernement in 1738–52. Large sums were spent on developing a major military and naval base at Louisbourg on Cape Breton Island, which was founded in 1720 in order to support the French presence in the Newfoundland fisheries, and to serve as a halfway port between France and the French West Indies.[34] Québec was extensively fortified, with both redoubts and a series of walls. Walled in 1688, Montréal was given new walls the following century. There were also large numbers of smaller fortifications, each of which could still represent a major change in the local distribution and representation of power.

To Europeans, power was territorial. Territoriality required knowledge – locational specificity – and the construction and acquisition of that knowledge were parts of a more general process by which the Europeans sought to understand the world in their own terms.

Terminology can convey different meanings here and elsewhere; for example, instead of 'understand' it is possible to use the term 'grasp'. Thus, in the nineteenth century the physical geography of the world was measured – seas charted, heights gauged, depths plumbed, rainfall and temperature graphed. All was integrated, so that the world was increasingly understood in terms of a European matrix of knowledge. Areas were given an aggregate assessment – for example, wet, hot, mountainous, forested – that reflected and denoted value and values to Europe. Similarly, regions were grouped together, most prominently as continents, in response to European ideas. Thus, for example, the South Atlantic world of the west coast of Africa, Brazil, the Guianas and the West Indies, was subordinated to a European model in which Africa and the New World were separate.[35] At a smaller scale, modern territorial divisions, for example between the USA and Mexico, affect perceptions of earlier regions. However, just as European perception of other areas and peoples was heavily influenced by earlier views, not least the classical legacy, so, as they came into contact with new peoples, they were also influenced by interlocutors. Thus, pre-existing antagonistic relations between native peoples, and the resulting perceptions, could greatly affect the European newcomers.[36]

Whatever the nature of indigenous spatiality, it was subordinated to imperial cartography after the arrival of European power. The maps that were produced for European governments and purchasers ignored or underrated native peoples and states, presenting Africa and other areas as open to appropriation. This mapping helped to legitimate imperial expansion by making the world appear empty, or at least uncivilized, unless under European control. The drawing of straight lines on maps, without regard to ethnic, linguistic, religious, economic or political alignments and practices, let alone drainage patterns, land forms and biological provinces, was a statement of political control, and an exercise of its use to deny existing indigenous practices and to assert the legitimacy only of the new, and only of a new that derived directly from European control.

Before turning to another end of knowledge, the improvement of commerce, and then the process by which territorial power was spread, it is appropriate to consider attitudes towards the non-European world, for these helped to mould the ends of power and were, in turn, moulded by them.

4

ATTITUDES

Introduction

Views on the societies, religions and cultures of distant areas, and on their actual or potential relationship with those of Europe were extremely varied. A large number of factors were involved in establishing perceptions of these areas, and in the subsequent discussion of them. The nature of the distant society, its religious, political and social organization and wealth were of importance, as were the colour and physiognomy of the population, and the ease with which unchallenged and interesting information could be obtained. The interests, commercial, strategic and religious, of European powers were of great significance in moulding attitudes.[1] Attitudes towards distant areas and their European links were often dependent on national preferences. It was relatively easy for a British or a Dutch writer to condemn transoceanic Catholic proselytism as cruel.

This focuses attention on the difficulty of judging attitudes. For example, because treatment of European expansion concentrates on peoples and societies that the Europeans came to dominate, and frequently exploit, there has been a misleading teleology of European supremacy. So it is necessary also to consider interactions with peoples, cultures and states capable of defeating Europeans, such as the Ottoman (Turkish) empire at the beginning of the period, in order, for example, to avoid the 'misleading conclusion of an inevitable English triumph and a ubiquitous English haughtiness'.[2]

The nature of this interaction is obscure for a number of reasons. First, there was the difficulty of discussing and conceptualizing what was poorly, if at all, understood outside the zone of interaction. Second, there was a habit of conceiving of the distant world principally as an extension of the near by, especially of its problems, configurations and patterns of causality. Thus, West Africa and the Indian Ocean were largely seen in terms of relations with other European powers, rather than as civilizations in their own right. Similarly, the Ottoman empire tended to be seen foremost as a sphere for commercial competition. As such, it was perceived and used to register particular interpretations of English/British and French economic strength and commercial politics, rather than to forward any understanding of Ottoman society and culture. This was indeed the perspective from, say, Marseilles or Halifax, and a concentration on the zone of interaction can serve to distract attention from the processes by which, and the purposes for which, images of abroad were constructed.

This chapter begins with religion, a crucial aspect of the European consciousness and world-view of the period, and one that is too frequently overlooked today.

Religion

Religion helped to define the world outside Europe. The part of it that was settled by Europeans could be seen in confessional terms and was also affected by similar religious movements, for example the Protestant evangelical proselytizing of the 1720s and 1730s, which had a major impact in British North America.[3] Furthermore, confessional links helped to join Europe and the colonial world. The extensive missionary effort towards non-Christians, both those within and those outside areas of colonial control, and the integration of the two, was an important effort and a link between Europe and the colonial world. Missionary activity attracted support from both clergy and laity. In the Catholic world the Papacy sought to organize missionary activity by the Sacred Congregation 'de Propaganda Fide', and religious orders, particularly Capuchins, Carmelites, Dominicans, Jesuits and Recollects, played major roles; part of a longer process reaching back to the earliest centuries AD. However, the Catholic rulers of France, Spain and Portugal sought to limit any control by Rome and, instead, to set ecclesiastical strategies within and from their colonies themselves. In Russia, where the Orthodox Church was very much under state control, missionaries were sent to Alaska.

In Protestant Britain there was a major missionary thrust. The Society for the Promotion of Christian Knowledge, founded in 1698, was followed by the Society for the Propagation of the Gospel in Foreign Parts, established in 1701, which was particularly active in Britain's New World colonies, sending large numbers of clergymen. The society was more successful among slaves than among Natives.[4] Later, these societies were joined by the Baptist Missionary Society (1792), the London Missionary Society (1795), the Scottish Missionary Society (1799), the Church Missionary Society (1799) and the Wesleyan Missionary Society (1813). The Church Missionary Society (until 1812 the Society for Missions to Africa and the East) in 1807 sent out Robert Morrison to proselytize in China, but he was not allowed to penetrate beyond the permitted foreign trading areas, and the situation did not change until after the Treaty of Nanjing in 1842. The British and Foreign Bible Society, established in 1804, spread the word in another way.

Individual missionaries played a major role in expanding the European presence. Robert Moffat (1795–1883), who became a missionary for the London Missionary Society in 1816, went beyond the frontier of Cape Colony, north into Namibia. Nine years later he laid out a new mission station at Kuruman. Moffat learned the Sechwana language and translated part of the Bible into it. In 1829 he erected a church and a schoolhouse at the mission. In 1830 the government allowed its printing office to be used to print Moffat's translation. Moffat was to be father-in-law to the great explorer of Africa David Livingstone. In the Pacific the first missionaries reached Tahiti in 1797.

The British were not the only Protestant missionaries: for example, Danish missionaries spread Protestantism in India and Greenland. Indeed, the first Protestant mission to India began at the Danish base of Tranquebar in 1706.[5] New England Congregationalist missionaries arrived in Hawaii in 1820 and the island was rapidly converted. The missionaries established schools, trained native teachers and provided literacy, but they also sought to transform society, and have been blamed for cultural decline and demoralization. Under Kamehameha II (r.1819–25), who aligned himself with the missionaries, temples and images of gods were destroyed while the religious taboos that had provided social parameters were abolished.[6]

Missionary activity was not always welcome, as the British discovered in India (where there were also effective indigenous Christian sects),[7] and this created problems for colonial administrators. Most, in Asia, arrived at a solution that privileged Christian activity, while allowing the native population and other immigrant groups the exercise of their religions. The situation was harsher where the natives were seen as primitive, as in Africa and, even more, Australia.

The most prominent missionary effort, until the suppression of the order by Pope Clement XIV in 1773, was that by the Society of Jesus, and this indicates the difficulty of separating religious from other factors, for the Jesuits were not just a religious order, skilled in self-publicity and the most meticulous historians of their own activities, who ran missions in Asia, Africa and the Americas. The society was also an intellectual enterprise that provided and supported leading explorers, scholars and scientists, and a massive business enterprise, owning land, slaves and trading and manufacturing concerns, and investing money for others. The drive to make converts and to further the mission was linked to their business interests.[8]

The Jesuits also revealed a different attitude to the native population than that shown by most Europeans. In South America they created *reducciones*, frontier settlements, where natives grew crops and tended animals under Jesuit supervision. These far-flung settlements were eventually seen as an infringement on governmental sovereignty, as no Spaniards other than Jesuits could enter the mission zone, but they also represented an anchoring of the European presence and, more specifically, helped define the Spanish position against Portuguese expansion. Indeed, the *reducciones* resisted the slave-traders from São Paulo (in Portuguese-ruled Brazil) known as Paulistas or *mamelucos*, who had done much to lower native numbers. In Amazonia the Jesuits also established mission settlements, such as Abacaxís. Other missions were established by the Calced Carmelites, Franciscans and Mercedarians.

The growing determination of European governments to control their colonies and their profits in the second half of the eighteenth century led to the end of the Jesuit missions. This also drew on a sense that the Jesuits were a sinister and unwelcome influence in European government. In 1754 Portuguese and Spanish troops enforced an agreement between their governments on the border between Paraguay and Brazil that transferred mission territory, and in 1767 the Jesuits were expelled.[9]

The Jesuits had played a major role throughout the Catholic world. They arrived in Pondicherry in India in 1689, where the French had established a base in 1673, and built a large church there in 1699. By contemporary European standards, the Jesuits had an acute awareness of non-European cultures, and were particularly important in spreading knowledge about Asia,[10] publishing a large number of reports, such as Du Halde's *Description . . . de la Chine* (1735). Their determination to learn languages and not infringe native customs helped overcome one of the leading problems for Europeans in their quest to understand the non-European world, linguistic ignorance. In China Jesuit missionaries sought to accommodate Christianity to Chinese customs, particularly ancestor-worship, as part of an attempt to create a dialogue with Chinese culture, but also to show how the Christian message completed Chinese culture. However, their Franciscan and Dominican rivals accused the Jesuits of accepting pagan rites, and both their practice of accommodation (syncretism) and the Chinese rites were condemned by papal pronouncements (in 1704, 1715 and 1742).[11] The Jesuits duly desisted, showing the limits of syncreticism in this period, but also the extent to which contact with non-Europeans tested European assumptions and forced them to consider how best to respond. To illustrate the range of Jesuit activity, in 1672 Charles Albanel reached James Bay, the southern extension of Hudson Bay.

Elsewhere, the tradition of conquest for Christ remained strong, and difficulties experienced in proselytism led to a harsh attitude that also justified imperial expansion. State and Church could be closely linked. When, for example, Nojpeten, the capital of the Maya people known as Itzas, was stormed in 1697, Martín de Ursúa, the interim Governor of Yucatán, ordered his men to plant the flag with the royal arms of Spain and religious standards among the Itza temples 'in which the majesty of God had been offended by idolatries'. Ursúa thanked God for his victory and then joined soldiers and Franciscans in destroying a large number of 'idols'. This was religious war against opponents presented as guilty of human sacrifice, cannibalism and killing priests.[12] Five years earlier, when Santa Fe was regained by the Spaniards after the Pueblo rebellion of 1680, there had also been a reimposition of Catholic control: Franciscan priests absolved Natives of their apostasy and baptized those born after 1680, with the governor serving as godfather for the children of the prominent. In the first clash for control of Lower California, the battle for Loreto Conchó of 1697, a well-armed Spanish missionary party fought off a Native attack. Victory was followed by the spread of Christianity; as elsewhere during the Iberian conquest of Latin America, smaller, weaker native groups proved more receptive to conversion.[13]

The same was true in the eastern Aleutian Islands where massacre by Russians and European diseases had led to a dramatic fall in the population. Mass conversions of the Kodiak Aleutians began in 1794. On the other side of the

Pacific, the Spaniards had established a mission on Guam in 1668, the first European post on a Pacific island distant from East Asia. This mission was supported by troops, and the island chain was renamed the Marianas to signify the role of religion. Spanish missionaries from the Philippines reached the Palaus in 1710, but a hostile response cut short the opening.

Spreading the faith was seen as a reason why European expansion succeeded: it fulfilled God's purpose, and in return deserved benefits such as trade and land. Rather than interpreting religious explanations of, and calls for, European expansion as anachronistic, it is important to note their continued vitality, which looked towards both the role of missionaries and religious conceptions of a European civilizing colonial role in the nineteenth century. Religious discussions of empire could take a number of forms. For example, in 1762 Arthur Dobbs, Governor of North Carolina, sent the government a memorandum in which he called for liberating and improving the New World by free trade and Christianization. Britain was then at war with Spain, and Dobbs suggested that the British

> publish manifestos in the Spanish tongue on landing . . . declaring the Spanish colonies free states to be governed by laws framed by themselves after the model of British liberty under the protection of Britain as a perpetual ally with a free trade most favourable to Britain . . . to retain, as cautionary pledges of the future friendship and fidelity of those colonies, Vera Cruz, Havana, Portobello and the isthmus of Darien, Cartagena, Hispaniola and the other Spanish islands. Spanish Florida to be entirely ceded to Britain . . . to send missionaries to civilize and Christianize the natives where the Spaniards have no settlements and to form them into regular polities under the direction of governors truly Christian and educated for that purpose in Britain at the expense of the public.[14]

It would be unwise to minimize the extent to which warfare with the Turks and with other Islamic powers, principally the Barbary States of North Africa, played a continuing role in sustaining hostility to Islam, and thus a sense of the non-Western world as hostile. This was particularly true of the Catholic and Orthodox world, but far less so of its Protestant counterpart, which was not so threatened by Turkish power. Wars with the Turks were presented as crusades and seen as the struggles of Christian Europe, rather than as simply of concern to the particular states at war. In 1668–9 Louis XIV of France sent troops to help in the defence of Venetian-ruled Candia in Crete. However, the island, invaded by the Turks in 1645, finally succumbed in 1669: the siege of Candia had been an epic struggle that had been followed closely in Europe, especially in Italy. The same was true of the Turkish siege of Vienna in 1683. The relief of the city was widely greeted throughout Europe. The failure of the Turkish siege of Corfu in 1717 made less of an impact, but was still of great interest in Italy.

The crusading attitude receded from the mid-eighteenth century, in large part because of the long period of peace between Austria and the Turks from the Treaty of Belgrade of 1739 until 1788. Furthermore, due to the advance of the frontier of Christendom into the Balkans in the war of 1716–18, Turkish successes in the conflict of 1737–9, while serious, did not threaten the heartlands of Christian power.

However, even from 1740 to 1788 there was a series of institutions and events to remind Christians of their ancestral opponent: for example, attempts to raise funds to buy back Christians captured by Barbary privateers; although the *Pères trinitaires* only redeemed Catholics. There were also several thousand captured Muslims used as slaves in mid-eighteenth-century Italy, mostly on the galleys. The Order of Malta, a sovereign Catholic crusading order that ruled that island, had branches throughout Catholic Europe, especially in France. Earlier, Louis XIV had taken seriously his role as Protector of the Order.[15] More generally, the Very Christian King of France was the Protector of the Catholics in the Turkish empire.

Turkish themes became more important in the creative arts and the Turks provided knowledge of inoculation, although Turkey might have become less viable as a point of comparison for writers about Europe. However, Turkey continued to play a major role in affecting public perceptions about a hostile world on Europe's immediate frontiers. More generally, negative attitudes towards Islam helped colour responses towards not only Turkey but also other Islamic societies, especially those of North Africa.[16] A study of images of Islam in the work of French writers of the early eighteenth century notes that the limited good that writers found in it appeared to derive entirely from Christianity or Judaism.[17] Mohammed was still widely regarded as a fraud.

This is an important reminder of the need for caution in exaggerating the impact of new concerns with the outside world. In particular, there is a danger that a focus on Protestant Europe, more specifically on Britain and the United Provinces, and especially on mercantile interests and related lobbies and 'discourses', will lead to a misunderstanding of the placing of the outside world by Europeans, and an underrating of different attitudes.

The influence of distant areas

Aside from stressing the vitality of religious approaches towards the outside world, it is necessary to note the extent to which European opinion was not engaged with this world. This was not only true of Eastern Europe, but even of major imperial states. For example, the landed nobility was crucial to power in France, and the role of land in elite identity was underlined under Napoleon by his reliance on a new service aristocracy who were provided with estates. The nobility was far more interested in the army than the navy, and in the land rather than trade or empire. These values affected French society as a whole. The loss of Canada in 1760 and Louisiana in 1763 was criticized in mercantile circles in the Atlantic ports, but had only limited impact elsewhere, not least because they were seen in fashionable circles as barren and profitless. Aristocratic families had scant presence in French North America.

The cultural influence of distant areas was often dependent on the extent to which they could be used by writers and others to make comments on their own countries; while in economic terms trade with colonies was the means by which merchants transformed themselves into landed gentry. The goal of merchants was not focused on the wider world, but on the means of enhancing social status in Europe and the colonies.

As a source of motifs, distant areas, especially the Orient, were important, but artistically their impact was not generally significant. If European settlers absorbed to a small extent the local styles, devices and instruments in architecture and music, these were of limited consequence in Europe, although, in the late eighteenth century, a *chinoiserie* movement was all the rage in the decorative arts, especially furniture, tapestries and paintings. William Chambers (1723–96), who, very unusually among those who worked in the arts, had travelled to China, both built in Oriental styles in the gardens of the palace at Kew and published his *Designs of Chinese Buildings* (1757), the first record by a European architect of Chinese architecture, and a *Dissertation on Oriental Gardening* (1772).[18] Sometimes, Oriental motifs were seen as curiosities akin to the animals that were obtained for menageries, such as those Louis XVI obtained from Algiers in the 1780s, including four ostriches,[19] or the giraffe which was brought to Paris in the 1820s, exciting immense curiosity as it crossed France.

In contrast many writers were willing to create and use a literary image of particular distant societies. In part this was based on knowledge of their practices and, to a lesser extent, literature. Confucius was available in translation. In 1734 George Sale published an English translation of the Koran, arguing that 'to be acquainted with the various laws and constitutions of civilized nations, especially of those who flourish in our own time, is perhaps, the most useful part of knowledge'.[20] This was not, however, intended by Sale to suggest any equivalence. Instead, he was certain that Providence had reserved the glory of the overthrow of Islam to the Protestants.

Noble savages

Most European intellectuals, particularly prior to the mid-eighteenth century, had a very limited knowledge of distant cultures, and throughout the period very few had travelled outside Europe. Dependent for their knowledge on the writings of others, they could be misled by inaccurate information, such as the Patagonian giants reported by John Byron on his circumnavigation of 1764–6, or unduly influenced by particular impressions.

The island of Tahiti in the Pacific, described by Bougainville and Cook, was presented as an earthly paradise, a Garden of Eden without Christianity. Aside from the beauty of the island, the pleasantness of the climate, the quality and exotic nature of the food, and the sexual freedom of the inhabitants all attracted attention. Tahiti was named New Cythera by Bougainville after the fabled realm of Aphrodite; his naturalist wanted to call it Utopia. In his *Supplement au Voyage de Bougainville* (1773), Diderot presented the Tahitians as noble primitives whose moral openness was a worthy counterpoint to the artificialities of European culture and the restrictive strictures of Christianity. Thus, and this point attracted considerable attention, sex was possible without sin, and promiscuity could be part of a benign moral order.

The painters who accompanied Cook, such as William Hodges and John Webber, provided a powerful visual image of the South Seas. They were responding both to the desire for pictures in published accounts and to the determination to record biological and ethnographic information accurately. It has been suggested that Alexander Buchan's painting of the Patagonian Onas in 1769 may be the first contemporary visual record made by Europeans of their meeting with non-Europeans. However, it is misguided to suggest that the engravings produced to illustrate distant places and peoples were necessarily the same as field sketches: there were changes, although it is misleading to see these in terms of some conspiracy. Instead, there was a degree to which works were changed to conform to stylistic norms.

The process of illustration was not restricted to the Pacific. Hodges (1744–97) was draughtsman on Cook's second voyage. After he returned he was employed by the Admiralty in finishing his drawings, and in superintending their engraving. Hodges also painted in India between 1778 and 1784 and in 1793 published an account of his *Travels in India*. His Indian paintings had already been engraved for a British market fascinated by distant lands. The excitement and exotic aspects of the sub-continent were also captured by other painters, such as Johann Zoffany, who spent from 1783 until 1789 in India.[21] The Pacific, as in Hodges's *Tahiti Revisited*, offered a vista of paradise, and of truly noble figures, as in Joshua Reynolds's portrait of Omai, a Pacific islander brought back from Cook's second expedition.[22]

The seductive portrayal of innocent children of nature was true only in part, but it served to challenge conventional European views and to help in the redefinition of what was considered to be natural behaviour. Expeditions that visited both Alaska and the South Pacific contrasted the inhabitants of the latter favourably with the former. The Pacific islands appeared to offer a primitive but beneficent social harmony that challenged civilization and Christianity and made a mockery of the notion that the strictures of the latter were moral and necessary. Thus, exploration in overturning earlier fantasies about the Antipodes provided a site for a new idyll.

Alternative readings of the Pacific islanders were at first downplayed. Wallis's expedition had in fact discovered not a primitive Utopia but a complex society with rulers, aristocracy, private property, priestcraft and feuding. Cook also stressed the presence of private property, law and social ranks, and thus of a civilization whose fundamentals were similar to those of Europe, albeit with major differences, such as the absence of Christianity. More pointedly, the discovery of human sacrifice put the stress on savage, and on a savagery without appeal, and the killing of Cook in 1779 further contributed to a sense of brutishness. One of Lapérouse's captains, Paul de Langle, was killed by Natives on Samoa, and Lapérouse was sceptical about the notion of the noble savage. A process of mutual disappointment with contact between Europeans and islanders became more insistent.

Yet favourable accounts still appeared in print. George Keate's *Account of the Pelew Islands, from the Journals of Captain Henry Wilson and some of his officers, shipwrecked there in the Antelope in August 1783* (1788) was a considerable success, with five London editions by 1803 and French (1793) and German (1800) translations, an indication of the extent to which knowledge of British maritime endeavour was widely disseminated. Wilson and his crew found a friendly reception, and brought back to Britain the 'Prince' Lee Boo, who became a celebrity before dying of smallpox in 1784.[23]

Whether or not European commentators presented the South Sea islanders in a benign fashion, they tended to have few doubts about Europe's contact with them. In his *The History of the Decline and Fall of the Roman Empire* (1776–88), Gibbon (IV, 168–9) was convinced of the general benefit of European expansion:

> every age of the world has increased and still increases the real wealth, the happiness, the knowledge, and perhaps the virtue of the human race. The merit of discovery has too often been stained with avarice, cruelty and fanaticism; and the intercourse of nations has produced the communication of disease and prejudice. A singular exception is due to the virtue of our own times and country. The five great voyages, successively undertaken by the command of his present Majesty, were inspired by the pure and generous love of science and mankind ... introduced into the islands of the South Sea the vegetables and animals most useful to human life.

In his acceptance of the harshness of 'discovery', Gibbon revealed enlightened susceptibilities, but his account was also Eurocentric: savages were to receive gifts. Cook introduced pigs and possibly the white potato as well as exotic weeds to New Zealand. Leaving aside the serious issue of ecological imperialism,[24] a present-minded critique of Gibbon's account might emphasize the possibilities of a more multifaceted treatment of human happiness and progress, and would contrast his relative openness to the value of non-European religion, especially Islam, with a failure to appreciate other aspects of the cultures of those he termed barbarian.

The presentation of South Sea islanders as noble savages benefited from the novelty of European contact with them. There was a longer and more complex discussion of the Native Americans. They could be seen as virtuous primitives or as degenerate, the latter a theme of the influential French naturalist George-Louis Buffon (1707–88). In a pioneering anthropological study which influenced Rousseau, *Moeurs des sauvages americaines comparée aux moeurs des premiers temps* (1724), Joseph Lafitau, a French Jesuit who had spent some of the 1710s among the Iroquois, presented the Native Americans as a living model of human society in its primitive form.[25]

The cult of the noble savage, whether found in the South Seas, among the Native Americans, or located in the myths of national history, such as the primitive Goths, was but one instance of the use of comparison as a form of judgement. Though certain writers employed fantastical journeys, such as to the moon or Lilliput, most relied on contemporary societies that, supposedly, could be reported objectively and which anyway were known to exist. The Orient was the most important region, at least in the first half of the eighteenth century. Africa and the Pacific were then mostly unknown to Europeans, as was the interior of North America. They did not appear to contain developed societies and cultures comparable to those of southern and eastern Asia. In Central and South America, the developed native societies that were known to the Europeans had been brought under Spanish control, the Mayas of the Yucatán being finally conquered in the 1690s. When Voltaire presented a perfect native South American society in *Candide* (1759), his Eldorado had to be located on a plateau surrounded by unscalable mountains and reached by his hero only after twenty-four hours on an underground river.

Responses to the Orient

In contrast, Persia, India and China, especially the last, had long been familiar and were to be employed by writers such as Montesquieu and Lyttelton, who published letters supposedly from a Persian in Europe to a compatriot at home in 1721 and 1735, respectively. Similarly, Oliver Goldsmith used a fictional wise Chinaman, Lien Chi Altangi, in his *The Citizen of the World* (1762). French Jesuits in early eighteenth-century India had already been struck by the similarities between French and Indian societies, the caste system, and the hierarchical distinctions and psychological barriers of societies or orders. Russia could serve as a similar frame of reference for Europe at the beginning of the eighteenth century, but it was a measure of the perceived Europeanization of the country that it lost this role.

The Orient was unsettling and also stimulating precisely because it presented developed civilizations that seemed equal or superior to that of Europe and owed nothing to what were regarded by Europeans as central to modern civilization, particularly Christianity, the religious framework of morality, and the classical legacy of Greece and Rome. The vitality of medieval Islam had long ensured that the achievements and ideology of Christian Europe were seen as relative, and that the pluralistic nature of world civilization had been grasped. This process was taken much further as a consequence of the European voyages of discovery. Considerable knowledge was acquired and this played a major role in the development not only of opinions about the non-European world, but also in comparing it with Europe. These opinions came to play a greater role in European intellectual life, especially as they were disseminated in books. Herbelot de Molinville's *Bibliothèque orientale*

(1697) was a particularly important work in organizing knowledge, although, in more recent days, it has been criticized for Eurocentricism.[26] Because of conflict between Christianity and Islam, not least the Crusades, Islamic culture could be depicted as anti-Christian, infidel and demonic. Oriental culture entailed no such conflicts and therefore was seen as neutral, which could make it unsettling.

Such knowledge and opinion played a role in debates within Europe. For example, some discussion of Louis XIV's revocation of the Edict of Nantes in 1685 stressed the relative freedom of thought prevalent in Mughal India, an Islamic state.[27] Similarly, British Deists were able to praise Islam as showing signs of 'natural' religion: that is, an uncorrupted monotheism. This could be contrasted with the Christian Churches.[28]

In contrast to Islam, Chinese society was not Judaic in its origin, nor obviously dominated by revealed religion and monotheistic theology. The comparative challenge it could be made to pose was indicated by Voltaire's *Essai sur les Moeurs* (1756), which continued the writer's campaign to scour history and the world in order to establish standards by which contemporary France could be judged.

The eighteenth century, however, witnessed a gradual shift away from the Orient as a point of reference for European writers. Usbek and Rica, the two Persian visitors in Montesquieu's *Lettres Persanes* (1721), could serve to comment on Pope Clement XI as a 'conjurer who makes people believe that three are only one; that wine is not wine and bread not bread', a sweeping attack on transubstantiation, while Selim, their counterpart in Lyttelton's *Letters from a Persian in England, to his friend at Ispahan* (1735), could be used to cover an attack on the leading British minister Sir Robert Walpole, closing with the reflection: 'if slavery is to be endured, where is the man that would not rather choose it, under the warm sun of Agra [India] or Ispahan [in Persia], than in the northern climate and barren soil of England?' However, Persia was in decline, and the 1720s and 1730s were a period when the chaos caused by civil war there was widely reported in the European press, sufficiently so for a leading British racehorse to be named after Nadir Shah.

Ottoman defeats between 1683 and 1718 reduced Turkish prestige. Turkey was believed to be in decline, and the ambivalent Turkish stance towards Christian Europe, in particular the borrowing of military technology and experts, reduced its possible usefulness as a source of alternative values. The British writer Henry Fielding, in his play *Rape upon Rape or the Coffee-House Politician* (1730), satirized the fears of Politic, who is so concerned about reports of international developments that he neglects threats to his daughter's virtue. His first soliloquy is devoted to the Turks: 'I cannot rest for these preparations of the Turks . . . Should the Turkish galleys once find a passage through the Straits [of Gibraltar], who can tell the consequence?' (I, iii). He returned to his concern in the following scene, and again in the next act (II, xi):

I dread and abhor the Turks. I wish we do not feel them before we are aware . . . what can be the reason of all this warlike preparation, which all our newspapers have informed us of? . . . Is the design against Germany? Is the design against Italy? – Suppose we should see Turkish galleys in the Channel? We may feel them, yes, we may feel them in the midst of our security. Troy was taken in its sleep, and so may we . . . should the Turks come among us, what would become of our daughters then? . . . and our religion, and our liberty? . . . Give us leave only to show you how it is possible for the Grand Signior to find an ingress into Europe. Suppose, Sir, this spot I stand on to be Turkey – then here is Hungary – very well – here is France, and here is England – granted – then we will suppose he had possession of Hungary – what then remains but to conquer France, before we find him at our own coast . . . this is not all the danger . . . he can come by sea to us.

This was at once resonant of past fears and also satire.

Egypt, which was a largely autonomous part of the Turkish empire, was seen as an example of fallen greatness, and thus a dramatic instance of the bankruptcy of non-European cultures. The scholars who accompanied Napoleon to Egypt in 1798 greatly advanced knowledge of ancient Egypt and its civilization. Napoleon hoped that the scholars would not only acquire knowledge but would also further his wish to establish a benevolent and progressive administration. Organized in the Institut d'Egypt, the scholars made little impact on Egyptian culture, but they helped to increase and satisfy European interest in Egypt. Major publications included the *Voyage dans la Basse et la Haute Egypt, pendant les campagnes du général Bonaparte* (1802) by Baron Dominique Vivant Denon, which created an *égyptomanie*. It was reprinted in over forty editions and translated into English, German and other languages. The *Description de l'Egypte* that resulted from the expedition appeared in twenty-one volumes from 1809 to 1822.

Egypt fused the widening interest in antiquity with the interest in the East, and was to be a rich source of cultural and intellectual inspiration. However, this was an interest in Egypt past. The *Description* presented Egypt as having declined since antiquity, the Egyptians as timid, passive and indifferent, and their rulers as barbaric and superstitious. Clearly, it would benefit from French rule.[29] 'Jewels', such as obelisks, could be plucked from such a decayed civilization and used to enhance European townscapes.

The obvious weakness of the Mughal empire after the death of Aurangzeb in 1707 made India seem weak and in disorder. Modern scholarship has questioned the degree to which the crisis of Mughal power or, more generally, the problems of eighteenth-century India was a sign of degeneracy, but many European commentators were apt to suggest decline. They were less awed by the Marathas than they had been by the Mughals.

A sense of a new triumphant deity in India, or at least destiny, was offered by the cartouche to a map of India published in 1782 by James Rennell, former Surveyor-General of the Bengal Presidency, after his return to England. It showed Britannia receiving the sacred scriptures of India from a Brahman. Four years earlier, Spiridion Roma had been commissioned by the directors of the East India Company to paint the ceiling of their Leadenhall Street headquarters. His *The East Offering its Riches to Britannia* showed India and China, both as women, indeed presenting their riches.[30]

A sense of Indian political weakness was compatible with growing European cultural interest in the sub-continent, but most commentators who were willing to adopt a favourable view saw India in terms of a glorious past, akin to classical Greece, rather than an advancing modern society. That did not necessarily encourage a determination to change Indian society. Warren Hastings, Governor of Bengal from 1772 to 1774 and in 1774–84 the first Governor-General, believed that each society had its own politico-cultural genius, and that it should be adhered to, not violated. This conservative notion of institutional authority, which did not encourage any attempt to impose British laws and institutions, was qualified under Marquis Cornwallis (Governor-General 1786–93), particularly in his creation of the Permanent Settlement in Bengal in 1793. However, by the early nineteenth century British policy had reverted to its earlier conservatism, with a strong willingness to preserve 'ancient' institutions seen, for example, in the careers of Sir Thomas Munro (Governor of Madras 1819–27) and Charles, Lord Metcalfe, who had a series of posts in India in the first half of the century. Munro was responsible for strengthening the position of Native judges and for confirming the role of local courts of arbitration, and he emphasized the value of using Natives in government. He understood and appreciated Indian customs.

From the mid-eighteenth century more was published on India, and information became more rapidly and regularly available. Thus, Henry Vansittart's *Narrative of Transactions in Bengal, 1760–1764* was published in 1766. Sir William Jones, who made his reputation translating Persian works in the 1770s, producing a *Grammar of the Persian Language* in 1771, mastered Sanskrit in the following decade, and translated several Hindu classics. Founding the Bengal Asiatic Society in 1784, he studied Indian languages, literature and philosophy. This engagement with India was particularly the case with the British and, to a lesser extent, the French. Britain's ever closer involvement in India brought first-hand acquaintance with contemporary Hindus and Zoroastrians who were found to have some of the same components in their faith as were present in Judaeo-Christianity, for example the story of a great flood. These contacts with non-Christian societies offered plenty of ammunition for critics of the Churches. The Scottish Deist Alexander Dow, author of the *History of Hindustan* (1766–72), who was anxious to demonstrate the moral superiority of Hinduism to Christianity, was opposed by both Jones and a former army chaplain, the Reverend Thomas Maurice, author of *Indian Antiquities* (1793–1800).[31]

Japan and Korea, in contrast, were able to preserve a self-imposed isolation. Japan, with its population of about 30 million in 1800, was unwilling to trade with Europeans, except through a small artificial island in Nagasaki harbour.

Only China appeared territorially powerful. Between 1680 and 1760 the Manchu dynasty conquered Taiwan, Outer Mongolia, Tibet, the Amur valley, eastern Turkestan, Dzungaria (Xinjiang), Tsinghai and southeastern Kazakhstan, a formidable amount of territory that brought rule over a large number of non-Chinese peoples. Nevertheless, China participated in the general lessening of approval that marked European intellectual attitudes towards the Orient in the second half of the eighteenth century, and even more in the early nineteenth. The Oriental powers were increasingly seen as weak, regarded as especially stagnant domestically, and as unable to offer the intellectual dynamism and respect for the individual that were sought by European commentators.

Chinese culture was criticized by Rousseau and Diderot, who refuted notions of Chinese superiority. The end of the Jesuits' mission in China and the growth in trade ensured that relations with the empire were more frequently seen in commercial terms. China became another market, rather than a model. Furthermore, the varied intellectual developments within Europe in the late eighteenth century, especially primitivism, neo-classicism, Romanticism and Hellenism, left little room for intellectual or cultural interest in China.[32]

North America

The relative shift in interest from the Orient, first to the Pacific islanders in their supposed 'state of nature', and then to the civilized, and yet reputedly free and egalitarian, American settlers, who rebelled against George III in 1775, was a response both to a general shift in sensibility and to the tyranny of fashion that increasingly influenced informed circles. Furthermore, prior to the revolution, British America had been understood by Europeans as very different to their societies. Ignoring the hardship undergone by Natives and slaves, they saw it as a new land of liberty and of freedom from many of the burdens of the Old World, albeit one that was culturally backward.

There was cause for at least the first two arguments. Modern social historians have not shown that contemporary participants in the intellectual construction of America were wrong in any of their major claims. As contemporaries almost universally attested, the societies of colonial British and revolutionary America, in comparison with those of Europe, did indeed have significantly higher proportions of property holders, higher rates of family formation, broader opportunities for achieving economic independence and personal 'empowerment', less poverty, fewer and less rigid social distinctions, and less powerful and obtrusive political and religious establishments.

The notion of America as a land to which freedom was natural underwent a powerful revival among European commentators during the era of the American Revolution, when American exceptionalism took on political weight.[33] Of course, just as not all 'progressive' writers had praised China, so doubts were expressed about the paradisaical qualities of Tahiti and the Potomac. The Hessian soldiers sent to fight the Americans were not alone in their conviction that the American treatment of their slaves formed a hypocritical contrast with their claims of the equality of man.[34]

Nevertheless, for many, America came to occupy the place of China, Christian Schubart writing in his *Deutsche Chronik* in 1777: 'Oh, you beloved America, you are still the hobbyhorse upon which we journalists can canter at ease.'[35] American independence provided a concrete instance of the possibility of a completely fresh start, as well as a citizens' army and a written constitution. It offered an exciting perspective, bringing change and democracy from the realms of Utopian fancy, revealing the weakness of the old order, and showing that internal strife could produce radical reform, rather than simple anarchy.

However, independent America was not the equivalent of China in offering a potential comparison with European civilization. The American War of Independence, the greatest transoceanic military commitment by any European power in the period, was a civil war not only within a political entity, the British empire, but also within the Christian European community. The war also upset Protestant apologists, such as Granville Sharp, in that it involved Protestants fighting Protestants, and thereby weakened the faith in the face of the Catholic enemy. Far from broadening the knowledge of other civilizations, independent America could be taken to be an alternative model for Europe from within the European world. It was also a model for future British colonies, especially the 'white' dominions.

Controlling non-Westerners

Another theme of the late eighteenth century, agitation for the abolition of the slave trade, revealed that, in an age when European empires were extending their sway, attitudes towards other peoples were complex, and a sense of fellow humanity, always present in the Christian message, was not absent. Indeed, it echoed throughout the period. A sense of humanity affronted, and morality breached, by slavery can be seen in the tale of 'Inkle and Yarico' published in the leading English periodical the *Spectator* on 13 March 1711:

> Mr Thomas Inkle, an ambitious young English trader cast ashore in the Americas, is saved from violent death at the hands of savages by the endearments of Yarico, a beautiful Indian maiden. Their romantic intimacy in the forest moves Inkle to pledge that, were his life to be preserved, he would return with her to England, supposedly as his wife. The lovers' tender liaison progresses over several months until she succeeds in signalling a passing English ship. They are rescued by the crew, and with vows to each other intact, they embark for Barbados. Yet when they reach the island Inkle's former mercantile instincts are callously revived, for he sells her into slavery, at once raising the price he demands when he learns that Yarico is carrying his child.

This was but a stage in a tale that had surfaced in Richard Ligon's *History of the Island of Barbadoes* (1657), but it was the most influential stage. The *Spectator* was published in all the major European languages, and the account of it was taken up by a number of prominent writers. Although Goethe never wrote his planned play on the subject, other German writers, including Christian Gellert and Salomon Gessner, tackled it. A French adaptation, *La Jeune Indienne*, by Sébastian-Roche Nicolas Chamfort, was successfully staged at the Comédie-Française in 1764. The period of the story's greatest currency was when the abolition of the slave trade was a central theme in public debate. Thereafter, it rapidly declined.[36] Abbé Raynal's influential *Histoire philosophique et politique des établissements et du commerce des Européens dans les deux Indes* (1770) became, especially in its 1774 and 1780 editions, a channel for the expression of progressive ideas, such as free trade, colonial rights, anticlericalism and anti-slavery.[37]

However, this sense of fellow humanity was far from uniform. The Dutch Reformed Church, the established Church in Cape Colony, argued that slaves were not entitled to enter the Church, and that conversion to Christianity would not make slaves akin to Europeans because they had been born to slavery as part of a divine plan. As a result, the settlers opposed missionary activity among their slaves; the same was also true of plantation owners in the West Indies.[38]

In addition, in so far as it existed, the sense of fellow humanity was predicated on European cultural assumptions. Foreign cultures were intellectually categorized in European terms, and presented thus in print and picture. This was a matter of perception as well as of intellectual comprehension: the imagined Orient affected attitudes and policy more than the experience of the Orient. As far as colonies were concerned, the *philosophes* (influential, progressive eighteenth-century French intellectuals) and other intellectual groups agreed with colonial administrators as to the need to civilize savages, as native peoples were all too often depicted.

Independence did not improve matters. For example, the development of a concept of just wars in the USA, in which seeking alternative means of resolving conflicts before embarking on wars was advocated, was of limited assistance to the Native Americans. The notion of 'Manifest Destiny' provided a justification for American expansion, with quasi-religious and moral overtones. For Jefferson and other American patriots, Natives were at an earlier stage of historical development and could only share in the future of North America if they changed 'into civilized republicans and good Americans'.[39]

On the other hand, non-'white' subjects of European powers who were not slaves were increasingly granted civil rights if they were prepared to adopt European practices such as Christianity. There was a movement from simple economic exploitation to closer connections and to notions of responsibility. In New France (Canada), there was a measure of enculturation and assimilation of Native Americans, and the French made efforts to incorporate free Africans as subjects, as with Louis XIV's *Code Noir* of 1685[40] and as citizens with the abolition of slavery in 1793–4. In 1761 Asian and East African Christian subjects of the Portuguese crown were given the same legal and social status as Portuguese whites, on the grounds that subjects should not be distinguished by colour. It was made a criminal offence for 'whites' to insult 'coloured' subjects. Repeated in 1763, these regulations were given teeth when new officials were sent to the Portuguese Indian colony of Goa in 1774 with instructions to favour Indian clerics. Pombal, the leading Portuguese minister, explicitly cited the classical Roman model of colonization. Citizenship was to bring equality. If there was no question of giving Hindus, Muslims, Buddhists, Negroes and Mulattos equal status within the Portuguese empire,[41] there was little different from the position in Europe where the rights of heterodox Christians or of Jews were generally limited.

If pressure for emancipation and equality was predominantly legal, and did not extend to economic opportunities, this again was similar to the moves against serfdom in Europe. Economic equality did not hold the same place on the moral agenda, a circumstance that was understandable in the light of the ideology and social assumptions of the age. More specifically, extended rights for non-whites in Goa, a long-established colony, where syncreticism and mutual interest were both important, provided no guidance to the treatment of slaves and Native Americans in Portugal's leading colony, Brazil. Furthermore, if new issues, such as emancipation and colonial independence, became prominent in the European world from the late eighteenth century, they did not immediately alter the essential governmental, political and commercial nature of transoceanic imperial activity.

Engagements with the outside world

Yet, to end this chapter in such a way would be unsatisfactory if it led to a neglect of genuine attempts to come to terms with a very different world. They can be presented as compromised by the inherent prejudices and suppositions of the European vision, but such an approach is less than fair to the variety of relationships that spanned the divide with non-European peoples. This can be seen not only with leading intellectuals, such as Sir William Jones, but also, more generally, with the attempt to create effective structures for ruling non-Europeans and for understanding their cultures. One such individual, Sir Robert Chambers (1737–1803), and his role in the creation of British judicial authority in Bengal, has recently been the subject of a biography. He was one of the four judges sent to Calcutta to inaugurate the Supreme Court funded under the East India Regulating Act of 1773. Eventually Chief Justice, Chambers played a prominent role in the development of Anglo-Indian law, which was no mere enforcement of its English counterpart. Furthermore, Chambers was interested in Indian culture, becoming President of the Asiatic Society in 1797 and building up a fine collection of Sanskrit manuscripts.[42]

At the same time, a less favourable account of the development of Anglo-Indian law has been offered. It has been argued that this process stemmed from the East India Company's involvement with fiscal and judicial administration, but that it included a misunderstanding of indigenous legal practices and an implementation of English legal terminology and property and inheritance law. The replacement of local judicial powers by those of colonial agents was eased by the introduction of legal codes and it has been argued that the collaborative nature of colonial rule in this respect was very much slanted towards British power.[43] It has also been suggested that, far from seeking to impose European law on India, British intellectuals had a healthy respect for Hindu and Muslim laws and thought them the equal of, and in some ways similar to, British common law. Cultural curiosity was compatible with hostility and expropriation. Jefferson was very interested in Native American linguistics, but also insistent that the Native Americans, the 'merciless Indian savages' of the Declaration of Independence, make way for settlers, in pursuit of America's destiny.[44]

Knowledge of non-European cultures was linked to a relativism that was willing to concede values and virtues to these cultures, although this was structured in accordance with the views of the European narrator or viewer. Thus, Samuel Johnson's *Voyage to Abyssinia* (1735) set out to revise the Catholic original on which it was based in order to show that the Abyssinian (Ethiopian) Christians were not heretics but adherents of the religion of their ancestors, a view that accorded with the interests of the anti-papal Church of England in the Primitive Church. Johnson, often seen as the quintessential Englishman, was clearly interested in Abyssinia, publishing in 1759 his *Rasselas, Prince of Abyssinia*. His engagement with the world outside Europe included tracts about policy, especially *Thoughts on the late Transactions respecting Falkland Islands* (1771), as well as employing Barber, a black servant, who was handsomely provided for in his will.

A more vivid engagement was offered by George Stubbs (1724–1806), a very popular British painter of racehorses. Visiting Italy in the mid-1750s, he made friends with a Moor and visited Ceuta with him. From the walls, he saw a lion seize a white Barbary horse, and this powerful scene provided the subject of numerous of his pictures, including *A Lion Seizing a Horse* (1764) and *A Lion Devouring a Horse* (1770). Once engraved, these proved popular prints. These works can be variously interpreted, and clearly Stubbs's skills, which derived in part from his anatomical expertise, explain part of their attraction. Nevertheless, there is a sense of observing the savagery of the non-European world that locates the focus of contemporary impact. This was a world in which animals were still powerful, and, apparently, many of the people were in some way akin to animals. Such attitudes suggested that Europeans were best placed to define and spread civilization.

5

TRADE

World trade had been transformed by the age of European expansion from its outset. This statement can be qualified by noting the continuation of earlier patterns of trade in the Indian Ocean, and South and Southwest Asia, and by throwing doubt on the extent to which the Portuguese, and later the Dutch, changed trade links there,[1] but no such qualification can be offered in the case of the New World. This entered global trade as a result of European exploitation, and came to play a major role in it. This role derived from the production there of bullion (gold and silver) and of non-manufactured products for Europe's consumers, especially fish, timber, tobacco, rice, indigo, sugar and coffee. In turn, the colonies in the New World became major markets for European manufactured goods and for slaves brought from Africa. The bullion imported from Latin America served to pay for Europe's imports from other areas, especially the Middle East and East Asia.

That was the bare bones of European trade with the outside world in 1650–1830, but this brief statement testifies neither to its importance nor to its diversity and changes. The importance of trade affected both Europe and much of the populated world. It helped pay for the British subsidies that funded opposition to France, financed the extension of slaveholding plantation economies throughout the Caribbean and in the newly independent United States, and ensured, for example, that coffee producers in Martinique could compete with others in Yemen to serve the French market. It was also linked to the movement of disease between parts of the world.

Trade helped restructure much of the European economy. It accentuated the development of the Atlantic seaboard and led to a relative downplaying of other regions, especially other spheres of economic activity, such as those around the Mediterranean and the Baltic, except in so far as they could benefit from this Atlantic trade.

Transoceanic trade and the acquisition of bases and colonies were seen as inherently competitive. In part, this competition was a product of already powerful rivalries within Europe, but colonies and transoceanic trade added a new dimension. Jean-Baptiste Colbert, who in 1669 was appointed to the new post of French Secretary of State for the Navy, was motivated by a desire to challenge and emulate, if not replace, the profitable and powerful maritime position of the Dutch. This level of government-driven competition was characterized by initiatives taken at state level. For example, French West India and East India companies were founded in 1664, and the Dutch were driven from Cayenne (later French Guiana) on the northern coast of South America the same year. The first French trading base in India was founded at Surat in 1668, Pondicherry following in 1674, and in February 1669 the first East India Company ship returned from India to France, bringing pepper, saltpetre and indigo. In 1670 Colbert sent an expedition on a fruitless attempt to found bases in Hudson Bay. In 1757 Malachy Postlethwayt argued in his book *Great-Britain's True System* that France's strength was the consequence of its trade:

> The great advantage gained by the French from such an extraordinary increase of their trade, is apparent from the great sums they draw annually from other countries, in return for their American products, as well as for their cambrics, tea, brandy, wine, and other numberless manufactures . . . This is the source of treasure, whereby they maintain such powerful armies, and afford such plentiful subsidies and pensions to several powers in Europe.[2]

War directly affected trade. Dutch primacy in world trade in the 1650s owed much to the earlier successful assault on Spanish and, even more, Portuguese interests, and in turn it had to be protected from the English in the First Anglo-Dutch War of 1652–4. Conversely, the Dutch position was hit by the Franco-Dutch war of 1672–8. The number of ships sent annually to the French East India Company by the Dutch fell after 1676, and by 1680 the company had ceased paying dividends.

The Dutch remained important traders, especially in South Asian waters, where the East India Company profitably linked trading zones and interests, but elsewhere there was relative decline, especially in the slave trade. The Dutch lost their territorial presence in Brazil in 1654 and in North America in 1674, and, although they continued to profit from trade and investment in areas they did not control, the British reaped greater benefits. In the eighteenth century Dutch commercial interests had to adjust to French and English power.[3]

French trade was also affected by war. After the Nine Years War ended in 1697, transoceanic trade from the French port of Saint Malo expanded greatly.[4] However, the resumption of war in 1702 hit France's transoceanic activities, for example the Newfoundland cod fishery. Again, French trade with Asia fell in 1744–63, in much of which period France was at war with Britain. Falling trade hit the accumulation of profits necessary to encourage and finance fresh activity. The French East India Company had a major loss of assets as its ships and commercial installations were destroyed in war. It incurred a heavy debt, and collapsed in 1769. The company was in no position to compete with its British rival.[5]

Trade protection was important in the development of navies. It focused on the wartime protection of commerce from European opponents, but also involved resisting the privateering forces of non-European states, especially the Barbary powers of North Africa. European powers dispatched expeditions to show the flag and deter the North Africans from privateering, but these had little lasting effect. Occasionally, privateering bases were attacked, but they generally proved difficult targets. For example, the French bombardment of the Moroccan privateering bases of Larache and Salé in 1765 achieved little. The following year the French sent a nine-ship squadron to intimidate the rulers of North Africa.[6] In the case of the Dutch, attacks by the Barbary states led them to send men-of-war twice yearly to escort merchantmen to Italy and the Near East. In addition there were efforts to show the flag and to chase privateers. Formal conflicts included war with Algiers in 1716–26, 1755–9 and 1792–4, and with Morocco in 1715–52 and 1774–7.[7]

Trade encouraged interest in colonies, although most of the trade with Africa and Asia was conducted via trading bases or small territorial enclaves, which were very different to the large settlement colonies of the New World. The enormous wealth that colonies did, could, or were believed to bring was a major reason for European interest in them. In what was still in many respects a pre-statistical age, one contemporary estimate valued France's domestic exports at £11.5 million in 1787, while the exports from its colonies to France averaged over £8.25 million between 1784 and 1790.[8] It was not surprising that transoceanic trade was seen as a solution for national indebtedness, nor that so many individuals pressed to share in the wealth it created. It is also unsurprising that powerful interests resisted abolitionist pressure to end the slave trade. Thus, in France in 1789 the Club Massiac was formed to resist the Amis des Noirs. The club had branches in major ports, including Nantes, Bayonne and Bordeaux.

Imports of colonial and transoceanic goods rose markedly in the period. This was part of a general expansion in trade and shipping, but transoceanic commerce was particularly important as a source of profit and for the multiplier effects produced by re-exports. Whereas in 1660 Marseilles imported only 19,000 quintaux (100 kilograms to a quintal) of coffee of Yemeni origin from Egypt, in 1785 it imported 143,310, of which 142,500 came from the West Indies. The Europeans had taken over the bulk of world trade in coffee. Introduced to Martinique and Guadeloupe in 1725 and to Saint-Domingue in 1730, French West Indian coffee was more popular than that produced by the Dutch in the East Indies, and it swiftly became the principal global source. In 1770 350,000 quintaux were produced and in 1790 over 950,000. Most went to France and much was then re-exported, from Marseilles principally to the Turkish empire, reversing the trade flow at the start of our period.

Not all goods enjoyed comparable growth, but increases in sugar, tobacco, cotton and rice imports were marked. They were principally obtained by the Western European powers. Their import, re-export and processing became a significant source of wealth to ports such as Bordeaux, Bristol, Glasgow, Le Havre and Nantes. These were not the only ports involved, and towns that today might not be seen as transoceanic centres played a prominent role in the Atlantic economy. Cork was important in the provisions trade to the West Indies and Newfoundland. In the mid-1740s Whitehaven annually imported 9–10 million pounds of tobacco, making it briefly the second largest tobacco-importing port in Britain after London. Much of the imported tobacco was re-exported to France and the United Provinces.[9] The value of British re-exports rose from £2.13 million in 1700 to £2.30 million in 1720, £3.23 million in 1750, £4.76 million in 1780 and £4.83 million in 1790. In 1778 the largest French colony in the West Indies, Saint-Domingue, exported 1,634,032 quintaux of sugar.

Colonial goods were also exported from Latin America. Thus, sugar, tobacco and hides were exported from the Portuguese colony of Brazil, and the export trade grew thanks to cotton exports from the 1760s and coffee from the 1790s. From Spanish America, cacao, tobacco, cotton, coffee, sugar and indigo were exported from Venezuela, hides from the Plate estuary, tobacco, sugar and hides from Cuba, and sugar, dyestuffs, cacao and, in particular, silver from Mexico. These were not static trades. Indeed, the economy of Latin America was dynamic, and this dynamism had an impact on social structures, not least on the development of regional elites that were to play a major role in winning independence.

The opportunities offered encouraged powers to attempt to develop colonial production of raw materials, and, in areas outside territorial control, to try to gain a share in transoceanic trade, principally by the foundation of chartered trading companies, to compete with long-established companies, especially the British and Dutch East India companies.[10] Indeed, the Indian trade was important in helping Britain finance the Nine Years War (1689–97) and the War of the Spanish Succession (1702–13).

Attempts in the mid-seventeenth century to found trading companies, by both major powers and humbler counterparts, such as Duke Jacob of Courland, were revived after the lengthy wars of the period 1688–1714. The second French East India Company, founded in 1719, closed part of the gap on its Dutch and English rivals. Whereas one French ship had been sent to India on average every two years in 1600–64 and three or four annually in 1664–1719, the annual average in 1720–70 was ten or eleven. A major home base was developed in Lorient from 1724, and especially in the 1730s.[11] The Ostend Company, based in the Austrian Netherlands, the Swedish East India Company, and its Prussian counterpart based at Emden in East Friesland, were, like other such efforts, initially heavily dependent on the capital, contacts, expertise and shipping of established transoceanic trading circles. The first four ships of the Emden company were purchased in Amsterdam and England. The Ostend Company, and its counterpart the Trieste Company, which was designed to develop trade with the Levant, reflected the ostentatious commitment to trading companies of Emperor Charles VI (r.1711–40), the ruler of the Austrian Habsburg territories.

The range of activity possible is suggested by the Swedish company which was created at the start of the century and received a royal charter in 1731. Trading with China, via Canton, where the Chinese channelled overseas trade, it was part of a global economic system, exporting Spanish silver coins obtained at Cadiz, and importing tea, porcelain and silk. Investors received high dividends, and the trade of the company increased from an annual average of 1,600,000 rixdollars in 1738–40 to 2,290,000 in 1744–6.[12]

The new companies competed for European markets and helped to depress prices, making goods from the Orient more affordable, just as colonial goods were also becoming so. In 1753 the price of tea at Hamburg, one of the leading European markets for transoceanic goods, fell as a result of sales there of cargoes imported by Danish, Prussian and Swedish companies. Transoceanic goods also stimulated internal European trade as they were transported to consumers, and increasingly so as they became less expensive.

It was hoped that great wealth would flow from transoceanic trading companies. This was seen as a benefit both for economies and for public finances. It was no accident that the two biggest financial schemes of the first half of the eighteenth century were both associated with such companies: the British South Sea Company and the French Mississippi Company. The latter was founded in 1717 to exploit the economic potential believed to be present in Louisiana. In 1719, renamed the Company of the Indies, it absorbed all the other French oceanic trading companies, took over the national debt and became responsible for collecting taxes. Speculation in the shares of the company, and the inherent weakness of the financial plans focused on it, led to a crash in 1720, but the scheme reflected the lure of easy profit from the tropics.[13]

Transoceanic areas became significant markets for European goods. This was not so much true of East and South Asia, the most populous areas in the world, as there was well-established local production and the taste for European manufactures was limited. As a consequence, specie had to be exported to Asia to pay for goods, especially spices and Oriental luxuries, such as ceramics.[14]

The case was different in the New World. Colonies with a large European population and relatively high wage rates were willing and able to purchase European manufactured goods in return for their bullion, plantation crops and other products. Bullion came from the Spanish and Portuguese colonies. Silver came from Spanish America, particularly northern Mexico. Gold was also mined in Spanish America – in Colombia – but there were substantial developments in Brazil: major discoveries of gold in the Minas Gérais province in 1693–5 were followed by finds in the Cuiabá, Goias and Mato Grosso regions, and by discoveries of diamonds in the Rio de Frio area in the 1720s.

The struggle to supply goods to the Spanish empire was as sharp as that to sell colonial goods to Europe, the two being intertwined. In mercantile and, increasingly, political circles international disputes, such as the War of the Spanish Succession, took on the appearance of struggles to control markets.

These were especially important to Britain and France, each of which had developing industries seeking new markets. In 1741–2 Bordeaux annually exported over 8 million livres' worth of produce, principally wine and textiles, to the French

West Indian colonies, and the figure for 1753–5 was over 10 million. For French manufacturing towns, such as Elbeuf, the Spanish empire was an important market. The population of Nantes rose considerably after 1730 as the New World market for its cheap silks grew.[15] In 1762 Choiseul, the leading French minister, feared that if Britain conquered Mexico it would provide a market for their manufactures and ruin much of France's.[16]

New World markets were also important to Britain. In his *Tour of Scotland 1769* (1771) Thomas Pennant recorded of Kendal how trade encouraged industry, leading to the integration of numerous areas into a global economy:

> The number of inhabitants is about seven thousand; chiefly engaged in manufactures of . . . a coarse sort of woollen cloth called cottons sent to Glasgow, and from thence to Virginia for the use of the Negroes . . . the manufactures employ great quantities of wool from Scotland and Durham.

Although Irish exports of wool and woollen textiles to foreign and colonial markets were banned in 1699, in order to help British competitors, the percentage of Irish exports going to the New World as a percentage of total Irish exports rose from about 6 per cent in 1698 to 20 per cent in 1784.

In return, trading powers needed New World bullion. Although, in return for imports of cotton, calicoes, pepper, saltpetre and wood from India, the French sent alcohol, cloth, gold thread and iron, nevertheless the far greater value of the imports had to be made up with bullion, which in 1725–70 was at least half of the value of the cargo from France. As a consequence, the French were worried about the Spanish *flota* from Veracruz. The bullion this brought helped drive the engine of the French world economy. In 1727 the French were very concerned when Spain imposed a high *indulto* or duty on the cargo of the *flota*. A negative trade balance with France led to French towns like Toulouse becoming major centres for dealing in Spanish coin.

Spanish silver was also important to the British, although they sought to gain it from trade, legal or illegal,[17] directly with the Spanish colonies, rather than via Spain. The major stake of the British in the Portuguese economy from the 1700s also ensured that they were the principal international beneficiary of the gold brought back from Brazil.[18] Portuguese gold and silver coins circulated in England. Spanish dollars, overstruck as worth 4s 9d, were common in Scotland in the second half of the eighteenth century.

It is worth noting the human hardship that was part of what is often described blandly as a global economy. All too frequently description of such hardship is restricted to the plantation slaves, but many others also suffered difficult and dangerous working conditions. This was true of transport – the sailors and those who are more commonly overlooked who carried heavy loads on their backs or guided mules along precipitous paths and across dangerous rivers. It was also true of mining. Indeed, the harshness of conditions in the Mexican silver mines led in

1766 to an organized withdrawal of labour in order to obtain change, a novel practice.[19]

In 1701, soon after he came to the throne of Spain, Louis XIV's grandson, Philip V, gave the French Guinea Company for ten years the privilege of the *asiento de negros*, the right to provide slaves to the Spanish colonies. This was a lucrative opening into the protected trade of the Spanish empire. In 1701 French warships were also given permission to sell goods there. Queen Anne told Parliament in October 1705, 'Nothing can be more evident than if the French king continues master of the Spanish monarchy, the balance of power in Europe is utterly destroyed; and he will be able in a short time to engross the trade and wealth of the world.'

Conversely, in 1708 the Archduke Charles, the British-backed Habsburg candidate in the War of the Spanish Succession, promised Britain the *asiento*. When the war ended with the Peace of Utrecht of 1713, Philip V, who had been confirmed as ruler of Spain, gave in to British pressure and conceded the *asiento* for thirty years. He also gave the South Sea Company the right to send an annual ship to trade at the time of the great annual trade fairs, a major blow to the Spanish trading monopoly which was reorganized in 1717 when Cadiz was established as the monopoly port for all trade to and from the New World. This was designed to prevent the evasion of royal duties.[20] However, illicit trade with the colonies hit demand for exports via Cadiz.

Competition for the Spanish market affected British and French traders. While France, thanks partly to cheaper sugar from her newer West Indian plantations, increasingly beat Britain in the European re-export trade, Britain was more successful in obtaining colonial markets for her manufactures. This was partly due to political factors. The French were disappointed by the unwillingness of their Spanish allies to open up their empire to French commercial penetration. In contrast, in the first half of the eighteenth century Portugal and its Brazilian empire took significant quantities of British products, particularly textiles, paying for them with Brazilian gold, which helped to keep the British financial system buoyant and to finance British trades elsewhere that showed a negative balance, especially that with South Asia. Financial buoyancy was particularly important in long-distance trade, in which new ships lasted only for two or three voyages, financial returns were delayed, and merchants needed to obtain long-term credit on favourable terms. Insurance was also an issue, as distance was one of the major determinants of rates.[21] Britain and the Dutch had more sophisticated credit systems than the French (who had a weak banking sector), and this was important to the development of the Atlantic commercial system.

Much of the French economy was undercapitalized. In the 1780s many of the Bordeaux merchant firms trading with the West Indies were financially weak, with a limited margin of security and little liquid money; and this was the most profitable large-scale transoceanic French trade of the period. Although French overseas trade increased greatly in peacetime, investment and profitability at the level of individual traders and companies were frequently low.[22]

French defeat in the Seven Years War (1756–63) was also significant. France lost Canada to Britain and, at the close of the war, ceded Louisiana to Spain, to compensate Spain for ceding Florida to Britain. Neither Canada nor Louisiana was as yet well populated or a significant market, but both possessed considerable potential. The French traders who continued to develop the river routes from the Great Lakes were now working for British entrepreneurs. Later employers were not necessarily British, but they were not French. In 1786, Pierre Vial opened a trail from San Antonio to Santa Fe, and in 1792 from there to St Louis, but he was now in Spanish service as Don Pedro Vial. Jean Baptiste Truteau, who explored the Missouri valley in 1794, did so for the American Missouri Company.

Trade was central to Britain's North American colonies; indeed, external trade accounted for nearly 20 per cent of total income at the end of the colonial era. No such thing as a colonial economy developed until the end of the era, after coastal trade had helped integrate the colonies; instead, there were sets of 'colonial economies', each linked more closely with London than with each other.[23]

Britain's trade with her North American colonies was very badly disrupted during the American War of Independence (1775–83), but thereafter, in defiance of traditional mercantilist assumptions that linked commerce to politically controlled markets, trade rose. Average annual British exports to North America rose from £0.27 million in 1701–5 and £1.3 million in 1751–5, to over £2 million in 1786–90. The newly independent state was populous, still needed access to Britain's credit (often generously supplied), and lacked the range of British industrial production. This was particularly fortunate for Britain, as the 1780s witnessed difficult industrial and commercial conditions in Western and Central Europe which provided added incentives for the expansion of foreign trade to cope with industrial expansion and the contraction of internal markets.

Disappointed by the return from their assistance to the Americans during the War of Independence,[24] the French were especially hopeful of Russia, with which a commercial treaty was negotiated in 1787. However, although trade with Russia grew, she did not become a leading commercial partner. This was but part of a more general disappointment experienced by Western European merchants who had hoped to create new markets further east. Instead, they were affected by a range of problems including poor communications, the over-extension of credit to Russian buyers, the rarity of 'sound money' in Russia, the limited number able to purchase imported goods, and a series of political problems beginning with the outbreak of a Russo-Turkish war in 1787.

Hopes of trade with Russia via the Black Sea were part of a more widespread French search for commercial and strategic advantage, especially on the overland route to India and around that axis. There was an increasing awareness of the strategic importance of Egypt, which looked towards Napoleon's invasion in 1798. In 1785 the French signed an agreement with the beys who wielded most influence in Egypt, opening the Red Sea route to India to trade via the Isthmus of Suez. Marseilles merchants sought to exploit this, although the French East India Company opposed attempts to establish an Egyptian company.[25]

The French were less successful in negotiating with Persia and with the Iman of Oman, but were energetic in both areas. An embassy under the Count of Ferrières-Sauveboeuf was sent to Isfahan in 1784 in order to develop trade links. In 1785 the French East India Company was refounded.[26]

Further afield, the French played a role in Cochin China, the area around the Mekong delta, where a civil war was in progress. By the Treaty of Versailles of 1787 with N'guyen Anh, one of the claimants, France acquired a claim to bases in Cochin China, and a valuable possibility of increased trade with China opened up. In practice it proved impossible to implement the treaty, because France lacked the resources to send assistance. In place of royal forces N'guyen Anh received only a small number of Frenchmen, hired thanks to the help of French merchants.[27]

Problems in European markets led to an emphasis on the value of transoceanic markets and this looked towards the situation during the French Revolutionary and Napoleonic wars (1792–1815). Then the value of the European market for Britain was lessened by conflict. Furthermore, the opportunities created by American independence were repeated as the Latin American Wars of Independence led to a breaching of Spanish monopolies and to greater opportunities for foreign, especially British, merchants. This helped to underwrite British finances.

Commercial and colonial competition played major roles in relations between European powers, although it is important not to adopt a simplistic account of the role of transoceanic interests. Europe was insulated to a degree from the wider world, especially in the first seventy-five years of our period, partly because several of the major powers were not maritime states, but also due to the marginalization of commercial considerations by royal and aristocratic policy-makers. In the 1690s the increased prominence of the Spanish Succession in European diplomacy helped to direct political attention to the fate of the Spanish colonies, but these colonies played little role in the subsequent war and were not the essential topic of the peace negotiations.

In addition, colonial disputes could be settled, neglected or exacerbated in order to facilitate diplomacy centred on European issues. Dutch troops aided Portugal in the war of independence against Spain in the 1640s at the same time as the two powers fought in Angola and Brazil. Conversely, France and Portugal reached agreement in their 1697–1700 dispute over Maranhão (Brazil north of the Amazon) only after the Spanish Succession came to the fore.

If the Spanish Succession raised political interest in the New World, there was thereafter no continuous curve of rising interest, as in 1713–37 alliances or understandings between the major maritime powers, especially the Anglo-French alliance of 1716–31, helped to keep the peace or to reduce tension. From the late 1730s, however, the situation changed and transoceanic interests came to play a greater role in government concerns. For example, the major role of Portugal in Britain's Atlantic economy helped encourage French (or French-supported Spanish) invasions in 1762, 1801 and 1807, and ensured British concern for Portuguese independence, or at least for the security of Brazil.

At the same time, economic opportunity and the way in which this interacted with, and was mediated through, political cultures and governmental structures played a major role in explaining why particular initiatives for colonial advantage were taken, and, more generally, the balance of activity between particular options. This was readily apparent in the case of France. With its major production of sugar and coffee, the West Indies was far more important to the French colonial (and metropolitan) economy than Canada, and the French also devoted more political and military effort to preserving their position there.

There was also an active French governmental encouragement of the colonial production of export goods. For example, Fort Rosalie (Natchez), a fortified trading base on the Mississippi upstream of New Orleans, was founded in 1716 and developed as the centre of the tobacco industry. This was hit by a native rising in 1729, but in the 1730s the French Minister of the Marine, Maurepas, supported a revival of tobacco production in order to lessen imports from British North America, as well as the development of cotton production in Louisiana.[28]

There were also British efforts to encourage the production of naval stores in North America. This was intended to reduce imports from the Baltic, which were a drain on bullion and also potentially vulnerable in wartime. Thus the production of tar, turpentine, pitch and hemp from the pine-forested coastline of North Carolina was encouraged. North American naval resources were also used in the form of American-built ships. These made up an appreciable portion of the British merchant marine by 1774.

Alongside government emphasis on the export of products that would assist imperial economies, there was the development within colonies of manufacturing to supply local needs. Thus, furniture, metalwork, pottery, textiles and tools were manufactured across the colonial world. Although luxury goods were imported into the colonies, and non-luxury items could be imported for those willing to purchase them, the bulk of the world of goods did not come from Europe. Instead, native peoples, slaves, poor 'whites', and many of their more affluent counterparts were served by local craftsmen. In addition, in so far as such craftsmen were unable to supply local needs, these were met in large part not by goods from Europe, but by production elsewhere in the colonies. Thus, important inter-colonial trading networks developed. They received less governmental attention than those between colonies and Europe, but were of great significance.

This was more the case for the British colonies in the New World than for the French, but far more so for their Spanish counterparts, because trade with Europe was proportionately more important for British and French New World colonies than for the Spanish colonies. Mexico City, Lima and Guayaquil (in modern Ecuador) were centres of major trading networks within Latin America. In part, this involved the movement of food and drink, the production of which was specialized, such as wine from southern Peru, cacao from Ecuador and Venezuala, and sugar from Mexico and Cuba. Equally, for reasons of distance, some goods could as readily be shipped to European markets as to elsewhere in Spanish America, for example hides and salt beef from the River Plate. Furthermore, this agricultural trading economy was dynamic. Thus, the export of hides developed not only from what was to be Argentina, but also from the Jesuit missions in Paraguay and Brazil. Some of the production of such goods, as of plantation products, such as tobacco and sugar, was for consumers in the New World. Thus, demand in the New World for cacao was greater than in Europe, and Mexico in particular consumed a large quantity.

There was also a development in industrial production for sale within the colonies, for example of Mexican textiles. Specialization and the development of a transport and financial infrastructure had led by the start of the period to a growth in such trade that challenged exports via Seville. This shift helped to increase wealth and employment within the colonies. As a consequence, real wages in parts of Latin America probably increased in the seventeenth century. Industrial production also helped fund demand for food, and thus to improve the prospects of the rural economy, and of trade in food and specialization in particular crops.

At the same time, it is necessary to note the powerful barriers to economic development within the colonies. These included the skewed nature of affluence, with much of the colonial population having little disposable income, and the nature of environmental obstacles. Rivers were generally without bridges and their fords and ferries were vulnerable to spring spate. Coastal trade was affected by prevailing winds and currents, such that, for example, there was little trade between the Amazonian centre of Belém do Pará and Brazil (instead both traded with Lisbon), and internal routes were often long and arduous, irrespective of the terrain and vegetation. Travel to these areas today, for example to the eastern shore of the Chesapeake, with its numerous inlets and large number of lakes, as well as wide rivers and dispersed settlement, throws light on the difficulties of communications in the past. These problems increased the cost and unpredictability of trade within and between colonies.

State efforts in developing export trades from colonies were important because the role of government was central to much European transoceanic expansion. This was particularly true of France, Portugal and Spain, and less so of the Dutch and the British. The French case is particularly important in our period because this was an age when competition between Britain and France was crucial to the future of the European world. This struggle was more than one between two European states; it was also central to the character of the transoceanic project.

The general regulatory framework within which the French colonists and merchants were expected to operate was stronger and more intrusive than in the case of their British counterparts. This has led to claims that government heavy-handedness hindered entrepreneurship, a charge that has focused on the case of monopoly chartered companies, which were seen by successive governments as ways to harness and control private enterprise. The British had such companies, and the East India Company, chartered in 1600,[29] and the Hudson's Bay Company, chartered in 1670, were particularly important in their area of operation, but overall the role of companies was less important in British than in French trade. Nevertheless, there was criticism of the companies. For example, the Hudson Bay Company was attacked for allegedly failing to uphold national interests in the face of French competition and for a lack of interest in expanding into the interior of Canada. This criticism led in 1749 to a parliamentary inquiry, and in 1752 to an unsuccessful attempt by London merchants to obtain trading privileges in Labrador.

Other privileged companies, such as the British Royal African Company, faced similar criticism. Their monopolies aroused anger in those excluded from their benefits, principally the merchants of secondary ports. In addition, demands for governmental assistance, such as those from the Royal African Company, were resented. Criticism of the East India Company led in 1698 to the establishment of a new East India Company as well, but in 1709 the two companies merged. This did not end concern about the role of the company, nor indeed the problems of deciding how best to manage the Asian trades.[30] It was hoped that the embassy of George, Lord Macartney, which left London for Beijing in 1792, the first British embassy to China, would obtain commercial advantages. Government initiative was felt to be especially necessary because the East India Company was opposed to any initiatives that might affect the monopoly of its factory [trading base] at Canton. The company was also criticized for failing to aid the export of British manufactures to the Orient, although its advice on exports was sought by the government.[31]

The monopoly of the Dutch East India Company was challenged when Roggeveen sailed into the Pacific via Cape Horn. His voyage was supported by the Dutch West India Company but, irrespective of whether this route breached the monopoly, the ships were seized at the East India Company base at Batavia. The West India Company never achieved the success of its more prominent rival and went bankrupt in 1791. The Russian American Company sought to limit the spread of information about Arctic discoveries.

In the absence of reliable statistics and an effective state machinery for regulation, the French government created regulatory bodies or turned to existing ones, rather than establishing a general supervisory regime and permitting free trade within it. The most recent comparative study of European commercial enterprise in pre-colonial India suggests of the French that

> in so far as state support involved state management to a degree not encountered in the case of any other East India Company, it constituted in the long run more of a liability than an asset and may perhaps legitimately be held largely responsible for the eventual failure of the French enterprise in Asia.[32]

However, it is necessary to qualify any simple impression of mercantile enterprise being crushed by an oppressive state (or an overly clear-cut comparison with a more effective, because freer, British commerce). First, it has been argued that private (i.e. non-company) French merchants were more dynamic and less constrained by the regulations than is generally appreciated.[33] Second, it would be misleading to suggest that merchants were necessarily opposed to regulation. Instead, both economic interest and political culture attracted them to it. For example, far from advocating free-trade policies, the deputies of the French Council of Commerce established in 1700 (who were selected by the leading commercial towns) were protectionist in outlook, and their pleas for liberty were based on the traditional support of rights and privileges. The deputies sought both a symbiotic relationship between government and commerce and, on an individual basis, state support for specific privileges. For example, in 1700 only six French ports were allowed to trade with the French West Indies.[34]

However, then, and more generally, the ambiguities and tensions latent in any symbiotic relationship were exacerbated by the continual struggle by interested parties for privileges. The existence of a vast network of interests, institutions and corporative regulations made it necessary for industrial and commercial concerns, especially new ones, to seek privileges.

The process of regulation did not only affect transoceanic trade where there was a case for company organization in order to support the expensive fixed facilities of forts, for example in West Africa, India and Canada. Regulation was also true of overland trade from France's colonies, and, in that, contrasted greatly with the position in the British colonies. This was readily apparent with the fur trade in North America. From 1632 until 1681 travel without permission in the Canadian interior was prohibited, leading to the illegal trade of the *coureurs de bois*, unlicensed fur traders. In addition, monopolistic practices and taxation were burdens on the fur trade, making French products in Canada more expensive. The interior trade was not liberated until 1681, although it was still regulated thereafter by means of a system of permits. Liberalization led to a large supply of beaver in Montréal. The response was not an acceptance of the opportunities and problems of the free market, but rather more regulation. In 1696 a royal edict closed most interior trading posts and ended the permit system. The angry *coureurs de bois*, unable to trade with Montréal, instead sold their furs to the British. The permit system was restored in 1716, a liberalization in French terms, but still one that restricted the fur trade and also made it easier to force the traders to pay taxes.[35]

A mercantilist regime and ethos also prevailed in Louisiana. In addition, these French colonial regimes were shot through with profiteering and clientage by officials. Although that can be seen as free enterprise and as a way to harness individual energy and private resources, it was also potentially detrimental to both government and trade.[36] Governments sometimes felt it necessary to take over bases run by chartered companies. In 1663 Louis XIV dissolved the Company of New France and took over the administration of its colony. In 1767 the French government took over control of Mauritius and Réunion, and started to improve their defences and increase their garrisons, in order to develop the islands to support intervention in India. This had not been the priority of the East India Company. Relations with overseas agents were also a problem for the French in

West Africa, for example for the Compagnie du Sénégal in the late 1780s.[37] The growing power of the British East India Company from the 1750s created problems, as the British government sought to ensure that legal rights to territories lay with the crown not the company.[38]

A suspicion of merchants was also common among French diplomats. Envoys at Constantinople, such as Bonnac and Villeneuve, preferred a regulated trade, rather than liberty of commerce, which they referred to as disorderly. The Marseilles Chamber of Commerce clashed with Villeneuve. Benoît de Maillet, consul at Cario 1692–1708, was contemptuous of French merchants, while the agreement by which French merchants were invited back into Palestine in 1790 by the governor was denounced by the consul in Syria and Palestine, Jean-Pierre Renaudot, as demeaning, and he complained that the merchants had come to terms against his wishes.[39]

Suspicious and often poor relations between government and merchants were not the only aspects of the commercial world that created tension. There was also a clash between governmental efforts to prevent colonists (and their home population) from trading with foreign merchants and the attempts of their people to do so. This was particularly pronounced where the economic interests of colonists could not be met within the regulated protectionist systems of imperial government. The Spanish empire was the most prominent example. The populace of Latin America were able to obtain cheaper European (and North American) goods as a consequence. The supply of these goods affected not only the economies of Latin America and Europe, but also, more specifically, the European colonies who played a role in supplying Latin America either as sources of supplies or as entrepots, such as the Dutch islands of Curaçao and St Eustatius, or British-ruled Jamaica.

British trade in North America was far less regulated than that of France, although, like that of the French, it depended on co-operation with the Natives. British merchants increasingly traded among Native groups west of the Appalachians. In the 1720s they established temporary posts on the upper Ohio and on an eastern tributary of the Wabash. In 1725 the Iroquois permitted the Governor of New York to construct a stone fort at Oswego. This was the first British base on the Great Lakes, and it served to extend their trading network, for example into southern Ontario. Rum was available, and inexpensive, at Oswego. Further south, in the 1740s, the Miami were increasingly drawn to the British by trade.

Although direct government intervention might be less important than with French trade, the general context within which British trade flourished owed much to government action. This was particularly so in wartime. Thus, the British capture of Louisbourg in 1745 allowed them to blockade the St Lawrence, destroying the basis of the French fur trade. Native alliances were sustained by presents and trade goods. British fur traders were now able to undersell the French dramatically, and this encouraged both the Miami and the Huron to break with the French.

The fur trade did not provide the wealth of Latin American bullion, but it is a reminder of the variety of economic links, and accompanying relations with non-Europeans, that characterized European expansion. Another good example of this variety is provided by fishing. Europeans, particularly English, French, Basque and Portuguese, fished off North America, especially Newfoundland, and heavily salted the cod they caught, taking it to European markets; although the number of Portuguese ships, also of Spanish Basque ships, declined in the late sixteenth century. This trade had a number of permutations, with ships in the eighteenth century increasingly based in Newfoundland. In 1675 about 1,700 English fishermen overwintered there. Furthermore, New Englanders came to play a bigger role in the fishing. The numbers involved in fishing were considerable: in 1664 Le Havre sent 97 fishing boats to Newfoundland, Les Sables-d'Olonne 73 and Saint-Malo 61. The numbers of workers involved in processing the cod, including collecting the oil from the livers, was large, but the absence of a significant Native population and the unsuitability of the climate for slaves led to a reliance on Europeans. As with the triangular trade that underlay slaving, the Newfoundland trade involved a number of flows, including salt from Western France, and from Setubal in Portugal. Most of the cod caught by English fishing boats was sent directly to Iberia and Italy, although the cod oil went to England.[40]

Trade with Europeans provided opportunities to the Natives of North America,[41] but also posed serious threats to them. It would be mistaken to imagine that European traders introduced the temptations of commerce to Native peoples who had not hitherto taken part in long-distance trade. However, European traders changed the character of trade. Violence could play a role, although, again, this was not absent from pre-contact trade.

On the northwest coast of North America after 1785, where British, American and Russian traders competed, relations with natives, initially cordial, soon became strained, with mutual distaste periodically exploding into violence, mainly owing to fraud and kidnapping by white traders. Hostilities usually ended in a stand-off, although the natives suffered more casualties thanks to greater Euro-American firepower. Trade was both destructive and enriching for the natives, who were already decidedly mercantile before white contact. The traders wanted sea-otter pelts and offered trinkets, beads, copper, iron, firearms, textiles and alcohol. Aside from coastal trade, the Montréal-based North West Company developed trading networks in the interior, making extensive use of waterway systems. Trade brought much prosperity, but also the disruption and suffering of alcoholism, firearms and smallpox.[42]

There was similar disruption in Australasia and the Pacific. In the latter sealers, followed by whalers, depleted animal stocks and also hit island societies with new diseases. Sealers were particularly found round New Zealand and also in the Hawaiian and Marquesas islands. The first New Zealand sealing operation was established in 1792 and the first British and American sealing stations began operating on the east coast of New Zealand in 1802. The search for seals led to the 'discovery' of sealing islands, such as Antipodes Island in 1800, Auckland Island in 1806, and both Campbell and Macquarie islands in 1810.

Other voyages sought to supply the new British colony in New South Wales. Until the Australian colony could feed itself, traders imported pork from Pacific islands, especially Tahiti. Other goods were also sought across the Pacific. In Hawaii, where the sandalwood trade flourished in the 1810s and 1820s, traders from New England co-operated with the king and the aristocracy to force people to cut sandalwood in the wet uplands, a process that affected traditional subsistence patterns. From 1820 sandalwood traders arrived in Fiji and from 1825 the Solomon Islands attracted traders in turtleshell and mother-of-pearl.

In addition to disease and alcohol, traders brought firearms. They had a disastrous impact in New Zealand. The 'Musket Wars', which began in 1818, killed nearly a quarter of all Maori males.[43] In Australia disease quickly followed the settlers. Smallpox hit the Aborigines of coastal New South Wales in 1789.

Not all European pressure was so insistent. In October 1793 Captain John Hayes hoisted the British flag on the northwest coast of New Guinea, and took possession on behalf of George III of what he called 'New Albion', the first European post on the island. This was a privately funded expedition, in search of valuable nutmeg, backed by two British merchants in Bengal. The local Papuan people were welcoming, but the Governor-General of India, Sir John Shore, and his council, sceptical about the economic prospects, refused to support the new settlement at Fort Coronation, and in 1795 it was abandoned.[44]

Despite this case, disruption characterized the European impact not only on societies that had limited experience of conquest, but also on those with considerable experience, for example in India. Alongside the emphasis on British imperialism as a syncretic system, dependent on the co-operation of local elites,[45] with a consequent stress on consensus and continuity, it is possible to emphasize its coercive character, and thus to stress force and discontinuity.

In Bengal, where the East India Company gained effective authority in 1765, it can be seen as a new force trying to define mutually beneficial commercial links, but the emphasis can also be on an exploitation that brought high taxation, deflation and famine.[46] British administration of Bengal revealed the different attitudes of the natives and the British to authority and profit. This was shown in financial control over markets and trade. The idea of a capitalistic market economy, it has been suggested, was more important to the British (an argument that may underrate the role and sophistication of Indian banking networks), and the entry of the East India Company into regional trade, it has been argued, involved force: the colonial confrontation was thus partly a prolonged contest over the habits, terms and meanings of goods, markets and people, which constituted a vital link between authority, patronage and material culture in Bengal. Once company power was forcibly established, a process that began in 1757, there was an alteration in the political economy of trade, as control over customs was monopolized. The authority of local landed chiefs was banished from rivers, ferries and tollways, and intermediate writs over markets were ended. As a consequence, the colonial marketplace was opened up to the freer flow of imperial commodities and investment. The gathering of information was central to this policy. Long-distance trade rose and prices became more uniform. Published lists of prices challenged the immense variety of wholesale and retail rates that had once characterized markets where trade was subject to different political authorities.[47] It was not only local chiefs who suffered: the treatment of native labour by the company was also harsh.

At the same time, although the British organized/taxed/exploited (each of these descriptions is appropriate but, if only one is used, a single, misleading resonance is struck) trade, this process could only work, as earlier with European penetration of South Asia, if it satisfied non-Western interests and attracted their merchants. In 1772 Dean Mahomet, an Indian in the service of an officer of the Bengal army, found that in Calcutta 'the greatest concourse of English, French, Dutch, Armenians, Abyssinians, and Jews, assemble here; besides merchants, manufacturers, and tradesmen, from the most remote parts of India'.[48] However, as British power increased, the terms of this relationship were more slanted to the benefit of the British than had hitherto been the case. Mutual interest was capable of many definitions.

Similarly, there were large colonies of Chinese background at Batavia and Manila, the centres of Dutch and Spanish activity in Asia. The relationship between colonial rulers and non-local inhabitants, such as the Chinese, was sometimes poor. There was often suspicion, as in Batavia, where the Chinese were treated harshly from 1722, while they in turn evaded immigration quotas. The situation boiled over in 1740 when Dutch fears of a rising, and Chinese fears of expulsion, led to a crisis that got out of hand. About 10,000 Chinese were slaughtered in the ensuing massacre, and the surviving Chinese joined the Javan opponents of the Dutch, provoking fresh massacres. Nevertheless, the crucial role of the Chinese in the economy of Batavia was such that, in subsequent censuses in 1778 and the 1810s, they comprised a large percentage of the population.[49]

There were also severe problems in the Spanish-ruled Philippines: Chinese trade and its impact on that between Manila and Acapulco was seen as a potential threat to the latter, and thus to the articulation of the Spanish empire in the Pacific. Orders for banishment of the Chinese were issued in 1709, 1747, 1755 and 1769, and there was a massacre in 1763, reputedly of 6,000 Chinese. In practice, the authority of the Spanish state at such a distance was only episodic.

Before turning to consider the issue of regulation and constraint in migration and settlement, it is important to note the degree to which transoceanic trade affected the material culture of Europeans and their diet and health. By supplying new products, or providing existing ones at a more attractive price, or in new forms, this trade both satisfied and stimulated consumer demand. This process was not restricted to the western littoral of the continent, but was spread throughout Europe by mercantile activity that responded to markets encouraged by both demand and emulation. If falling prices and the greater availability of goods, such as calicoes and sugar, were significant, so also were the varied means, including the development of the press and other advertising media, by which fashions could be encouraged and retail services publicized. Transoceanic trade provided goods designed to stimulate: sugar, tobacco, and caffeine drinks: tea, coffee and chocolate. As none of these was 'necessary', this was very much consumerism. Tea arrived in Western Europe in 1610 and coffee about five years later.

The dynamic of the global economy was linked to shifts in taste. Thus sugar came to be much more important in the response of individuals to food and drink, partly replacing honey as a sweetener. Opium, then used as a medicament and painkiller, was another import, although the East India Company developed its production not to serve European but rather Asian markets. In particular, its sale to China helped to pay for imports of China tea to Britain.[50]

From 1717 British ships began a regular cycle of trade direct to China in order to obtain tea, and whereas in the 1720s almost 9 million pounds of tea were landed, by the 1750s more than 37 million pounds came to Britain, the price falling by roughly a half over that period. In 1772 alone the British imported 12 million pounds of tea, and in 1791 they bought 17.25 million pounds at Canton.[51] The China trade (like whaling) also led the Americans into the Pacific: in 1784 the American *Empress of China* made its first voyage to Canton, sailing via the Cape of Good Hope.

Europe's diet was changed by the import of sugar, just as this trade transformed the areas devoted to sugar plantations[52] and drove the slave trader. The average retail price of sugar fell considerably in the second half of the seventeenth century, and the addition of sugar to drinks increased their popularity. Chocolate was altered by sugar, making it a sweet rather than a bitter drink, and encouraging the growth in exports to Europe of its main ingredient, cacao. As production increased in the New World – the French establishing cacao plantations on Martinique and Guadeloupe in the early 1660s, the Portuguese following in the late 1670s, and the Dutch (on Surinam) and English (on Jamaica) in the 1680s – prices fell, and this encouraged consumption.[53] As the consumption of caffeine drinks rose, so demand for sugar increased.

Bordeaux's imports of sugar, indigo and cacao from the French West Indies tripled in 1717–20, the beginning of a massive increase in re-exports to northern Europe. Sugar output from Saint-Domingue doubled in the 1730s. From the low base at the close of the War of the Spanish Succession in 1713, French Atlantic trade may have increased by 600 per cent by 1744.[54] Once the War of Austrian Succession (1740–8) ended, French trade resumed. In 1749 large quantities of French sugar and coffee reached Hamburg.[55] During the war, French trade there had been hit very badly and was forced to rely on neutral shipping. After the Treaty of Versailles in 1783 French sugar exports again boomed, although they collapsed in the early 1790s. In 1788 Saint-Domingue exported 1,634,032 quintaux of sugar, more than that from all the British sugar islands.[56]

Another aspect of material culture that was affected by the non-European world was furniture. Mahogany and other exotic woods were used to enhance the range and appeal of European furniture.[57] Similarly, cotton fabrics imported by East India companies were both attractive and could be used to provide for a mass market, styles otherwise restricted to more expensive silks and brocades. Processing colonial goods brought many jobs, for example in sugar refining at Orléans, further accentuating the extent to which the value-added stages were all under European control.

Yet, at the same time, the economic possibilities presented by Europe's commercial position in the world were limited by technological and, to a lesser extent, organizational limitations in industry and transport, as well as by the political economy of tariffs and other restrictions on economic flows within Europe. La Rochelle was typical of several Atlantic ports in having only an enclave economy with only a limited impact on economic activity in its hinterland,[58] while in the 1780s the major industrial centre of Lyon did not benefit greatly from the activity in the French Atlantic ports. Elsewhere, such trade brought crucial investment capital. For example, although the extensive sugar and tobacco trades based on Glasgow were enclave activities that had little direct effect on the rest of the economy, the profits gained from them acted as stimuli for other economic sectors: those from the tobacco trade substantially funding the development of the chemical industry in west-central Scotland. Similarly, the liquidity of banks such as the Edinburgh-based Royal Bank was increased by the profits of the tobacco merchants.

Alongside the impact of trade in high-value products, it is also worth noting the transformation of the European diet that resulted from the transplantation of New World crops into Europe. The result was a rough dividing line on the 55th parallel running through Bordeaux. North of that line the potato fed Europe, while south of it maize did so. By the mid-eighteenth century these crops had transformed the food supply in Europe and greatly helped to reduce the incidence of famine.

Oceanic trade helped to transform aspects of European life a long way removed from military and political history. Yet there was no compartmentalization. Just as wars affected the flow of goods, so this flow in turn partly depended on the factors that contributed to slavery and the slave trade; while, by the end of the eighteenth century, the latter was to play a part in Europeans' awareness of their role in the wider world that had been lacking at the outset of our period.

6

MIGRATION, SETTLEMENT, SLAVERY AND COLONIES

and that the country . . . may be dignified by us . . . we of our grace
. . . call it the Province of Carolina.

Charter granted by Charles II to the Lords Proprietors
of Carolina, 1663

Migration and settlement can be discussed in terms of the contrast probed in the previous chapter between more and less regulated political cultures and governmental practices. That will be the theme of the first section of this chapter. Yet, it is also necessary to consider involuntary migration and settlement, in particular the slave trade and slavery.

The principal division in European overseas expansion was between regions where Europeans were numerous, if not a majority, and those where they were an obvious minority. Essentially, this was a division between the western and eastern hemispheres. The distinction is clear if the possession of particular states is considered. Spanish settlement and exploitation of the Philippines was far less than that of Mexico or Peru, a contrast that owed most to distance, but much also to climate, the absence of bullion, and Spanish determination that the trade of the islands should be subordinated to the Spanish imperial economic system. Similarly, the Portuguese colonies in Africa and Asia were less populous than Brazil. Demographically, the European world was the western hemisphere and Europe: an Atlantic world.

Settlement in the eastern hemisphere

The Pacific and Indian oceans were too distant to trade with easily for other than high-value goods; emigration thither in large numbers was not practical; local states were more powerful; and there was no basis for a substantial slave economy comparable to that based on the large number of slaves transported from West Africa and Angola to work in the plantations of the western hemisphere.

Europeans were preponderant in the eastern hemisphere in only a few areas. One which experienced the shift from trading station to settlement colony was the Cape of Good Hope. Founded in 1652 to supply the ships of the Dutch East

India Company en route to and from the Indian Ocean, the colony expanded with scant support from the company, although it controlled the economy, especially trade. Whereas the company withdrew its trading base in Natal at Delagoa Bay (established in 1719) in 1730, settlers, attracted by well-watered lands and a temperate climate, spread out from the Cape. The Hottentots and Bushmen did not offer effective resistance, and in 1760 the Orange River was crossed. This was an unregulated movement that was opposed and only grudgingly accepted by the company. Indeed, the settlers were moving outside its effective control. This was clearly a factor encouraging movement, but so also was the availability of land and the good rainfall that helped crops. It was not until the Boers (Dutch settlers) came into contact with the Xhosa, a migrating Bantu people, in 1779 that the situation changed, as a formidable opponent was encountered. By then there were about 12,000 people of European descent in the colony, compared to only 350 settlers (not company employees) in 1695.

Few other areas in the eastern hemisphere had a climate suitable for European settlement and agriculture. This was a particular problem in Africa, where south of the Sahara many of the native powers were weaker than their South Asian counterparts. However, aside from opposition to European coastal settlement, which could be considerable and successful, as the rulers of Dahomey showed, there were major difficulties in establishing positions. Prevailing wind and ocean conditions limited access to the coast south of the Gulf of Guinea and in, and south of, the Mozambique Channel. In addition, much of the coastline was not easily accessible, a particular problem with the extensive coastal lagoons and swamps of West Africa. Elsewhere, especially on the coasts of modern Mauritania, Namibia and Somalia, there were problems with desert conditions. Penetration inland in Africa was variously hindered by deserts, tropical rainforest (with its attendant diseases) and, less frequently, mountains. The harsh ecology was amply demonstrated by the average annual death rate of Royal African Company factors between 1684 and 1732: 270 per 1,000.[1]

A differently harsh environment was that of Siberia, although conquest in the late sixteenth and early seventeenth centuries ensured that Russian settlements were located across its vast expanse. European diseases, especially smallpox, helped limit the indigenous population.

Australasia had seemed unwelcoming to Dutch explorers, although Cook's account of his visit in 1770 suggested that it was fertile and could support settlements. The British decision in 1786 to found the colony of New South Wales at Botany Bay was primarily taken for strategic reasons and to provide a penal establishment. In January 1788 the first settlers were landed. Besides supporting a penal colony, the British also hoped for geopolitical advantage: aside from beating the French, they planned a base that would project their power into the southern hemisphere and would provide naval supplies.[2]

Initially, the high hopes were to be disappointed, as the harsh climate and difficult ground vegetation created problems, as did scurvy. A failure to provide and produce sufficient supplies ensured that until the Second Fleet arrived in 1790 there were grave difficulties. Thereafter, the situation improved: more fertile soils were cultivated, and Port Jackson on Syndey Cove (the latter named after the Home Secretary) became an important calling-place for whalers and sealers.[3] New Zealand was not settled by Europeans until the following century.

In more tropical waters in the eastern hemisphere there was no opportunity to develop plantation societies comparable to those in the western. The European presence in the East Indies was far more limited, and dependent on local co-operation, than that in the West Indies. The Dutch East India Company introduced coffee into Java in 1696, and also imported pepper, sugar and indigo from there. By 1723 Java produced 12 million pounds of coffee. Cloves, tea and coffee came from Ambon. However, due to political problems and distance, these trades could not match those from the West Indies, and the heavily regulated nature of the East India Company, which wanted limited supplies at high prices, not massive quantities able to compete on world markets at low prices, did not help. Although the Dutch had bases in Sumatra, Borneo and the Celebes, Java was the only major island on which they were a territorial power. The development of this power was not in accordance with the wishes of the directors in Amsterdam, but a response to the initiative of local officials. Javan peasants under the control of local chiefs served the same function as black slaves in the western hemisphere.

Similarly, Madagascar was no Cuba, but instead an island where the European coastal presence was very limited. However, in the Indian Ocean the French introduced sugar cultivation to the Île de France (Mauritius), which they had seized in 1715, and coffee was exported from Réunion, claimed in 1642. In 1769–72 French expeditions acquired clove plants on Ambon and introduced them to Mauritius. Nevertheless, the French islands did not produce the goods and silver to trade with China that the British gained from India and its trade.

The voyage round the Cape of Good Hope between Lisbon and Goa usually took six to eight months in either direction, as did the crossing from Manila to Acapulco, the route followed by the Manila galleon that was authorized to trade between the Philippines and Mexico, and that was an important link in the world movement of silver. Distance required resources and postponed returns. The greater distances of the Indian Ocean and the Pacific were one of the reasons why European activity there was for long more institutionalized than in the Atlantic world, and more dominated by government, much of it in the shape of chartered companies, which can be seen as delegated government as well as a form of mercantile organization. This institutionalized character ensured that initiatives from European centres were important, and if they were not sustained this could affect activity in the Indian and Pacific oceans. For example, in 1670 the French sent a large squadron to the Indian Ocean, instructed to found fortified establishments near the Cape of Good Hope, on Ceylon (Sri Lanka) and in the East Indies. The subsequent failure to reinforce the expedition has been held responsible for the weakness of France's position in the Indian Ocean later in the century.[4]

Competition between European powers often took precedence over rivalry with non-Europeans; it certainly has to be borne in mind in order to offset any emphasis on Europeans versus non-Europeans. For example, in 1672–8 France was at war with the Dutch, and this affected the French attempt to develop their position in the Indian Ocean. In 1674 the French captured San Thomé on the Coromandel coast of India from the ruler of Golconda, but the pressure of France's European commitments led to a failure to send necessary reinforcements, and in 1674 an alliance of Golconda and the Dutch forced the French at Masulipatam to surrender.

Settlement in the Atlantic world

Although competition between European powers could hinder their expansion, it could also encourage it. For example, the short-lived establishment of the French base of Fort St Louis on the Texan coast in the 1680s provoked a series of Spanish expeditions into Texas and along the Gulf of Mexico. More generally, competition between Britain and France in North America and India encouraged expansion by both powers. Similarly, Britain, Russia, Spain and the USA were all encouraged in their schemes in the northern Pacific by concern about the possible hopes of the others.

Distance was less of a problem in the Atlantic world. The English/British Atlantic 'shrank' between 1675 and 1740 as a result of significant improvements, such as the development of postal services, and the introduction of the helm wheel soon after 1700, which dramatically increased rudder control on large ships by removing the need to steer with the tiller. The average annual number of transatlantic British voyages doubled in this period and the number of ships that extended or ignored the 'optimum' shipping seasons also increased on several major routes. Average peacetime passages from England to Newfoundland were five weeks, from the eastern Caribbean colonies to England eight weeks, and from Jamaica to England fourteen.[5]

Partly as a consequence, the number of European emigrants to the New World far outnumbered those to Asia and Africa. This emigration accentuated the impact of earlier migration and increased the number and percentage of non-Natives in the New World, a process that also owed much to the factors causing a fall in the Native population, particularly disease. In central Mexico the percentage of the population who were Natives in 1646 was 87.2, while Spaniards, whether born in Mexico or immigrants, amounted to 8 per cent, *mestizos* (mixed) were 1.1 per cent, and *pardos* (wholly or partly black) 3.7 per cent. Compared to the 1560s, this represented a rise in the percentage of every category, especially the *mestizos*, bar the Natives. This trend continued, so that in the mid-1740s the respective percentages were 74 and then about 9 each. As far as the whole of Mexico was concerned, the population in 1810 has been estimated at about 6,121,000: 3,676,000 Natives, 1,107,000 Spaniards, 704,000 *mestizos* and 634,000 *pardos*.[6] For Spanish America as a whole in 1800, there are estimates of a total population of 16.9 million, of whom 3.3 million were Spaniards, 6.1 million *mestizos* or *pardos* and 7.5 million Natives.

Such figures are open to qualification, not simply in terms of counting numbers but also of categorization, as it is important to give due weight to the extent and impact of mixed unions. Thus, many listed as Spaniards contained some Native blood. The same was true of the *pardos*. Nevertheless, the extent to which the 'Native', that is pre-European contact, population had declined in relative importance was clear. This was even more true in the West Indies. Disease continued to hit Native peoples hard, with smallpox wiping out half of the Cherokee in North America in the late 1730s.

The ethnic composition of the colonial population varied greatly, and this was important in creating the character and culture of specific colonies and possessions. For example, there was a higher percentage of Spaniards in central Mexico and Peru than in Central America or New Granada (modern Colombia and Ecuador). The dynamic nature of this ethnic composition could also have an impact on social structures and attitudes. In particular, it was necessary to decide how best to respond to the percentage of mixed-blood people, which in some colonies increased greatly. This was especially true of Spanish America, but less so of British America as, although the numbers of mixed-race people there rose, their overall impact was lessened by the high rate of migration from Europe and by the relatively high survival rate among 'whites' on the mainland colonies, which ensured a reasonable gender balance.

Appearance helped to determine responses to those of mixed blood. Individuals who looked European were more likely to receive favourable treatment than those who looked African or Native. This has been referred to as a pigmentocracy, and there were terms for the products of particular unions – for example, a *castizo*, the child of a Spaniard and a *mestiza* (Spanish and Native); but there was no precision in gradation. However, there was a tendency to social allocation based on pigment that reflected racist assumptions and influenced the different access of mixed-blood individuals to economic and other opportunities. Thus in Santa Fe Spaniards of pure blood were the top stratum of society.

Most European migration to the colonies was within imperial systems,[7] for example Portuguese to Brazil, which ran at about 5,000 people a year in the 1760s, and totalled about 400,000 in the century. The pace of settlement was especially high in the British colonies. This reflected the slowdown in European population growth from the early seventeenth to mid-eighteenth century, a deceleration that was particularly marked in Spain and Portugal, the extent to which the British colonies in the New World were both newer and provided opportunities for agricultural and urban settlement, and also the consequences of British population growth in the eighteenth century, not least the pressures created in areas of Scotland and Ireland where there were few new economic opportunities.

The absence of large-scale settlement distinguished the French from the British in North America. This was paradoxical, as France had the largest population in Western Europe and was the most densely populated of the major European states.

However, neither Louisiana nor the St Lawrence valley in New France were as promising for settlement as many of the British colonies, particularly for the cultivation of grain. In addition, there were no Canadian agricultural exports in the seventeenth century and only a limited expansion over the next century. As a consequence, agricultural prices declined in the second half of the seventeenth century. Fur, which dominated exports from Québec, was not a source of much employment for colonists.[8] The 'Illinois Country' – the mid-Mississippi valley – was more suitable for grain, and 'a sort of terrestrial paradise',[9] but it was too distant to spur large-scale trade or immigration.

Furthermore, the element of opportunity in the British as opposed to the French colonies was as much set by the more liberal attitude of successive British governments to the composition of the immigrant population as by environmental factors. The British were especially tolerant of religious groups outside the established Churches. New France, France's principal settlement colony, contained some Protestant and Jewish merchants, but it was overwhelmingly Catholic.[10] Huguenots (French Protestants) were not allowed to settle there, and, instead, went to British North America. French colonial policy was to found Catholic colonies in North America, and religious exclusion played a major role, in particular in the attitude of Louis XIV (r.1643–1715) to colonialism and colonial trade.[11] This institutionalized a strong Catholic presence, and thus affected the subsequent history of New France.

By 1666 there were only 3,200 French inhabitants in New France. In the 1660s and early 1670s the government sent both money and settlers, including *filles du roi*, mostly orphans, whose immigration was subsidized in 1663–73 in order to offset the overwhelming preponderance of men. Colbert wished to develop the St Lawrence valley as a source of food and industry that would complement the fishing off Newfoundland and the colonial goods from the West Indies, producing mutually supportive and profitable interactions in the French colonial world. Indeed, grain, fish and timber were exported from New France and Newfoundland to the West Indies.

However, by the end of the seventeenth century, although the number of French inhabitants had risen to about 10,000, there were about 210,000 Europeans in British North America. This was despite the fact that Britain's population was only about a quarter that of France and that much of the French population was ready to migrate within France. In Britain there was a willingness to emigrate to, or act as an entrepreneur in, distant areas which was much more limited in France. Most French emigrants went to the West Indies, especially Saint-Dominigue.

The disparity with Britain became more marked during the eighteenth century. New France had about 56,000 inhabitants of French origin in 1740, whereas British North America had nearly a million people of European background. In part this reflected the English conquest of the Dutch colony New Netherland, which had already conquered that of Sweden, New Sweden, in 1655. New Amsterdam had become New York: taken by the English in the Second Anglo-Dutch War, it was retaken in 1673, but finally left to England under the treaty of

1674. The major reason for the rise in the population of British North America was a willingness to accept both a high rate of migration from the British Isles and non-British emigrants. An Act of Parliament of 1697 which allowed people to seek work outside their own parish if they carried a certificate made the poor more mobile and encouraged the migration of indentured servants to America[12] and the West Indies.

It is too easy to lose sight of the latter. Between 30,000 and 50,000 white migrants arrived in Jamaica in the first half of the eighteenth century: the cultivated area there increased greatly. But for disease, this migration would have led to a British New World demographically dominated by the West Indies. If migrants there had multiplied at the same rate as emigrants to the mainland, their population by 1760 would have been nearly 3 million, compared to only 1.7 million in British North America. If the rate had been the same as that of migrants to the southern plantation colonies, the figures would have been equal. Conversely, death rates comparable to those in the British West Indies would have left a mainland population of less than 200,000 in 1760, of whom only about 50,000 lived in the northern colonies. In Jamaica white death rates were higher than those of slaves, and this ensured that the colony could not become a settler society with a large native-born population. Yellow fever was a particular scourge, which was especially virulent in those previously unexposed to the disease. It first struck in 1694. Malaria was also a serious problem.[13]

Whereas in the seventeenth century English migrants dominated emigration from the British Isles to the New World, in the eighteenth there was also extensive emigration from Scotland and Ireland.[14] In return for their passage, indentured servants bound themselves to service for a number of years. Demand for these servants reflected economic developments within the colonies, such as the price of tobacco.[15]

Emigration to the British colonies from outside the British Isles affected both the general character of the colonies and particular localities. Germans were particularly concentrated in Pennsylvania, but not only there. In North Carolina in 1710 a group of Swiss and German immigrants established the town of New Bern, which was so successful that it became the capital of the colony in 1770. By then, maybe as much as 30 per cent of the colony's population was of German descent, although immigration from Germany was soon to fall as a result of the War of American Independence and of the greater appeal of Russia.[16] Religious refugees were particularly encouraged in Georgia, enabling the fledgling colony to anchor Britain's presence between Carolina and Florida, and to develop strong links with the Native Americans of the southeast of the modern USA. Many of these refugees came from the Archbishopric of Salzburg, indicating the importance of European colonization for ordinary people far distant from the Atlantic coast. Under the Plantation Act of 1745 it was possible for all bar Catholics to become eligible for naturalization after seven years in a British colony.

The impact of migration was accentuated by the European diseases that killed Native people, particularly smallpox. The two ensured that the British increasingly outnumbered the Natives close to the Atlantic, although in South Carolina the European population was probably outnumbered by the Cherokee as late as 1730, and both were outnumbered by the African slaves, who themselves were hit hard by smallpox.

Defeat also had a crucial demographic impact on Native numbers. North Carolinan victory over the Tuscaroras in the 1710s led the number of the latter to fall from 5,000 to 2,500. Many took refuge with the Iroquois and those that remained were grouped by the colonists in a reservation, which by 1760 contained only about 300 people. From 1715, most of the Yamasee were killed or enslaved by the colonial militia.

Such losses helped to ensure permanent moves forward in the frontier of European control. This brought new land for settlement. Thus, after 1730, as readily cultivatable land grew scarcer in Maryland, Pennsylvania and Virginia, settlers travelled down the Great Philadelphia Wagon Road, through the Shenandoah valley and the James River and Roanoke Gaps, to enter the Piedmont of North and South Carolina. This was a migration stream that was different in its composition from that which supplied people to the Tidewater or coastal plain of both colonies, and it drove up the population. That of North Carolina rose from 30,000 whites and 6,000 blacks in 1730, to 255,000 whites and 10,000 blacks in 1775. The combined population of blacks and whites (but not Native Americans) in Georgia was estimated as 23,375 in 1770 and 33,000 by 1773.[17]

The French proprietary companies that administered Louisiana from 1717 until it reverted to crown control in 1731 sought to encourage immigration. John Law saw this as crucial to the prosperity of the colony, and there was both voluntary and forced immigration. The former, however, proved largely unsuccessful as far as French settlers were concerned, although there was an important German immigration.[18] By 1763 there were about 4,000 whites and 5,000 blacks in the colony.

Only about 11,370 French people settled in New Canada between 1608 and 1759,[19] and only about six or seven people per million left France for New France each year. Most of the indentured labourers who were sent to work in New France went back to France at the close of their service.[20] The climate was discouraging, as was the shortage of readily cultivatable land, and neither New France nor Louisiana had positive connotations in the minds of the French people. The colonies were associated with indentured labour, hostile environments and savage Natives. In his *Description de la Louisiane* (Paris, 1688) Louis Hennepin, a missionary who had accompanied La Salle, described Louisiana as the future breadbasket for the French empire, a fertile area able to produce wine and foodstuffs for the French West Indies. Reality proved otherwise. Similarly, about 9,000 French colonists were shipped to Cayenne in South America in 1763–4, but the colony was badly hit by disease and poor management. Thousands died and a large debt was accumulated.[21]

The situation was different as far as North America and the British were concerned, although environmental opportunities were clearly important. Thus, for all the large numbers of settlers sent to the British colonies on the eastern seaboard, the 'houses' of the Hudson's Bay Company – Rupert House founded in 1668, Moose Factory in 1673, Fort Albany in 1679 and York Factory in 1684 – contained only a handful of men.

The overall disparity in numbers between British and French North America had obvious implications for the size of forces that could be raised locally and for the extent of the local market. The alternative to European immigration was a demographic strategy based on assimilation, whether by enculturation of and intermarriage with Native Americans (as was, in small part, attempted in New France and Louisiana) or, more controversially, by seeking to incorporate free Africans as subjects (as with Louis XIV's *Code Noir* of 1685 and, more boldly, with the abolition of slavery in 1793–4). These strategies were controversial, and their impact varied. They were more successful in creating a situation open to loyalism and French cultural influences in New France and Louisiana than in Saint-Domingue, where the French presence was so heavily associated with slavery,[22] but in all three cases French control collapsed when the French state was unable to sustain it.

Slavery

Slavery is one of the most emotive issues in history. To point out that it has been a constant for most of human history and that it has been practised by many societies[23] is not intended to minimize the suffering and impact of the Atlantic slave trade, which had fundamental effects on Africa, the New World and European imperialism. These effects reach to the present day, nowhere more than in the continued relevance of slavery for modern debate over racism and its impact.

Historically, there was no necessary relationship between slavery and racism. Indeed, enslavement was frequently a penalty for illegal behaviour. There were white slaves in this period, most obviously those who manned the oars of Mediterranean galleys.[24] Yet there was a deeper identity of racialism and slavery, for enslavement was frequently the response to the 'other', to other peoples (irrespective of their skin colour) and other creatures. Thus, treating conquered peoples and their offspring as slaves seemed as logical to many as treating animals such as horses as slaves. The latter, beasts of burden, were also the creation of God, but their very openness to enslavement apparently demonstrated a natural and necessary fate.

Enslavement was not the only way in which force played a major role in the migrations of the imperial world. The dispatch of convicts to provide a labour force was also important. It was used, for example, by the French in Cayenne, and also by the British. Concern in Britain about rising crime after the War of the Spanish Succession (1702–13) led to the Transportation Act (1718) which, for the first time, allowed for transportation not only as part of the pardoning process in the case of capital offences, but as a penalty for a wide range of non-capital crimes, including grand larceny – the theft of property between a shilling (5 new pence) and £2. Parliament went on to pass another sixteen Acts between 1720 and 1763 that established transportation as a penalty for crimes from perjury to poaching. As many as 50,000 convicts were transported from the British Isles to America and the West Indies in 1718–75: well over 30,000 from England, with more than 13,000 from Ireland, and nearly 700 from Scotland to America. The shipboard mortality rate was about 14 per cent, a British counterpart to the cruel treatment of Africans sent as slaves. Most of the convicts sent to America went to Virginia and Maryland, with most of the rest sent to Pennsylvania; very few were sent to New England.[25]

After the War of American Independence, transportation came temporarily to an end and a substantial number of major offenders were released back into the community, leading to a crime wave. After considering transportation to Africa, Australia was founded as a penal colony in 1788.

It was not only criminals who were forcibly sent to the colonies, but also other undesirables. Thus, in 1749 Parisian vagrants were seized, and some were sent to Cayenne. Prostitutes were also forcibly sent from France, while in 1767 reformed prostitutes were sent from Britain to help populate East Florida.[26]

There was also a harsh treatment of non-European, non-slave workers in plantation economies, as is seen, for example, by the Dutch in the East Indies. This harshness led to the movement of cultivators away from areas controlled by the Dutch. Natives were used in what was in effect slavery in Mexico. They were bound to the land on which they worked by debt and other pressures.[27]

Aside from obtaining slaves from Africa, they were also seized from Native peoples. For example, Native slaves and forced labour were important in Amazonia for the collection of cacao, sarsaparilla and other forest products. In contrast, the Brazilian plantations relied on slave labour from Africa. Smallpox had devastated many Native populations, and this and other diseases continued to do so. In 1743–9 possibly half the Native population of the Amazon valley fell victim to measles and smallpox.[28] Other Native peoples resisted European depredations more successfully.

As a consequence, slaves were mostly brought from a distance. There was, for example, a small movement of slaves by sea from the Indian Ocean to the Dutch colony at the Cape of Good Hope; and by 1800 there were nearly 17,000 slaves there. However, slaves taken from Africa to the New World were by far the most significant numerically, economically and culturally.[29]

Whether brought from abroad or born in the colonies, slaves were more malleable than indentured servants. The slave trade had initially been dominated by the need to supply the Portuguese and Spanish colonies with labour, but as the Dutch, French and British expanded their colonial presence so they played a more direct role in the trade and not, as hitherto, simply one of selling to the Portuguese and Spanish colonies. The first slaving voyage from Bordeaux sailed in 1672.

Providing slaves to the colonies of other powers remained important, although the Brandenburg and Danish companies were unable to make money doing so. In 1717 the two forts that the Brandenburg Company had on the Gold Coast were sold to the Dutch. In succession three Danish West Indian Companies failed to make the necessary profits; the Danes owned several small islands in the West Indies, but lacked a large market. In contrast, in 1701, as a sign of closer Franco-Spanish relations, the French Guinea Company was granted the *Asiento* contract to transport slaves from West Africa to Spanish America for ten years, a lucrative opening into the protected trade of the Spanish empire. The victorious British gained the right in 1713 at the close of the War of the Spanish Succession. In the closing decades of the slave trade in the nineteenth century, slavers from elsewhere, for example from Newport, Rhode Island, profited from demand in Brazil and Cuba. However, for Britain and France, the core trade was that of selling slaves to their own colonies.

The slave trade altered the demography of the Atlantic world, with a major movement of people from Africa to the West Indies, South America and the southern colonies in North America. During the eighteenth century, for example, the French colonies obtained 1,015,000 slaves from French sources, and in 1788 the French West Indies contained 594,000 slaves, many harshly treated. In 1687 Saint-Domingue contained 4,500 whites and 3,500 blacks; in 1789 28,000 whites, 30,000 free blacks and 406,000 slaves.[30] In the Anglo-French peace negotiations of 1761–2 that eventually led to the Peace of Paris of 1763, the French were keen to regain the slave port of Gorée, which the British had captured in 1758. John, 3rd Earl of Bute, George III's key adviser, noted, 'When Choiseul [the leading French minister] gives up Senegal and seems facile on Goree [both French posts], it is with an express proviso that the French be put in possession of a sea port on the Slave Coast.'[31] The 1780s was the peak decade for the receipt of slaves by the French West Indian colonies: nearly 30,000 annually. The numbers sent to Saint-Domingue rose from 14,000 annually in 1766–71 to 28,000 annually in 1785–9.[32] Thereafter, insurrection and war dramatically cut the movement of slaves to the French colonies, but, there was still no sign that slavery had passed its peak. Indeed, demographic growth in Europe was fuelling demand for plantation goods and continuing to provide emigrants to the New World, but not to compete for work with the plantation slaves.

The British transported even more slaves than the French. Between 1691 and 1779 British ships transported 2,141,900 slaves from African ports, and British colonial ships took another 124,000. In 1750–79 there were about 1,909 slave-trade sailings from Liverpool, 869 from London and 624 from Bristol.[33] In 1725 Bristol ships carried about 17,000 slaves and between 1727 and 1769 thirty-nine slavers were built there. By 1752 Liverpool had eighty-eight slavers, with a combined capacity of over 25,000 slaves. Most of the slaves transported by the British ended up in their Caribbean colonies, but the number in their possessions in North America rose from about 20,000 in 1700 to over 300,000 by 1763. In addition, the British transported slaves to the colonies of other powers.[34]

There were also important trades in slaves controlled by Portugal and the Dutch. The Portuguese benefited from their control of the coast of Angola and from the fact that their colony of Brazil offered an expanding market for slave labour, both on plantations and in mining. The Portuguese had more bases further north in Africa, especially in Portuguese Guinea, and even traded along coasts where they did not have bases. Angola supplied about 2 million slaves in the eighteenth century, mostly to Brazil. The Dutch had bases on the Gold Coast, but lacked a market comparable to Brazil or Saint-Domingue. Instead, they sold to all they could reach through entrepots in Curaçao and Saint Eustatius. More generally, new areas of European control were swiftly supplied with slaves: the first ones reached the French colony of Louisiana in 1719. Slavery also grew in areas seeing economic expansion. Thus, by 1800 about 15 per cent of the 800,000-strong population of Venezuela were slaves working in the plantations.

The slave trade was integral to the Atlantic commercial economy and also very important to the entrepreneurial circles and the financial world of the Atlantic European states. For example, in Britain it would be mistaken to imagine that only Liverpool, Bristol, Glasgow and London were involved in the slave trade; so also were smaller ports such as Lancaster, Poole and Whitehaven.[35] Returns from slave-trading ventures were sufficiently attractive to keep some existing investors in the trade and to entice new investors to join up. However, on the whole, the slave trade did not bring great profits, which may explain why the majority of British and Dutch ships involved made only one voyage in the trade.[36] Whitehaven merchants largely abandoned the trade after 1769. There were also problems for more prominent slaving ports, for example Bristol in the early 1730s. The trade was risky and expensive to enter, and concern about profitability was a major factor in the pronounced variation in the number of voyages per year from individual ports. Nevertheless, returns from the slave trade could enable men of marginal status to prosper sufficiently to enter the merchant class. The triangular pattern of Atlantic trade – Britain to Africa to the New World to Britain – was often practicable for small-scale operators, and this was also true for merchants from other countries.

There was considerable flexibility in Atlantic trade, and the outlay of funds required was less than for the trade to the East Indies. For example, when sugar became harder to obtain from the West Indies, Lancaster traders found other imports in which to invest their proceeds from slave sales, particularly mahogany, rum and dyewoods. This enabled them to maximize their profits on each leg of their enterprise: particularly important for marginal operators trading in a competitive field. When competition did eventually make the slave trade less viable at Lancaster, the contracts and experiences forged by the African trade meant that other opportunities were on offer to aspiring merchants.[37]

At the individual level, the reality of slavery was of the trauma of capture and transportation, shock, hardship, violence and disruption. Individuals were taken from their families and communities. Many died in the process of capture, in the drive to the coast, in the port towns where they were crowded together in hazardous circumstances, on the ships that transported them across the Atlantic, soon after arrival. The entire process exposed slaves to unaccustomed levels and types of disease. There are no precise figures, but it has been suggested that maybe

10 per cent died on the Atlantic crossing. With time, the percentage who died fell appreciably, but this was due to shorter journey times rather than improved conditions.

Once arrived, conditions could be very bleak. Slaves lost their names, and their identities were challenged.[38] The labour regime in sugar and rice cultivation was particularly arduous and deadly; tobacco and cacao less so. Partly as a consequence, colonies that shifted from tobacco to sugar saw a marked increase in the slave population and less of a reliance on indentured labour: on Montserrat in the West Indies, 40 per cent of the 4,500 population in 1678 was non-white; but this grew to 80 per cent of the 7,200 population in 1729.[39] Hacking down sugar cane – crucial to the production process – was backbreaking work. It also required a large labour force, and slavery provided this more effectively than indentured labour, which was not only less malleable but less ecologically attuned to the working environment.[40] Slaves also had difficult and frequently harsh living conditions. Aside from the nature of their work, they were less well fed, housed and clothed than the white population, and, partly as a result of these conditions, were more affected by disease. This was particularly true of the West Indies,[41] but less so of the Chesapeake, where tobacco cultivation combined with a less difficult environment to produce less hostile conditions.

The profits and possibilities brought by slavery and the slave trade readily explain both, but it would be wrong to present the complex dynamics of enslavement simply in terms of rising demand for labour in the New World. Accounts focusing on European economic domination in Africa, and/or the gun–slave cycle, by which slaves were obtained in return for guns, are inadequate. It was not until after the Industrial Revolution had transformed maritime Europe's economy that traders could exert significant economic pressure on Africans. Furthermore, weapon sales do not provide the key. Instead, it is necessary to focus on the supply of labour as well as the means for satisfying demand, and also to offer a specific examination of the slave-supplying regions in order to suggest the danger of broad generalizations.

What emerges clearly is a politics of frequent conflict within Africa that produced slaves. A breakdown of order was instrumental in providing large numbers of slaves in Congo, while on the Gold Coast wars and banditry resulted in the sale of large numbers of slaves. In the Bight of Benin area, instability emerged from the expansionism of Dahomey, while near Angola the expansionism of the Lunda empire produced slaves, although fighting was also often linked to serious droughts, as in Angola in the 1790s. Enslavement was thus common, but the widespread belief among many Africans exported as slaves that they had been sold to cannibals to be cooked and eaten possibly expressed a wider opposition to the cannibalistic social politics of selling slaves to foreigners.

If so, it had little effect on African politics. African rulers proved more than willing to sell captives, and the slave trade would not have been possible without their active co-operation.[42] The European territorial presence in Africa was very limited. Indeed, the slave trade encapsulated much of the reality of the European impact in the world. It was destructive, served the needs of a European-dominated global economy, and would have been impossible without local support. The global economy pressed on the local, and the local served the global, and vice versa. In the Senegal River valley patterns of trade between the desert and the savannah were annexed to the Atlantic world as the export of slaves and gum arabic (a product used in textile manufacture that was the other major European-controlled export from this region) reconfigured local economies and interregional trade.[43] The cloth and metallurgical industries in West Africa were hit by European imports.

British posts in West Africa were not held by sovereign right but by agreement with local rulers: rent or tribute was paid for several posts. The Royal African Company and, from 1750, its successor, the Company of Merchants Trading to Africa, had a role similar to that in India of the East India Company in the early eighteenth century. As in India, limited sovereignty did not prevent active intervention in local politics. The interaction between the companies and the African states depended upon the ability of the companies' officials to maintain a beneficial relationship with numerous local caboceers (leaders) and penyins (elders) through an elaborate and costly system of presents, dashees (presents demanded by the Africans) and jobs. The companies served both private (through the slave and African trade) and public (by representing Britain in West Africa) interests.[44] Although Senegambia, the area conquered from the French in the Seven Years War was organized as a crown colony, while the Sierra Leone Company was chartered in 1791 to organize and expand the British presence around Freetown (which became a colony in 1807), the British territorial presence in West Africa along the coast, let alone in the interior, remained modest until the second half of the nineteenth century.

The need for local support was more generally true for European activity in this period. Any discussion of relations in terms of conflict alone is unhelpful. Economic, cultural, religious and political ties crossed European/non-European divides, turning them into zones of interaction in which symbiosis, synergy and exchange are analytical terms that are as helpful as conflict and war. Much of the violence across these divides involved an important measure of co-operation. However, if this helps locate the slave trade, it does not lessen its horror.

The majority of Africans transported in the eighteenth century went to the West Indies and Brazil; and fewer than a fifth to Spanish and North America. The work was punishing and many slaves died, but the flood of arrivals Africanized the areas to which they came. They used their African culture to adapt to the Americas. African 'nations' emerged in the New World, but they did not correspond well to political or social units in Africa, in that they were based on language alone, and this sustained African culture in America. Revolts and plots revealed the manner in which these 'nations' worked politically in America,[45] although ethnic ties and identities were eroded when the percentage of those born in Africa decreased in slave communities.[46]

Then, new ties developed. Initially, these were circumscribed by kinship and area, especially individual plantations, but in the second half of the eighteenth century the influences of evangelical Christianity, the American and particularly Haitian revolutions, and internal migration within North America, not least to towns where controls over slaves were weaker, helped lead to more widely based notions of black identity.

This process was mediated through the differing circumstances of slave life. Focusing on the varied demands of tobacco and rice cultivation and on related environmental and social characteristics, slaves in the Chesapeake were more affected by white life as a result of close proximity to owners in relatively small farms, whereas in the rice lands of South Carolina there were fewer, but larger, plantations, the percentage of slaves was greater, and the higher death rate ensured that there were more imported African slaves (as opposed to American-born slaves in the Chesapeake). As a consequence, in South Carolina slaves were more autonomous and more influenced by African culture and material life. Furthermore, in South Carolina relations between slaves and whites remained more antipathetical than where they lived in closer proximity,[47] although it is not easy to assess slave attitudes. The slave situation in Jamaica where slaves were also harshly treated,[48] was more similar to South Carolina than the Chesapeake. However, there was also a majority of immigrants among the whites in Jamaica.

In slave-holding areas there were both slave risings and the problems created by escaping slaves. There were slave risings across the New World: in South America, for example, in Surinam (Dutch Guiana) in 1731 and 1763, the West Indies and North America. In 1739 in the Stono rising in South Carolina a hundred slaves rose and killed twenty colonists before being defeated by the militia and their Native allies.[49] Circumstances, however, did not favour slave risings. The whites limited the availability of firearms to slaves. Thus, those plotting what was to be known as Gabriel's conspiracy in Richmond, Virginia, in 1800 had first to consider how they could acquire guns, horses and swords. The plan was betrayed by other blacks before the rising could take place.[50] There were also efforts to prevent slaves plotting. In Pensacola under British rule (1763–81) no slave was allowed to be out at night without his owner's written permission and meetings of more than six slaves were forbidden after 9 p.m.[51]

Flight was a more common form of resistance. It occurred not only in North America and the West Indies, but also in South America, where Maroons – runaway or in some cases freed slaves – settled across large areas, for example in villages known as *mocambos* in Brazil, and on Mauritius. In Jamaica unsuccessful operations against the Maroons, who controlled much of the interior, were followed in 1738 and 1739 by treaties that granted them land and autonomy.[52]

The impact of African nationhood within the colonial context was to be revealed most clearly with the rebellion that led to the creation of Haiti (discussed in Chapter 9). Here, we will simply consider slavery as part of the practice, politics and economics of settlement. It can certainly be readily located in terms of the competitive search for profitability that underwrote the Atlantic economy and provided much of its character. One central feature was that private enterprise was crucial to the growth of the slave trade, and the use of slaves, just as it was central to the employment of indentured labour. Slavery was part of an employment system that was capitalist. There was no state control of vast state forces comparable to that seen, for example, in the ancient world. This capitalism was also central to the slave trade. For example, in the case of Britain slavery was particularly important in the outports where the role and influence of regulated companies was weakest. The freeing of the African trade from the control of the Royal African Company by the Ten Per Cent Act in 1698 (thus named because the merchants had to pay a 10 per cent duty to maintain the company's forts) legalized the position of interlopers. This helped Bristol merchants develop the triangular trade in which they took textiles, alcohol, metal goods, guns and gunpowder to West Africa and used them to purchase slaves. The triangular trade was not the sole commercial system that was developed to help finance and exploit slavery. Supplying the slave plantations was also important. Thus, a trade in salt cod developed from Newfoundland to the West Indies and to Charleston.

The slave trade was not a constant. Flows varied as, more specifically, did the sources of slaves and their destination. Furthermore, the pattern was different for the various states that traded. For example, the Portuguese moved slaves from Angola to Brazil, first to the sugar plantations of the northeast, then from the 1710s to the gold and diamond fields of Minas Gerais, and in the late eighteenth century to sugar and coffee plantations near Rio de Janeiro. As with much else covered in this book, force has to be seen alongside co-operation: 'the slave trade was the result of a partnership between Europeans and elite Africans'.[53] The dominant influences in the politics and trade of Angola were 'Luso-African' families who spanned the Portuguese world of the coast and the African world of the interior, and whose kinship branches penetrated deep into the interior – into the families controlling African polities – and also into the plantation-owning families of northeast Brazil: 'These Luso-Africans personified the subtle continuum of identities through which the Africans and Europeans actually implemented the encounter of abstract cultures, economies, and societies in western central Africa in the seventeenth and eighteenth centuries.'[54] Similarly, on the east coast of Africa the Arab slavers, from ports such as Zanzibar, Kilwa and Mombasa, who dominated the slave trade in the region, depended in large part on local co-operation.

Another aspect of variety was provided by the differing needs for slaves. In South Carolina, Georgia and East Florida opinion among planters was divided. The better established commercial agriculture was, the more its participants wanted to reform or diversify it, especially to prevent greater dependence on slavery. Conversely, newer settlers welcomed such dependence.[55]

The circumstances under which slaves lived and worked also varied. Nevertheless, although some slaves, especially those who lived in towns (for example Port Louis on Mauritius) and skilled artisans, had a standard of living that was higher than that of many European peasants, the general pattern was very bleak. This was true for slaves working gold and diamonds in Brazil, as well as for their counterparts on plantations.

In 1686 the Papacy condemned the slave trade, which was seen as harming missionary activity, but whereas there was widespread disquiet in the seventeenth century about enslaving Christians, the plight of enslaved pagans received less attention. There was more concern about bringing Christianity to slaves and about treating them as fully human than about ending the slave trade, let alone slavery.[56]

In the eighteenth century, however, the cruelty of slavery was increasingly brought home in the culture of print. For example, Voltaire had Candide visit Surinam, which was colonized by the Dutch as a plantation economy. A Negro told Candide,

> Those of us who work in the factories and happen to catch a finger in the grindstone have a hand chopped off; if we try to escape, they cut off one leg. Both accidents happened to me. That's the price of your eating sugar in Europe . . . Dogs, monkeys, and parrots are much less miserable than we are. The Dutch . . . who converted me, tell me every Sunday, that we are all children of Adam.[57]

The last is a reference to Christian hypocrisy.

The brutal treatment meted out to disobedient slaves was a blunt instance of the violence that underlay European expansion; although it would be mistaken to imagine that such cruelty was only practised by Europeans. Arab slave traders were every bit as cruel. Furthermore, not that this extenuates the horror, the loss of population due to slavery from western Africa has been estimated as a little over 10 per cent between 1680 and 1860, a lower percentage than that which European diseases inflicted on the Natives in the New World.[58]

In his novel *L'An 2440* (1770) Louis Sébastien Mercier described a monument in Paris depicting a coloured man, his arms extended, rather than in chains, and a proud look in his eye, surrounded by the pieces of twenty broken sceptres and atop a pedestal with the inscription: '*Au vengeur du nouveau monde*'. This seemed as Utopian as the remainder of his work.

Treatment of Natives

As far as the Europeans are concerned, the treatment of slaves can be related to that of recalcitrant conquered peoples. For example, the French began a practice of burning prisoners alive after the Natchez rising of 1729.[59] Native rebellion against European control was difficult. In part this was because rebellion produced economic dislocation and occurred where ethnic solidarity and political practices had already been breached by European conquest and settlement. One of the largest conflicts with the non-European world was the general insurrection in Peru in 1780–1. Provoked by the rigorous collection of taxes, and headed by Túpac Amaru, a descendant of the last Inca rulers, the uprising was crushed. Over 100,000 people died in the conflict.[60] A century earlier the Native Americans in New Mexico had rebelled against Spanish oppression, led by a victim of Spanish attempts to suppress Native religion. The colony was not reconquered until 1692–6.

The often brutal treatment of individuals could be matched by an expropriatory attitude to possessions, including land, the basis of settlement. The extent to which Native rights to land were recognized varied greatly, in large part in relationship to the degree of acceptance of Native governmental structures. Rights were not seen to exist outside such a context, but Native practices and ideas did not always match European concepts, while European officials often exploited contrasts in order to advance particular agendas. A notion of land as empty was particularly seen in North America, and this encouraged wide-ranging claims without any reference to Native authorities.[61]

Thus, in 1663 Charles II granted to eight supporters the proprietorship of a province named Carolina, from the Atlantic to the Pacific, between 31° and 36°N, bounds extended in 1665 to 29° to 36°30'N; although this was intended to free the area from dependence on the colony of Virginia as much as to deny Native interests. Compared to that, the British government was being modest in 1748 when it gave the Ohio Company, a group of Virginia landowners and London merchants, title to half a million acres in the Ohio valley. The Natives were not represented in the 1782–3 peace negotiations that ended the War of American Independence and reapportioned their land. Similarly, Aboriginal land rights were ignored in Australia.[62]

New flora and fauna

Aside from people, the Europeans transported many plants and animals to their colonies. These were designed to help exploitation. Thus, horses, pigs and cattle were introduced to the Americas, as were food crops such as wheat, grapes, apples, peaches and citrus fruits. Closely linked to slavery, the cultivation of sugar cane was spread.[63] European animals harmed native wildlife and had an impact on the native vegetation; which, indeed, was not always appropriate to them. This, for example, can be seen with the introduction into Virginia of types of cattle from the British Isles. Cattle ranching was to prove much more successful round the River Plate.

Animals and plants introduced by the Europeans spread outside their area of control, and this greatly increased their impact. Natives living near Spanish settlements in New Mexico first acquired horses in the early seventeenth century. They spread north, by trade and theft, into the Great Plains and came to play a major role in hunting and warfare. The Apache and Comanche had the horse before the end of the century, the Cheyenne and Pawnee by 1755. In the eighteenth century more horses were acquired from Europeans trading from the St Lawrence valley. By the mid-eighteenth century they had reached the Cree.

Aside from the unintended environmental consequences of new plants and animals, there were also deliberate attempts to alter the environment, seen most clearly with deforestation. These had unexpected consequences for wildlife, soil quality and retention, and Native lifestyles. The ecological impact of Europeans was greatest in settlement colonies and inshore waters that were fished and hunted, and least in areas where trade predominated, although there could be an important impact in these areas, especially in the spread of disease. Aside from this functional distinction, there was also an environmental one: the Europeans and their animals, plants and diseases had more of an impact on temperate regions than in tropical ones, especially in tropical areas that were already occupied by developed societies with large populations.

Centres and peripheries

The treatment of slaves and of Native populations was not the only example of dominance over people in the world of European imperialism: much of the European settler population was poor, without privilege, and lacking in power. Many were indentured servants, wage labourers or peasants. Although they had opportunities to challenge their conditions by abandoning their employment or by labour protest, and cannot really be considered as white slaves, their circumstances were often difficult,[64] and it is important to remember the role of social tensions within settler communities alongside the race relations that attract so much modern attention. Thus, in British North America and the West Indies gentry clashed with yeomen. Furthermore, racial issues were often driven by social tensions within the settler community. Opposition to the import of slaves and a desire to drive Natives from the land both in part reflected the particular interests of poor whites.[65]

The relationship between colonists and home governments can be seen in terms of control. The American War of Independence (1775–83) was the most dramatic example of the clash between European governments and their overseas settlers in the second half of the eighteenth century, but it was followed in the early nineteenth by the Latin American Wars of Liberation. In the eighteenth century clashes reflected authoritarian tendencies in government, as well as the determination of European governments to retain control and to profit from their colonies, especially by controlling their trade. No eighteenth-century colonists were granted representation in European legislatures until after the French Revolution, when the French colonies were admitted to a national assembly.

It would be mistaken to imagine that there were no earlier clashes. Indeed, the history of England's North American colonies in the seventeenth century reflected the instability of the homeland. In both this was an era of rapid change that challenged existing ideas and institutions, and ensured that developments occurred against a background of instability and crisis. Rather than thinking primarily in terms of a tension between colonial autonomy and English authority, differing political positions spanned the Atlantic. Thus, in the 1680s James II's attempt to impose autocracy operated alongside the corporate ideal of colonial government. The overthrow of James in the Glorious Revolution of 1688–9 was popular with colonial elites not only because it promised to roll back Stuart autocracy, but also because it provided legitimation for America's evolving politics.[66]

In addition to changes in authority to match those in England, there was also conflict specific to the colonies. In 1676 there was a serious rising among the European population in Virginia: Bacon's Rebellion. When many of the militia supported the rebellion, the governor, Sir William Berkeley, turned to local loyalists, but he was unable to hold Jamestown, and the rebellion only collapsed when Bacon died.[67]

Less dramatically, governors clashed with assemblies which, on the whole, displayed more independence than the British House of Commons. There was a strong sense of local rights and privileges that were seen as the local and necessary encapsulation of British liberties.[68] In addition, resistance to the power and pretensions of governors was widespread and frequent. For example, in 1708 Sir Nathaniel Johnson, Governor of Carolina, imprisoned Thomas Nairne, the province's first Indian agent, for complaining about his abuse of commercial links with the Natives. The expansion of territorial claims and settlement was a particular source of dispute as it brought issues of both authority and interest into play. In 1771 a consortium of traders to whom the Cherokee owed money got them to cede, in return for ending the debt, a large amount of land along tributaries of the Savannah River in Georgia. Governor James Wright, however, argued that such a cession could only be legally conducted with the government. This occurred in 1773: the land was ceded to Georgia, which reimbursed the traders, intending to compensate itself by selling the land to settlers.[69]

Furthermore, the role of royal officials and linked interests, based in ports and colonial centres, in directing backcountry areas led to complaints, many of which focused on taxation. In North Carolina in 1766–70 the royal government was attacked by backcountry farmers who sought to 'regulate' local officials, but the Regulators' attack on regressive taxation and a lack of consultation was unsuccessful, and they were defeated in battle.

The tension between royal officials and others had its counterpart for the chartered companies. For example, the East India Company faced problems from the unofficial activities of agents, self-appointed or accredited. Thus, in 1785–6 local initiative in the shape of negotiations with the Sultan of Kedah by a merchant, Francis Light, led to the occupation of the island of Penang, renamed Prince of Wales Island, as a base on the route to China. The company was less than enthusiastic about this commitment, and was reluctant to help the sultan against his aggressive opponents.[70] More generally 'country' (private) traders were far more enterprising than the company.[71]

There were tensions not only in the British colonies. Louisiana was transferred from France to Spain after the Seven Years War but in October 1768 New Orleans rebelled against the Spanish governor after trade outside the Spanish imperial system or in non-Spanish ships was banned. Having expelled the governor and his men, the Louisiana Superior Council appealed to Louis XV to restore French rule. There was support in senior French circles for the idea of Louisiana as an independent republic under French and Spanish guarantee but, faced with Spanish determination to restore authority, the French did not act, and in August 1769 a Spanish force occupied New Orleans and executed the revolt's leaders.

This extreme example was an aspect of the problems created for European empires by taking over settlement colonies. One response was to encourage the expulsion of settlers. The French population of Acadia (Nova Scotia) was deported by the British as a security risk in 1755, to be followed after its conquest in 1758 by the population of Île Royale (Cape Breton Island). The population of Pondicherry, the major French base in India, was ordered to leave in 1761; the victorious British also destroyed much of the city. Settlers could also leave of their own accord, as the Spaniards did when Florida was ceded to the British under the Peace of Paris of 1763, and, in turn, the British did when Florida was ceded to the Spaniards under the Peace of Versailles of 1783.

Elsewhere, settlers remained, creating issues of how best to adapt policies and practices of government to those of very different backgrounds, as with the French settlers in Grenada and more significantly Québec. Conquered by the British in 1759–60 and ceded under the Peace of Paris of 1763, the French-speaking Catholic inhabitants were eventually granted rights under the Quebec Act of 1774 that compromised the notion of Protestant British nationhood and looked towards a new concept of British imperial identity. This was followed in 1778 by the Irish Relief Act.[72] Due in large part to a shared Protestantism, there had been less tension when New Netherland had become New York in the 1660s and 1670s, although there were tensions, including Leisler's Rebellion, in the crisis of authority caused by the Glorious Revolution.[73]

The majority of the officials in the settlement colonies were appointed by the home governments. They were generally natives of Europe and products of their patronage systems, and their appointment was often a blow to the interests and aspirations of the colonists.

Tension between home governments and colonists was not continuous. Links were generally close and many colonists were recent immigrants, dependent on their home countries for military assistance, and also part of an economic system that was organized to supply European needs. There was a shared 'mental space': colonial newspapers were frequently dominated by news of the mother country, and imported works were central to bookselling.[74]

Influenced by eventual independence, it is too easy to underrate the Englishness of early America and the English context of social development in the Thirteen Colonies, as if the conditions encountered necessarily implied a radical break with the past. For example, the evolution of Maryland and Virginia society is incomprehensible without an awareness of English social development. Most settlers were English by birth and upbringing. They established a society based on English laws, government and economic organization, and brought traditional English attitudes towards the social order and religious practices. However, in the case of Chesapeake Bay, immigration from England greatly slackened from the 1690s and social contrasts became more marked. This was linked to a demographic shift in which, thanks to a decline in death rates, the percentage of native-born inhabitants rose. This ensured a better balance of men and women, early marriages and thus more children.[75]

The benefit colonists derived from their government was that of protection not only from Natives but also from other Europeans. This was true not only of security from invasion, but also of commerce protection. The two were fused in the case of deterring raids, such as the French raid on Portuguese Rio de Janeiro in 1711. Furthermore, protection was required not only from attacks from the accredited forces of other powers, whether colonists or regulars, but also from independents, especially pirates. For them, both war and peace were periods of opportunity, and they were as willing to attack compatriots as the subjects of other rulers. This helped lead to a shift in British attitudes: piracy at the expense of compatriots was different to buccaneering at the cost of enemies.

Piracy was a particular opportunity and problem in the late seventeenth and early eighteenth centuries, not least as a consequence of demobilization at the close of the War of the Spanish Succession, but ebbed after firm British action in the 1710s and 1720s. In 1718 Blackbeard, who had held Charleston to ransom earlier in the year, died after being trapped on the North Carolina coast. Four years later another British warship defeated the two ships of Bartholomew Roberts off West Africa, killing Roberts. Piracy can be seen as an aspect of a wider proletarian hostility to the forces of power, profit and order.[76]

Tension between colonists and home governments tended to be most marked when military assistance was least required, for example in Spanish America, and also in British America after the conquest of Canada. Tension was also marked where the economy, as in both these areas, was more powerful and self-sufficient than it was, for example, in the West Indian colonies, which depended heavily on the sale of colonial products to Europe. The Dutch agricultural settlers in South Africa were as relatively heedless of their colonial rulers as the British North American settlers pressing to expand into areas reserved by London for the natives.

Government entailed the dissipation of authority over distance, and colonies provided only one instance of this. However, the strategic, financial and commercial issues and opportunities involved ensured that governments often put more effort into overcoming the effects of colonial distance than they did with many regions in their European dominions. Governmental pressure was facilitated and made more apparent by the preponderantly urban nature of colonial settlement. This owed much to the importance of overseas trade to the colonial economies, and to the use of Natives or slaves as the agricultural workforce in many areas. In Latin America the Native population was very largely rural, and the Spaniards and Portuguese were disproportionately present in the major towns. Old-established towns, such as Bahia, Boston, Goa, Malacca, Mexico City and Lima, and newer counterparts, such as Charleston, helped to give colonial society an urban stamp. Planned in 1680, Philadelphia had grown from a population of 2,500 in 1685 and 4,000 in 1690 to about 25,000 by 1760.

The urban character of colonial society had important consequences for its politicization. This was seen, for example, in the press. Newspapers were published in towns and their close links with their readership owed much to the latter's propinquity. English newspapers were shipped across the Atlantic, but as early as 1704 Boston had the *Boston News Letter*, the first regular newspaper published by authority, although in 1690 the unlicensed and swiftly suppressed *Public Occurrences Foreign and Domestic* had been published. The press communicated both pressures for Americanization and those for Anglicization, both a sense of distinction from Britain and yet being part of a transatlantic world, as indeed the press was. It was a component in a transatlantic information system and, more specifically, many printers crossed the Atlantic to the Thirteen Colonies.[77]

Increased colonial news in the British press reflected not only greater interest in the colonies, which can also be seen in the magazines, but also the growing ease of providing such news, due especially to the development of a colonial press. This provided a regular source for items of colonial news, reducing the significance of information provided by personal letters. By the 1780s, items were regularly appearing in British newspapers with acknowledgement to papers such as the *Calcutta Gazette*.

The more regulated French colonies lacked a comparable press. British occupation of the colonies of other powers was followed speedily by the launching of papers: the *St Lucia Gazette* (1780), the *Royal Essequebo and Demerary Gazette* (1796) in Guyana, the *Trinidad Weekly Courant* (1800), the *Cape Town Gazette, and African Advertiser* (1800), and the *Ceylon Government Gazette* (1802). The role of the press underlined the urban character of the colonial presence, but also offered a different tone to politics within that presence than one simply set by regulations.

An urban presence was also important in Siberia, although, as in North America north of the plantation line, the labour force was largely supplied from Europe, and thus the European population was widely dispersed outside the cities. During the reign of Peter the Great state undertakings such as mines were greatly expanded. The Russian population of Siberia rose from about 100,000 in 1701 to 700,000 by 1721. Mining and metallurgy developed, first in the Urals and subsequently in the Altay, creating important concentrations of people and resources that had to be fed and protected.[78]

In the New World governmental pretensions were strongest in the field of commerce: regulation was used to further mercantilist ends. The British Navigation System obliged colonists to supply Britain with goods that she could not produce herself, at the same time as they were given a monopoly of the British market, and were obliged to use their own or British ships for their trade. Other colonial powers, such as France and Portugal, devised similar systems. Spain's trade with Spanish America was directed from Cadiz.

In the second half of the eighteenth century the imperial powers sought to increase their power in their colonies. This can be seen in British policy in North America, where the controversial Stamp Act of 1765 in part arose from an attempt to rationalize the inefficient customs system in the British colonies, and to increase revenue. Charles III of Spain (1759–88) in Spanish America pursued a similar policy. The clash between *peninsulares* (natives of Spain) and *criollos* (creoles, American-born descendants of Spanish settlers) that matched tensions elsewhere (for example, in Angola and in the British colonies in North America and the West Indies) was exacerbated by Charles III's reforms. These can be seen as pragmatic devices by officials concerned to maximize governmental revenues, rather than the expression of a new enlightened ideology, but, whatever the pragmatism, a determined attempt to develop the yield from the colonial link reflected both the well-established aspiration to maximize return from the 'estate' of royal powers and a utilitarian search for economic benefit that would enhance the revenue stream. There was also a concern to strengthen the empire against Britain and France. The fall of Havana to the British in 1762 had come as a major shock. The likely nature of future external threats led to attempts to improve administrative structures. Thus, Miguel de Muesas, the reforming Governor of Puerto Rico from 1769 to 1776, sought to improve the ability of his territory to resist attack.[79]

Charles III's reforms generally ignored creole aspirations. This was true both of economic regulation and of political power. The former was motivated by a desire to help Spain rather than its colonies, and to exclude other colonial powers. As a consequence, trade between Spain and the New World was encouraged, especially by allowing ships to sail direct from Spanish ports rather than waiting for regulated convoys from Cadiz. Under the Free Trade Decree of 1778, a direct trade between Buenos Aires and Spain began, which was very important to the expansion of the River Plate region. Silver production was also encouraged. Measures were taken to restrict foreign ships trading with Spanish colonies. This process was explicitly seen as likely to strengthen Spain's control over its colonies. More specific steps were also taken. The role of creoles in government was restricted. Senior officials were mostly *peninsulares*. Administrative reorganization led to the creation of new territorial units and non-venal *intendancies*. The viceroyalties of New Granada and the Rio de la Plata were established in 1739 and 1776 respectively and based on Bogota and Buenos Aires. The first increased control over northwestern South America which could not be effectively governed from the distant centres of the viceroyalties of New Spain (Mexico) and Peru. The second was a reflection of the growing economic importance of the River Plate region, and also a response to the threat from Portuguese expansion from Brazil. The Captaincy-General and Presidencia of Caracas were established in 1776, the Audiencia of Cuzco in 1787.

The new administrative agencies were part of a marked increase in the presence of government. Thus, the new capital of Caracas had a central treasury, a high court of justice and a regiment of troops.[80] The deficiencies highlighted in the Seven Years War led Charles III to send regular regiments for garrison duty in leading colonial centres and to set in train the raising of large forces of militia. Combined, these forces provided government with security to introduce changes, including new taxes, although the militarization of political authority that emerged was to help ensure that the political culture of the Spanish colonies was different to that of their British counterparts.[81] Although the Latin American Wars of Liberation were not to begin until the early nineteenth century, and owed much to the Napoleonic subjection of Spain in 1808, separatist feeling was already developing in eighteenth-century South America.

Pombal, chief minister of Portugal in 1750–77, sought to alter the relationship between the mother country and its principal colony, Brazil. The development of gold-working there had helped lead to a measure of dependence on Brazil. Pombal tried to respond by co-opting and integrating Brazilians into the mechanisms of government in both Portugal and Brazil, but also by seeking to derive more economic benefit for the state. He founded chartered companies to monopolize the trade of the Amazon region and northeast Brazil, their exclusive privileges affecting not only British merchants but also Brazilian interests.[82]

These and other systems encountered resistance, both from colonists and from European traders excluded from their privileges. However, it would be mistaken to argue that all colonists resented and opposed the commercial regulations. Just as in Europe, central government demands and initiatives met with a measure of local support, and in different parts of the world, such as Java, various groups willingly co-operated with European intruders, so in the European colonies there was co-operation with, as well as resistance to, home governments. Rather than suggesting any inevitable clash, it is necessary to explain why the process of reaching and endlessly redefining a consensus that underlay and often constituted government in this period broke down in some areas.

The problems of control and co-operation were not restricted to settlement colonies. In northern India the British initially adapted themselves to the social system as they found it, conciliating the local elites of Muslim service gentry and Hindu merchants, and benefiting from their power.[83] This mutually profitable relationship (but see also pp. 72–3) lasted until the nineteenth century when attempts were made to control and change society in India. The government of the empire acquired there by the British East India Company was initially left to the company, and influence outside the areas beyond British rule was wielded by Residents.[84] However, it became apparent that the company could not cope with the burden and also obvious that the real and potential importance of the company to national finances required government intervention. For a while this was primarily set by financial constraints: government, Parliament and company wanted the cost of maintaining the empire to be less than that of the revenues from it.[85]

In the American colonies, in contrast, many problems stemmed from the fact that the powerful section of the population was European, part of a political community that was united as well as divided by the Atlantic. If American interests could lead colonists to clash with their home governments over the division of the profits and responsibilities of the Atlantic trading systems, European ideas could provide them with justifications for resistance. The abortive plot of 1787 to expel the Portuguese and declare Goa a republic was inspired by those Goan clergy who had returned from France with radical ideas. The republican conspiracy in Minas Gerias in Brazil in 1789 similarly failed, but also showed the impact of radical ideas. This process gathered pace as the European Enlightenment developed an increasingly radical side and even more so under the impact of revolutionary movements in America (from 1775) and France (from 1789).

In Spanish America and elsewhere the complex relationship between centre and periphery helped provide a dynamic for the development of a sense of separateness.[86] This was a reflection of what was a very different world. However much the key elements in the colonial population lived in port cities and took part in a world that spanned the oceans, they also faced the opportunities offered by their peripheral location and the challenges of the frontier. Thus, in Brazil the most successful families knew how to use both the world of the settled lands and that of the wilderness. Elite families sought to exploit the resources of the latter, to control the institutions of local government, and to become representatives of the kingdom, an always shifting combination.[87]

Frontier societies

It is too easy to overlook the role and importance of the frontier and of frontier societies, not least because records survive better for those of the colonial populations who lived in port cities and plantations, and they and their trade with Europe engaged most fully the attention of imperial government. Furthermore, frontiers, frontier zones, their economies and societies were inherently unstable and prone to be absorbed by the controls, practices and ethos of more colonized areas, especially as immigration gathered pace. Thus, in the lower Mississippi valley, a frontier exchange economy lasted into the 1760s when new rulers in Louisiana (Spain) and West Florida (Britain) took measures to increase the number of colonial inhabitants, both white settlers and black slaves. An export economy based on indigo, tobacco and timber developed.[88]

Despite changes that made frontier societies unstable, and the general process of what was seen as development (and can now be viewed more critically), it is necessary to note the importance of frontier society and the complex relationships encapsulated by that phrase, both between Europeans and non-Europeans, and between the former and their governments;[89] there were also important frontier societies spanning different non-European peoples.[90]

In what has been termed the 'middle ground' of shared cultural space between Europeans and natives,[91] individuals and groups played an active role in organizing relations, instead of being simply victims of a distant imperial power. Eric Hinderaker argued in his perceptive account of the Ohio valley:

> I treat empires more like processes than structures, and more as creations
> of the people immediately engaged in colonization than of policy

directives . . . The empires of the Ohio Valley were negotiated systems: individuals could shape, challenge, or resist colonialism in many ways. They were also sites for intercultural relations. In the Ohio Valley, Native Americans actively participated in the European imperial systems.[92]

A similar theme for an earlier period emerges in James Drake's account of the background to King Philip's war of 1675–6 in New England. Drake argues that

> the English and the Indians, as part of the same society with their polities interwoven, fought a civil war by fighting one another . . . Philip sought to preserve his people's sovereignty by incorporating them into the English political system. The English, in turn, viewed Philip and his followers as subjects.[93]

Many individuals prominent in the 'middle ground' were the product of European–Native marriages, which helped them act as translators and also enabled them to play a major role in trade. Such intermarriage was very important in such frontier areas as Hudson Bay and West Africa.[94] In turn, as more mixed-race children were born, so the prospects of marrying mixed-race women increased. However, as Hinderaker amply shows for the Ohio valley, the process of participation in imperial systems, like the 'middle ground', was both unstable and unequal. Thus, there was growing opposition in the British empire to what was seen as concubinage.[95]

Yet, it is also appropriate to note that in some areas frontier societies lasted for a long time without the radical changes seen in the Ohio valley, and the pace of European pressure was less insistent. There was a greater degree of stability in the frontier zones of Spanish America, whether in Chile, to the south of the Argentinian pampas, in Central America, along the northern edge of New Spain or, more generally, where areas of control slid into those outside control.[96] In 1766–8 the Marqués de Rubí inspected northern New Spain, coming to the conclusion that much was occupied by Spain only 'in theory' and that the frontier line was 'imaginary'.[97]

Such a situation did not necessarily encourage a flourishing frontier society, but where stability was combined with economic opportunity, as, for example, in Portuguese Asia, such a society developed. In this case it was closely linked to the autonomous settlements and trades developed by Portuguese and others who evaded official control. The processes by which frontier societies developed, or existing ones were altered by European participation, are often obscure and require research that is sensitive to non-European perspectives. Yet, this obscurity should not detract attention from an important aspect of the European impact on the wider world. This aspect was less dramatic than the migration, settlement, slavery and colonial control discussed earlier in this chapter, but is an important reminder of the diversity of the European impact and the ambiguous character of what is too easily described as colonial expansion and control.

Conclusion

The diversity of European expansion has to be emphasized, especially in the division between the tropical and non-tropical world. In the early-modern period, most of the wealth was concentrated in the tropical regions and most of the people went there as well. Geopolitics also focused on the tropics. However, in the tropics, most Europeans died, or at least could not form themselves into self-replicating populations, whereas in temperate America, where few Europeans went, they flourished, especially demographically. Another major difference was between colonization in the eastern and western hemispheres. In the former, the native inhabitants were more numerous and powerful, and therefore able to mount effective resistance to colonization.

7

WARFARE WITH NON-EUROPEANS, 1650–1750

The period 1650 to 1830 is framed by two very contrasting events, each of which revolved around a port – the central places not only in the interaction of Europe and the outside world, and in the dynamics of European imperial power, but also crucial sites for much of the non-European world. In 1650, Sultan Ibn Saif al-Ya'rubi of Oman captured the Portuguese base of Muscat, and went on to develop a fleet on the basis of the ships he seized in the harbour and the hybrid culture he took over in the town. In 1830 the French began their second overseas empire when they occupied Algiers with 37,000 troops.

These two events can be presented to imply a progression from failure to success, but it would be equally possible to imply the opposite by, for example, citing the successful and lasting Dutch occupation of Cape Town in 1652 and the destruction of the 5,000-strong British Royal African Colonial Corps under Colonel Sir Charles Maccarthy, Governor of Sierra Leone, by a larger, more enthusiastic and well-equipped Asante army on 21 January 1824. The governor's head, which became a war trophy and was used as a ceremonial drinking cup, was a particularly lurid instance of European failure. Maccarthy's replacement, Major-General Charles Turner, recommended total withdrawal from the Gold Coast, which had been placed under the governor when the government took over the Company of Merchants trading into Africa in 1821; but, instead, the British withdrew to hold only Cape Coast Castle and Accra.[1] Still, this was scarcely an episode that suggested European imperial success.

Rather than resorting to potentially misleading exemplars, it is appropriate to note that the impression of European triumph with and after the voyages of discovery and the *conquistadores* of the period 1490–1550 has to be heavily qualified. Indeed, the late seventeenth century presents several good examples to suggest that the process of European advance had run into major obstacles. As will be shown, this is not the same as arguing that it had stopped, but an awareness of these problems is both important in its own right and also throws light both on contemporary advances, where they did occur, and on subsequent changes.

1650–1700

Between 1650 and 1700 the process of European advance encountered major setbacks in East, Southeast, South and Southwest Asia, and East and West Africa. Combined with expansion in this period in the New World, especially North America, and in the Balkans, these setbacks indicated the diversity of the European military/political relationship with the non-European world. They also indicated the range of dynamic non-Western powers in the world. The late seventeenth century offered different suggestions about a shift in the balance between Christian European and non-Christian powers.

China

In East Asia the Europeans were checked on both sea and land by Chinese power. Europe's leading oceanic power, the Dutch, had a major presence in Formosa (Taiwan), whence they had driven their Spanish rivals in 1642. However, in 1661 Chen Ch'eng-Kung (known to Europeans as Coxinga), a Ming loyalist, who had been driven from his mainland bases by the advancing Manchus (who were completing their conquest of China), invaded with a force of 300 junks and 25,000 men. After a nine-month siege he took the major Dutch base, Fort Zeelandia, helped by the defection of some of the garrison, who then explained how it could best be attacked. Coxinga's success owed much to old- and to new-style weaponry. He used his shield-bearers as an aggressive assault force, but also had twenty-eight European-style cannon, some directed by Dutch renegades, and the fort surrendered after the walls of its Utrecht redoubt collapsed under heavy fire.[2]

The failure of the garrison, which indicated the limitations of what has been termed the European artillery fortress, was matched by a failure of European naval power. Dutch relief attempts from Batavia (now Jakarta) in Java, the major Dutch base in Asia, failed due to poor leadership, bad weather and insufficient troops. Squadrons sent to re-establish the Dutch position in 1662, 1663 and 1664 were all unsuccessful. The failure of the Dutch to sustain a military presence so close to China contrasted greatly with the situation two centuries later when, by the Treaty of Nanjing of 1842, the British were able to force the Chinese to accept their capture of Hong Kong. European powers never again established a presence on Formosa, and when it fell it was to the Japanese in the Sino-Japanese War of 1894–5.

Far from being a redundant empire, the Chinese had never held Formosa prior to the 1660s. Their expulsion of the Russians from the Amur valley on their northeastern frontier also advanced the frontier of effective Chinese control. The valley was seen as a source of food for Russia's Siberian settlements, and there was also interest in developing overland trade routes with China.[3] The Chinese response was vigorous, once the Manchus had completed their overthrow of the Ming dynasty and dealt with domestic problems. An initially successful Cossack force on the Amur was defeated by a Chinese fleet in 1658. In 1682 the Chinese ordered the Russians to leave the Amur valley, and in 1685 they successfully besieged the Russian fortress of Albazin. The Russians rebuilt it, only to lose it to a second siege in 1686. Both sides were equipped with cannon, but the Manchu allowed hunger, backed up by superior numbers, to do their work.[4]

In 1683–4 other Chinese forces attacked Russian positions to the north of the Amur basin, demolishing forts on the Zeya, Selemja and Tugur rivers and clearing the Russians from the coastal region. In 1689 a large Chinese army advanced as far as Nerchinsk. By the Treaty of Nerchinsk of that year the Russians acknowledged Chinese control of the Amur valley. However, Chinese demands for a Russian withdrawal beyond Lake Baikal and the cession of the Pacific coastline were unsuccessful. The Russians were ready to yield the Amur in order to obtain better relations with China, but they fully intended to retain Siberia, for it offered resources, prestige and a link to the Pacific. Nevertheless, the Russian advance towards China had been stopped.

Southern Asia

Another major European power was unsuccessful in Southeast Asia. In 1685 Louis XIV of France sent Abbé François-Timoléon de Choisy to Siam (Thailand) in an attempt to convert its ruler, Phra Narai, and thus enable Louis to present himself as a champion of the Church, a desire strengthened by his disputes with Pope Innocent XI and by Leopold I of Austria's successes against the Turks in Hungary. Choisy failed, and was also unable to gain the privileges he sought for missionaries and converts, while commercial hopes proved abortive. Nevertheless, a Siamese embassy was sent to France, and suggestions from Constantin Phaulkon, a Greek favourite of Phra Narai, that the French establish garrisons in Bangkok and Mergu to protect local Christians were taken up. In January 1687 Louis ordered the dispatch of troops and a new embassy. However, in 1688 a coup dashed Louis's hopes. Phra Narai fell, his adopted son and Phaulkon were killed, the French garrisons lost many men and were expelled, and the new monarch, Phra Petratch, put a stop to hopes of good (or indeed any) relations.[5]

Elsewhere in southern Asia, the Dutch had no success in conflict with the kingdom of Kandy in the interior of Sri Lanka, and in the Javan interior in 1678–81 faced problems due to logistics, terrain, the number of their opponents and the unreliability of their allies. The attitude of local powers was crucial. For example, the Dutch took control of the Makasarese fort of Ujungpandang on Sulawesi in 1669, but only in combination with a local ally: the Buginese. Another aspect of local intervention was shown in 1683 when Portuguese positions at Goa and Chaul, which were attacked by the Marathas, were saved by their fortifications and because the Mughals attacked the Marathas the same year. Less well-fortified Portuguese positions in the Bay of Bengal fell: in 1662 the ruler of the Indian state of Golconda captured the base at San Thomé.[6] The Portuguese had already been expelled from Ethiopia in 1636.

In 1686 the English East India Company found itself in a difficult position when the Mughal Emperor, Aurangzeb, vigorously pursued a dispute. A powerful force advanced against Hooghly, the English base for the Bay of Bengal, and the English, without cavalry or field guns, were pushed back, and evacuated by sea to Madras. Another Mughal force attacked Bombay, forcing the English to retreat into the fort and then surrender. The English were only able to continue trading after they apologized for their conduct and paid an indemnity.[7] Further east, in the Philippines, in 1662 the Spaniards lost their base of Zamboanga in Mindanao which they had captured in 1635. Although they were to reoccupy it in 1718, the picture was scarcely one of Western advance.

In the Persian Gulf a blockade by a Dutch East Indian Company squadron in 1684 was part of a process by which European commercial interests were defended, rather than an attempt to create a network of bases. The Dutch were able to capture the island position of Qishm, but restored it to Persian control in 1685 in order to forward negotiations. The Portuguese had similarly used a naval force in 1674 to secure their share in toll revenue.[8]

In Southwest Asia the Omanis created a formidable navy after their capture of Muscat. Benefiting from the use of European mariners, gunners and arms suppliers, the Omanis were also helped by the degree to which the extensive Portuguese overseas empire had already been weakened by persistent Dutch attacks. The Omanis attacked Bombay in 1661–2 and Bassein in 1674, and Diu was sacked in 1668 and 1676.[9] However, aside from at Diu, the Omani impact on India was limited. Although the Omanis had links with the Marathas, these contacts did not lead to concerted action against the Portuguese.

Africa

The Omanis also attacked the Portuguese on the East African coast, where the latter were short of men, ships and money. In 1661 the Omanis sacked Mombasa, although they avoided Fort Jesus, the powerful Portuguese fortress there. In 1670 they pillaged Mozambique, but were repulsed by the fortress garrison. Pate fell, but it was barely defended. Fort Jesus was eventually captured in 1698, but the siege had lasted since 1696 and the Omanis had no siege artillery. The Portuguese, instead, were weakened by the vitamin deficiency that causes beriberi and by diseases which killed nine-tenths of the garrison,[10] brutal evidence of the impact of disease on European positions in Africa.

Further south, Portuguese adventurers tried to gain control of the upper Zambezi, but could not prevail against larger forces that were well attuned to fighting in the region. The adventurers raised private armies from among their slaves and offered their services as mercenaries in the civil wars in Mutapa (modern Zimbabwe), sometimes with two adventurers serving on opposite sides. In exchange they were given what amounted to revenue assignments, which they then re-presented in Portugal as land grants, and they levered their way into having them recognized by the Portuguese crown. The adventurers never really operated independently in the local wars, always co-operating with an African ruler, whose authority they accepted and recognized. This form of shared power was not restricted to Africa, but was far more typical of the Europeans there and in South Asia than in the New World.

Shared power and delegated sovereignty could be means by which European power advanced, as with the French in India in the mid-eighteenth century and the British there in the second half of that century. However, no such advance resulted from Portuguese initiatives in East Africa. Instead, in 1693 Changamira of Butua drove them from the plateau and they retreated to Tete on the lower Zambezi. In Angola the Portuguese had successes, for example over Antonio I of Kongo at Ambuila in 1665. This has attracted attention, but Kongo was not conquered and the Portuguese attempt to intervene in the Kongolese civil war led to a disastrous defeat at Kitombo in 1670, which showed that there was little to be gained even against a weaker Kongo. In addition, a long series of wars against the kingdom of Ndongo ended in stalemate in the early 1680s, and central Angola was not to be conquered until the late nineteenth century. Portuguese policy throughout Central Africa shifted away from large-scale wars aimed at conquest. The period of quiescence from the 1680s in part reflected acceptance of the difficulty of carrying on wars against any determined resistance because of the need for extended supply lines.[11]

In North Africa the pace of Christian advance of the fifteenth and early sixteenth centuries was not resumed. Instead, under Sultan Muley Ismael (r.1672–1727), the Moroccans drove the Spaniards from La Marmora (1681), Larache (1689) and Arzila (1691), and the English from Tangier (1684), although the siege of Spanish-held Ceuta (1694–1720) was unsuccessful. European powers, however, maintained their ability to project naval power successfully, and in 1682, 1683 and 1688 Algiers was heavily bombarded by the French, as was Tripoli in 1685, while, under the threat of bombardment, Tunis in 1685 agreed to return all French captives. Nevertheless, this was a long way from the ability to project power successfully on land, the basis for any territorial control, let alone settlement colonies. The French were far distant from the situation in 1830 and 1881 when they occupied Algiers and Tunis, respectively.

The New World

Elsewhere, the Europeans were more successful. This was true of the Balkans and of the New World; although, in 1682 an attempt to crush the Western Iroquois and expand the power of New France (Canada) led to a humiliating climbdown after influenza and logistical problems weakened the French force.[12] Overcoming Native opposition in the New World often required co-operation with the Natives themselves, and also learning to adapt to their fighting methods. For example, in King Philip's War in New England in 1675–7 the English were outmatched in forest combat by Natives who had adopted firearms until they began to copy their enemy's tactics and to make good use of their Native allies. Their opponents suffered from Mohawk hostility, and from disease, starvation, lack of ammunition and relentless English pressure.[13] The defeated Natives became serfs to British settlers.[14]

Relentless European pressure could be brutal. In 1664–5 Louis XIV had sent 1,200 troops who helped encourage the Iroquois to the south of New France to terms. This was achieved by burning villages and crops. Similarly, the French devastated the Mohawk villages in 1693, and those of the Onondaga and Oneida in 1696.

In addition, the French, like other Europeans, anchored their presence with fortifications: in 1665–6 five forts were built along the Richelieu River, giving control over the route from the St Lawrence to Lake Champlain. In 1673 the establishment of Fort Frontenac, named after the governor, strengthened the French position on Lake Ontario. Forts St Joseph (1679), Crèvecoeur (1680) and St Louis (1682) consolidated France's presence between Lake Michigan and the Mississippi, Forts Ste-Croix (1683), St Antoine (1686) and La Pointe (1693) to the south of Lake Superior, and Forts Kaministiquia (1678), Népigon (1679) and La Tourette (1684) to the north of the Lake. In contrast, in Africa and South Asia expansion largely took the form of establishing coastal positions.

In Latin America Nojpeten, capital of the Maya people known as Itzas, the last unconquered powerful native New World kingdom, fell to Spanish attack in 1697, with very heavy losses among the defenders. This, however, was no easy conquest, for the Spaniards found it difficult to support their new position. They were helped, however, by the rapid decline of the Itzas under the pressures of Spanish seizures of food, terrible epidemics, probably influenza and later smallpox, the capture of much of their leadership by the Spaniards, and subsequent disputes among the Itzas. An Itzas rebellion in 1704 was ultimately unsuccessful, and the Spaniards were able to impose a measure of control thanks to moving the population into towns and Christian missions; those who evaded the control lived in isolated forest areas, but were no longer able to challenge Spanish dominance.[15]

The Balkans

Although developments in North America were pregnant with future importance, those in the Balkans were of more immediate consequence. The Ottoman Turks failed against Austria in 1683–99, but were still a force militarily. Indeed, the Ottoman empire had recovered after its own mid-seventeenth-century crisis to display considerable vitality from the 1660s. After formidable losses Crete was finally conquered from the Venetians in 1669, while the Poles were forced to cede Podolia in 1672, and in 1667–8 Turkish invasions of the eastern Ukraine pressed the Russians hard, although the war was indecisive. Nevertheless, the 1681 Russo-Turkish Treaty of Bakhchisarai recognized Turkish rights to the western Ukraine. In 1682 Turkish forces, operating against the Austrian Habsburgs and in support of the Hungarian Imre Thököly, captured Kosice, and Thököly was crowned King of Hungary.

However, the Turks found it impossible to mount a successful invasion of Austria. The Austrians, under Count Raimondo Montecuccoli, won the Battle of St Gotthard in 1664, a successful defensive operation which was the sole significant engagement during the war of 1663–4. In the following war the Turks advanced to besiege Vienna in 1683, for the first time since 1529. This seemed to threaten a major change in world power politics, but a Christian relief force attacked the Turks at the Battle of Kahlenberg and decisively defeated them. Turkish defeat owed something to divisions among their commanders that reflected an absence of common purpose and a lack of reliable command structures.[16]

The Austrians faced difficulties in following up their victory. In 1684 they besieged Buda, the key to Hungary, but the fortress was a strong one with powerful cannon, and disease and supply difficulties hampered the four-month siege, which was eventually abandoned. In 1686, however, a shell landed on the main powder magazine, blowing open a breach in the walls, and repeated assaults then led to the fall of the city. Eger fell in 1687, and Peterwardein and Belgrade in 1688; while Turkish armies were defeated at Szalánkemén in 1691 and Zenta in 1697. Further east, the Russians under Peter the Great entered the war. After an initial siege had failed in 1695, the next year Peter captured the important Turkish base of Azov.

The balance of initiative had shifted towards the Christian powers. By the Peace of Carlowitz (1699) and the Treaty of Constantinople (1700), the Turks lost much territory, including most of Hungary and Transylvania to Austria, the Morea to Venice, and Azov to Russia. The Khan of the Tatars' claim to an annual tribute from Russia was also repudiated.

Naval strength and European power projection

In the seventeenth century European naval power was far from absolute. European control over African, Indian and Indonesian (East Indies) coastal waters remained limited, and their warships suffered in clashes in these waters through a lack of manoeuvrability and through their deep draughts. Disparities in strength were most apparent on the open seas, where European warships were becoming more heavily gunned. Instead of using converted merchantmen, there was a reliance on purpose-built warships, and a professionalization of naval officership, senior ratings and infrastructure. A breakthrough in European iron gunfounding in the late seventeenth century aided production of large quantities of comparatively cheap and reliable iron guns. These replaced the more expensive bronze cannon that had generally been used hitherto and directly abetted the vast expansion of European battle fleets.

This process was linked to a strengthening of the European positions on major trading routes, and also to a growing ability to support and benefit from distant possessions. This ability was crucial to power projection in the eighteenth century and helped to distinguish the European maritime empires from other powerful states, such as China and the Ottoman empire.

Navies were expensive and an important aspect of the degree to which war, or more specifically military capability, increasingly became a matter of the intersection of capitalism and the state. This was central to the ability to marshal resources, and was focused and symbolized in institutions such as the Bank of England, which was founded in 1694. Thus, the military–financial combination of the early modern period preceded the military–industrial complexes of the nineteenth and twentieth centuries. An economic system stressing values of labour, thrift, efficiency and accumulation contributed to military capability. More specifically, the European industrial system appears to have been well adapted to producing and supporting a large number of warships.

It would be misleading, however, to push too far a notion of European exceptionalism. For example, a link between state development and military potential was provided by the need for a political–administrative structure capable of mobilizing large numbers in order to sustain firepower tactics based on large forces. This was definitely true of European states that created substantial forces in the second half of the seventeenth century, but was also the case elsewhere, for example on the Gold and Slave coasts in West Africa.

Similarly, the process of recovery from economic problems and the consolidation of governmental power that can be seen in Europe after the so-called mid-seventeenth-century crisis can also be seen elsewhere. It led to increased resources at the disposal of the state, and to an increase in the military activity of a number of powers: China, the Ottoman empire and Mughal India, as well as Austria, England, France and Russia. If some of this activity was directed against peoples with looser governmental structures, as with the Europeans in the New World and the Russians in Siberia, this was also true of the Chinese in Mongolia. States that had a degree of coherence, continuity and bureaucratic development had several advantages in conflict with peoples with looser governmental structures. These included not only structures for tapping the demographic and economic resources of their societies, but also access to information technology denied societies that lacked widespread literacy and a printing and publishing industry.

1700–1750

In the first half of the eighteenth century the pattern of the late seventeenth still largely continued, and European expansion was patchy. Again the principal contrast was between the situations in Asia and Africa, and those in the Balkans and the New World; although such a simple contrast requires extensive modification. In East Asia the Russians did not return to the charge against China. Far from contesting Chinese control of the Amur valley, they continued their earlier policy of accepting the major shift in Asian power politics that occurred as the Chinese overwhelmed Mongolia in the 1690s and the Dzhungars of Xinjiang from the 1690s to the 1750s. The Chinese also conquered Tibet. Further east, the Russians advanced across the North Pacific to Alaska, but not south to Sakhalin or Japan. Nor did the Dutch make any attempt to return to Taiwan.

In Southeast Asia there was no attempt to revive the French presence in Siam. The Dutch East India Company remained an important presence in Java, but far less so in most of the East Indies. In Java the company intervened in disputes in the kingdom of Mataram in the First and Second Javanese Wars of Succession (1704–8, 1719–23). Nevertheless, the Dutch army was weak and its ability to operate successfully away from coastal areas was limited, as was shown in the Third Javanese War of Succession in 1746–57, and in operations against Bantam in 1750. Dutch garrisons were forced to withdraw from Kartasura, the capital of Mataram, in 1686 and 1741. By a treaty of 1749, the Dutch acquired sovereignty over Mataram, but this authority amounted to little in practice. However, as a reminder of the need to judge success in terms of goals, it is important to note that the Dutch had little interest in conquering the interior and instead sought to ensure that the rulers there did not contest their coastal positions and trade.[17]

India

On the South Asian mainland the Europeans had mixed success. In 1718 unsuccessful attacks were mounted by English East India Company forces against Gheria and Khanderi, coastal forts on the Konkan coast of the Maratha naval commander Kanhoji Angria, who launched piratical attacks on the company's trade. Angria's ships avoided battle and the thick walls of his forts saw off poorly conducted attacks. A naval attack on Gheria failed in 1720, while in 1721 another of Angria's forts, Colaba, was unsuccessfully attacked: the land force was dispersed by Maratha cavalry and, despite the involvement of the Royal Navy, the naval bombardment failed to destroy the fort. The British made little impact until, after Kanhoji had died in 1729, his navy was divided between his sons, and a policy developed of seeking to exploit their rivalries and of gaining local allies against one of them.[18] Near by, the Portuguese were hard pressed by the Marathas in 1737–40; they captured Bassein in 1739 and Chaul in 1740, and nearly took Goa in 1739. The Marathas benefited from the support of disaffected peasantry. Also in India the Dutch were defeated by Travancore in 1741.

The French, however, showed far more dynamism in India, successfully operating as a player in the complex politics that followed the decline of Mughal power. In 1721 French merchants established a base at Mahé, and when they were expelled in 1725 the French sent a squadron from Pondicherry that forced their return and obtained new commercial benefits. Sent to Chandernagore in 1730, Joseph-Francis Dupleix founded an establishment in Patna which he saw as a base for trade with Tibet and Kashmir. Further south, Yanaon became a French base in 1731 and Karikal was seized in 1739. Pondicherry had grown to a population of about 120,000 by 1741.

Dupleix, who became governor in Pondicherry in 1742, was responsible for a distinct shift in French policy that also marked a major change in that of European power on mainland South Asia. There had earlier been schemes to conquer major areas, but he produced a workable political–military strategy to do so. Dupleix followed an expansionist and interventionist policy, becoming a player in the volatile situation created by the decline of Mughal power and, in particular, disputes over control of Hyderabad and the Carnatic. This entailed an interaction with Indian potentates in which the French, having proved their prowess, sought to profit from the situation, while at the same time they served the purposes of Indian allies.

This interpretation, which corresponds with much recent work on the rise of the British in India, can, however, as with the British, be counteracted by another view that stresses the alien character of French expansion and the discontinuities that it caused. This has implications for the perception of Dupleix. The former interpretation makes it easier to present his interventionist policies as an extension to France's coastal presence, while the latter view ensures that they are seen as a departure that was as potentially disruptive within India as it was to be costly to France.

In 1746, on the Adiyar River, French *sepoys* (Indians trained to fight in a European fashion) defeated the cavalry and elephants of the Nawab of the Carnatic. The French were drawn into the politics of the largest state in southern India, Hyderabad, where a succession struggle was in progress, from 1748. The Nizam (ruler), Nazir Jang, a protégé of the British, was defeated and killed by a mixed French–local force in 1749, and Charles de Bussy became the key adviser of his successors, first Muzzafar Jang and then, more particularly, Salabat Jang, who owed much of their power to French assistance. In 1750 Dupleix was appointed as the Nizam's deputy in the lands south of the Krishna River, and the French were rewarded with the trading base of Masulipatam and with the Northern Circars on the Bay of Bengal. A French protégé, Chanda Sahib, became Nawab of the Carnatic in 1749 and the revenues of the Carnatic were allocated to the French.

This level of intervention, let alone of success, was unmatched in South Asia and Africa in this period. The European presence in the Persian Gulf remained limited. Moves against French trade at the coffee port of Mocha in Yemen led to the dispatch of a squadron from Pondicherry in October 1736. Arriving the following January, the French bombarded the port, disembarked troops and seized Mocha. This led to the restoration of commercial privileges, but there was no permanent military or territorial presence.

Africa

In East Africa the Portuguese regained Mombasa in 1728, but the garrison capitulated to Omani siege in 1729 as a result of low morale and problems with food supplies. In West Africa the French in 1719 fortified Fort St Joseph to protect their trade along the River Senegal. They also constructed river boats for trade and protection. However, the French system of forts and boats depended on local co-operation.[19] Gifts of guns were used to expand French influence. Further east, Dahomey forces captured the French fort at Whydah in 1728 after blowing up the magazine. British cannon drove off Dahomey forces that attacked their fort at Glehue that year, but these forces had captured the Portuguese fort there the previous year.

In North Africa the Algerians captured Oran in 1708, at a time when Spain was convulsed by civil war and foreign intervention, but in 1732 a united and stronger Spain retook the port. The role of force in European relations with North Africa was shown by the frequent reliance on representation by naval officers. Thus, the British sent Captain George Delaval on two missions to the Emperor of Morocco. In 1700 he negotiated a treaty for the redemption of captives, and in 1708 an agreement not to molest each other's ships. Captain Padden concluded a truce with Morocco in 1713, and Commodore Augustus Keppel an agreement with Algiers in 1751, and in 1783 Commodore Sir Roger Curtis was ordered to renew the Anglo-Moroccan treaty of friendship, although instructed to discourage a return embassy as they were expensive to receive.[20]

The Balkans

European pressure was far more constant on the long land frontier that divided Christendom from its neighbours across Eurasia. This pressure was most insistent in southeast Europe, where there were two major wars between Austria and the Turks: in 1716–18 and 1737–9. In 1716, when the Ottomans besieged the Austrian general Prince Eugène in a fortified camp at Peterwardein (Petrovaradin), Eugène sallied out and defeated his more numerous opponents, killing possibly up to 30,000 Turks, including the Grand Vizier, Silahdar Ali Pasha. Eugène successfully combined battles and sieges, an ability that often eluded generals and that reflected his own skills and the capability of the Austrian army. In 1716 he marched on to take Temesvár, which controlled or threatened much of eastern Hungary. Although it had defied the Austrians in the 1690s, was well fortified and was protected by rivers and marshes, Temesvár surrendered after heavy bombardment. In 1717 Eugène crushed a Turkish army outside Belgrade, which led the city to surrender. The Peace of Passarowitz of 1718 left Austria with substantial territorial gains: the Banat of Temesvár, Little (Western) Wallachia and Serbia.

However, earlier that decade Peter the Great had failed when he tried to overthrow Turkish power in the Balkans. Advancing from Kiev in 1711, the 34,000-strong army marched through Poland towards Moldavia, but was badly affected by supply problems and Tatar harassment. This indicated the problems of campaigning on what was in effect a land ocean, a region without urban bases or a population from which supplies could be readily obtained. The speedy advance of a large Ottoman army limited Balkan support, and the Russians were hit by the failure of the Moldavian harvest. Advancing too slowly, Peter was outmanoeuvred, surrounded and, under fire and short of supplies, forced to sign a peace agreement.[21] The Turks were also able to hold off Christian naval forces in the eastern basin of the Mediterranean. In 1718, off Cerigo, the Turkish fleet had the advantage over an opposing Christian fleet, principally consisting of Venetian warships; the Christians lost nearly 2,000 men.

In the 1730s success on land was reversed. The Russians began by attacking the Turks in 1735. Their success reflected the degree to which they were able to exert their force in a hostile terrain and at a considerable distance. Invasions of the Crimea in 1736, 1737 and 1738 fell victim to disease, heat and supply problems, but the Russians were able to besiege Azov successfully in 1736, and Ochakov in 1737, and in 1739 to invade Moldavia, defeat the Turks at Stavuchanakh and capture Jassy. The importance of resources and organization were shown in 1737 when the force that advanced on Ochakov was supported by supplies brought by boat down the Dneiper, and thence by 28,000 carts. Equally, the ecological problems of imperialism were shown in 1738 when Ochakov was abandoned due to a plague outbreak that killed thousands.

The Austrians entered the war in 1737, but each campaigning year was unsuccessful for them. Poor command, inadequate tactics and disease culminated in 1739 with the surrender of Belgrade and the cession, in the Treaty of Belgrade, also of Little Wallachia and northern Serbia. The Russians, now isolated, were driven to make peace. Their gains in the southern steppe, and the retention of an unfortified Azov, still left them without a Black Sea coastline, let alone Moldavia.

Russian advances

If the 1730s indicated Turkish resilience, Russian campaigns further east indicated the difficulties of overland European expansion, but also the methods that could help provide success. Advancing along the Caspian Sea in 1722–3, the Russians hoped to benefit from civil war in Persia in order to gain control of the silk routes, annex territory and pre-empt Ottoman expansion. Derbent fell in 1722, and Baku and Rasht in 1723. The Russian advance was preceded by careful planning in which information was accumulated and used: naval and cartographical missions explored and mapped the coastline and an army officer examined the roads.[22] However, aspects of the campaign were mismanaged: logistics were poor, especially the supply of food and ammunition. In this sense more facets of warfare were becoming professionalized, but the key element of long-distance combat, logistics, remained poorly organized and in part arbitrary. The Russians found their Caspian conquests of little use: large numbers of garrison troops, possibly up to 130,000 men, were lost through disease, and in 1732, at a time of rising Persian power, the lands to the south of the Caspian were ceded by the Russians by the Treaty of Rasht. They were never to be regained. By the Treaty of Ganja in 1735, Derbent and Baku were also returned.

The Russians made more lasting gains to the northeast of the Caspian. The Bashkirs were suppressed in the 1730s and 1740s, and control over them was anchored by a new line of forts from the Volga to the new fort of Orenburg, built from 1733. Further east, an expedition sent to persuade the Khan of Khiva to accept Russian suzerainty, and thereafter to investigate the route to India, was attacked by Khivans, Uzbeks and Kazaks in 1717, and, although protected within their camp by firepower, the army was annihilated when it left camp. Yet further east, the Russian advance into the upper reaches of the Ob, where Biysk had been founded as a base in 1709, had led to a firm Dzhungar response, including the destruction of Biysk. Russian expeditions sent in 1715 and 1719 to discover gold sands in Dzhungaria were repelled.

The Russian response to challenges was to build. In reply to the Dzhungars a series of forts was built on the Irtysh, including Omsk (1716). The Russian position in the Altay foothills was protected by the Kuznetsk–Kolyvan' Line, designed to block Kalmyk raids. The Usinskya Line based at Troitsk (1743) was constructed along the River Uy to protect the agricultural zone to the east of the Urals. By the second half of the century, a chain of forts, over 4,000 kilometres in length, extended from the Caspian to Kuznetsk in the foothills of the Altay. They were more effective than the Spanish *presidios* in North America, not least because the Russians devoted more military resources to the task; five regular infantry regiments alone were added to the Irtysh Line in 1745.

As with the British, French and Spaniards in North America, the Dutch in Java, and the British and French in India, the Russians benefited from divisions among potential opponents. Rivalries between the Kazaks, Kalmyks and Bashkirs played a major role in enabling the Russians to conquer the last. The Kazaks turned to the Russians for military assistance against the Dzhungars in 1731, and the Kazak Younger Horde became a Russian vassal, followed by the Middle Horde in 1740.[23]

North America

Both fortresses and divisions between native peoples were of value to European powers in North America. The longest-established power, Spain, expanded the least in this period, and essentially sought to maintain its position against both Native pressure and that of France and Britain. In 1732 an expedition was launched against the Apache, while in 1721 another had re-established the Spanish position in East Texas, after its capture by the French in 1719. The French were the widest ranging of the European powers in North America in this period. In 1699 Pierre Le Moyne, Sieur d'Iberville, founded Fort Maurepas in Biloxi Bay, Mobile following in 1702, and New Orleans in 1718. Further north, the French had consolidated their position on the St Lawrence in 1701 when the Iroquois promised neutrality in the event of a future Anglo-French conflict. The same year, against the advice of the Governor of Canada, the Secretary of State for the Marine backed Cadillac's plan to develop a base at Detroit in order to secure France's position in the Great Lakes and also communications with Louisiana. Missions were established at Cahokia (1699) and Kaskaskia (1703) on the upper Mississippi.[24]

Expansion gathered pace after the War of the Spanish Succession. The French were dependent on Native co-operation: they traded extensively while their settlements relied on local allies, such as the Choctaws. Agreements and alliances in turn drew the French into local rivalries, for example supporting the Potawatomi against the Fox tribe of modern Illinois–Mississippi. A string of French–Native attacks were launched against the Fox – in 1712, 1715, 1716, 1728, 1730, 1731 and 1734. Governor Charles Beauharnais sought to exterminate the tribe. A heavy defeat was inflicted in 1730, and by 1738 the Fox, once 10,000 strong, numbered only a few hundred.[25]

The French advanced and solidified their presence with forts. In 1724 Fort d'Orléans was established on the north bank of the Missouri near its confluence with the Mississippi, but the initiative could not be sustained from distant Louisiana, a colony then in difficulties, and in 1728 the fort was abandoned. New France proved a better basis for expansion. Fort Niagara was rebuilt in the 1720s, and in the 1730s Pierre Gaultier de La Verendrye built a series of posts towards the sea then believed to be in western Canada. Fort St Charles (1732) on the Lake of the Woods was followed by Fort Maurepas (1734) at the southern end of Lake Winnipeg, and Fort La Reine (1738) on the Assiniboine River. Fort Bourbon (1739) took the French presence to the northwest shore of Lake Winnipeg, Fort Dauphin (1741) established their presence on the western shore of Lake Winnipegosis, and Fort La Corne (1753) near the Forks of the Saskatchewan, a crucial node of native trade routes first reached by French explorers in 1739–40. These explorations enhanced the French position in the fur trade, but did not bring the hoped-for route to the Pacific.

Further south the French expanded from Louisiana. Upstream from New Orleans, the Natchez initially accepted French trade and expansion, but in 1729 a French land fraud led to a Natchez attack in which over 200 settlers were killed. The Natchez did not receive the support of other tribes and in 1731 were crushed by the French and their allies, the Choctaws, in a campaign of systematic extermination. The rising showed the weakness of the colony, as it had been necessary to call in troops from France, and the cost hit the colony's proprietor, the Company of the Indies, leading the crown to resume control of Louisiana in 1731.[26]

The war with the Natchez led to a spread of French commitments. Having been driven back by the Natchez in an attempt to reach the Arkansas country in 1731, the French established a garrison at Arkansas Post in 1732 in order to keep an eye on the Chickasaws, rivals of the Choctaws, who traded with the British, and with whom the remnants of the Natchez had taken refuge. Chickasaw independence concerned the French, who in 1736 launched attacks from New France and Louisiana. Intimidated, the Chickasaws agreed a truce, but they remained aligned with the British, and in 1749 drove the French from their position at Arkansas Post.[27]

The British were also advancing from their colonies. The war with the French in 1702–13 interacted with tension and conflict with Native Americans, especially arising from the land hunger that the demographic growth of the British colonies exacerbated. The Tuscaroras responded to the advance of settlers by raiding settlements in North Carolina in 1711. Colonel John Barnwell led counter-attacks in 1711 and 1712, but did not win any decisive victory. In contrast, James Moore, with the support of a larger Native force, defeated the Tuscaroras in 1713: their fortified base of Neoheroka was stormed and nearly 600 were killed or enslaved. This defeat was followed by the advance of settlement to the Blue Ridge Mountains.

Provoked by exploitation by Carolina merchants and landowners, the Yamasee of the Lower Savannah River attacked South Carolina in 1715, raiding to within twelve miles of Charleston. Other tribes, including the Lower Creek, Cherokee and Catawba, provided support. The initial South Carolina military response was unsuccessful, but the Native alliance was not sustained. The Cherokee came round to help the Carolinians in 1716, and in 1717 the Creek deserted the Yamasee. Native disunity greatly helped the colonists. In 1711 the Yamasee had helped the North Carolinians.

British activity was a matter of initiatives by British-Americans. The British government took little interest in the interior of North America. In contrast, the French followed an active policy of expanding their power in the interior. The Peace of Aix-la-Chapelle with Britain (1748) was followed by a determined French effort to reimpose control in the hinterland of New France. Fort St Jean was rebuilt in 1748 in order to strengthen the French position near Lake Champlain: a new wagon road linked the fort to Montreal. Niagara was also rebuilt, and in 1750 the French erected Fort Rouillé (Toronto).

French power was also extended. In 1749 a small expedition under Céleron de Blainville was sent into the Ohio valley. It had little effect, bar burying lead plates asserting French sovereignty. Nevertheless, this expedition was indicative of a newly strengthened French imperial assertiveness. This was to contribute directly to the outbreak of the Seven Years War, which led to a major increase in the degree of European resources committed to North America and India, and to a considerable extension of European power there. Although the troops deployed were intended for use against other European states, they were drawn into conflict with real or apparent allies of the latter, and, more generally, helped advance European power and also ensure that it was measured in terms of territorial extent.

South America

South America is generally denied any military history between Pizarro's overthrow of the Incas in the 1530s and the Wars of Liberation in the early nineteenth century. This is misleading. The *conquistadores* had taken only a fraction of the continent, and conflict between Spanish and Portuguese colonists and Natives continued. The pace was set by colonial expansion. This was most notable in the early eighteenth century in Brazil as a result of the discovery of goldfields in the interior, including the Cuiabá goldfields in 1719.

The consequences of exploitation soon worried the Native Americans. A convoy of gold seekers in canoes was destroyed by the Paiaguá on the River Paraguay in 1725, and another was mauled the following year. The Paiaguá fired their bows more rapidly than the Portuguese their muskets, and they also made masterly use of their canoes, not least by leaping into the water and tipping them up to protect themselves from musket fire. In 1730 the annual flotilla carrying gold was ambushed and mostly destroyed on the way back from Cuiabá. Punitive expeditions achieved little in 1730 and 1731, but in 1734 the combination of surprise attack and firepower devastated the Paiaguá. Although the Paiaguá mounted successful attacks in 1735 and 1736, their casualties led to a slackening of activity, and they were also affected by disease and by the attacks of the Guaicurú Natives. By the 1780s the Paiaguá had been largely wiped out, but their story shows the danger of assuming a simple model of European military superiority.

Elsewhere, the use of native allies was important: Portuguese troops were unable to defeat the Caiapó, who ambushed Portuguese settlements and convoys, but the Bororo, in contrast, under the leadership of a Portuguese woodsman, António Pires de Campos, pressed the Caiapó hard in a bitter war between 1745 and 1751. The Portuguese ability to win and exploit local allies reflects the lack of Native unity. This, disease and the consequences of enslavement all helped the Portuguese far more than any success in contact warfare.[28]

Conclusions

The expansion and the warfare of the period showed the diversity of circumstances in which the Europeans operated. Expansion in North America indicated that it was possible, with a modest outlay of effort, to make major territorial acquisitions where the native population was relatively small. Conversely, where the demographic balance was very different, as in India, gains and influence depended on fitting into local power struggles. If the concluding theme was therefore one of variety, there was, even in North America, a need to adapt to and benefit from existing polities and peoples. This could entail co-operation, exploitation, or both, but the only blank spaces were on the map.

8

WARFARE WITH NON-EUROPEANS, 1750–1830

1750–89

The warfare of the 1750s is generally considered in terms of the Seven Years War (1756–63) between Britain and France, and their respective allies, but it was preceded outside Europe by conflict involving both states and non-European powers that not only helped to pave the way for war between Britain and France, but was also important for the wider military balance between European and non-European powers.

India, 1750–6

Conflict was most acute in India. There, Britain and France supported rival claimants to the Carnatic. In 1751 Chanda Sahib, the French-backed Nawab, besieged Trichinopoly, but the young Robert Clive led a diversionary force of 500 which captured his capital, Arcot, in a surprise attack, and then held the fort against a fifty-day siege by a force of about 10,000. After the siege was raised, Clive pursued the retreating besiegers and defeated them at Arní. He followed this up by defeating Chanda's son, Rájá Sahib, for a second time at Cáveripák.

These defeats wrecked the momentum and appearance of success on which Dupleix depended. Further north, he had pressed on to fight the Marathas, defeat of whom he saw as a prelude to an expedition to replace the Nawab of Bengal with a pro-French ruler. On the night of 3–4 December 1751 Bussy led a surprise attack by 411 Frenchmen and Hyderabadi forces that routed their army. However, Dupleix was wrong to expect a quick war. Instead it proved difficult to obtain any lasting victory over the Marathas, the lengthy campaign exhausted Hyderabadi finances, and the French were unable to concentrate their own or their allies' forces to fight Clive in the Carnatic. In 1752 both Chanda and a French force surrendered in the Carnatic, the latter to Stringer Lawrence, the able and energetic commander of the forces of the Madras Presidency of the East India Company. Lawrence created a company field army in the Carnatic, ensuring that the company was not restricted militarily to a few coastal positions, and enabling it to take a more active role in politics. By 1752, when Lawrence defeated French-trained *sepoys* at Bahur and established a garrison at Trichinopoly, his army amounted to 1,200 European troops and 2,000 *sepoys*. In 1753 the French besieged Trichinopoly, but Lawrence relieved it. The battles he fought in 1753, such as Golden Rock and Sugarloaf Rock, are now forgotten, but they reflected Britain's successful use of Indian troops, and secured the British position in a strategic area, greatly expanding their control southwest from Madras. Dupleix's failure to regain Trichinopoly and his demands for men and money led to his recall by the French company in 1754 and a provisional peace was reached with the British that winter.[1] Britain was left as the dominant power in South India, but the French remained influential in Hyderabad, much to the concern of the East India Company. Local support remained important: in 1756 the British co-operated with the Marathas in capturing Gheria and destroying the fleet of Tulajee Angria.

North America

Whereas conflict in India did not lead directly into world war, the situation was different in North America: royal authority was more directly involved than in India, where it was largely a case of the two East India Companies hiring out troops to rival Indians. In 1752–4 the French sent more troops into the Ohio valley, drove out British traders, intimidated Britain's native allies, and built four forts between Lake Erie and the junction of the Ohio and the Monongahela rivers, although this alienated many of the Native population and led some to seek British support.[2] Both sides were convinced that the other was stirring up Native hostility. The fur trade interacted with Native alliances and a dynamic French strategic policy.[3] Further north, French competition with the Hudson's Bay Company was part of an assertiveness also directed against Natives. The destruction of villages and crops, in which the French relied heavily on the Quapaws, forced the Chickasaws to terms in 1752.

The clash over the Ohio valley led directly to fighting between British colonial and French forces in 1754 and thence to war. This conflict also affected relations with the Natives, and was affected by them. For example, the defeat of Edward Braddock in 1755 by a French–Native force owed much to Braddock's refusal of support from Shingas, the Delaware chief who had sought a promise that the Ohio region should remain in Native hands. From a Native viewpoint, it was crucial to consider whether Britain or France posed the greatest threat to the Ohio hinterland. In 1758 the French position was weakened when Pennsylvania authorities promised the Native Americans that they would not claim land west of the Appalachians. The consequent shift of Native support obliged the French to give up the Ohio region, while John Forbes's success in capturing Fort Duquesne (Pittsburg) strengthened Native advocates of conciliation. Viewed from Europe, this was still a two-sided conflict, whereas on the ground the shifting support and fears of Native groups could be decisive. Equally, the victory of the British over the French, which culminated with the surrender of Montréal and the Governor-General of New France on 8 September 1760, left the Natives in a weaker position.

That year war had broken out between the British and the Cherokee, a generally pro-British tribe whose hunting lands in modern east Tennessee and west North Carolina were under pressure from the advancing frontier of British-American activity, control and settlement. Effective resistance thwarted an expedition of regular troops in 1760 and the Cherokee forced the besieged Fort Loudoun to surrender. However, in 1761 the British were able to mount a fresh invasion. Their mixed force – of regular troops, Carolina Rangers and allied Natives – displayed the variety of forces the British could deploy. A scorched-earth policy in which settlements and crops were burned was countered by Cherokee resistance based on highland hideouts, but food shortages and despair engendered by failure led the Cherokee in 1761 to agree terms and yield territory.[4]

India, 1756–66

In India the Anglo-French struggle was less central to that with native rulers, certainly outside southern India, where the French had been defeated at Wandewash in 1760 and had lost their last base, Pondicherry, in 1761. In June 1756 in response to the company's defiance of his authority, Siraj-ud-daula, the newly acceded Nawab of Bengal, stormed poorly defended and fortified Fort William at Calcutta after a brief siege. He confined his captives in the 'Black Hole', which, for the British, was to become a symbol of Indian cruelty and thus moral inferiority. A British expeditionary force under Robert Clive regained Calcutta and pressed on to defeat the Nawab at Plassey on 23 June 1757. One of his generals, Mir Jaffir, was installed as his successor, and Clive received over £250,000 from him.

The path from Plassey to British control of Bengal was not smooth: the British had to face both attempts to reimpose a Muslim ascendancy and the problems of establishing a stable regime there. In 1760 an invasion of Bihar by Shah Zodah, the eldest son of the Mughal Emperor, was defeated. The increasingly distrusted Mir Jaffir was replaced by his son-in-law, Mir Qasim, but he fell foul of the excessive financial demands of the company and the private interests of its avaricious officials. War broke out in 1763, but the British were helped by the earlier defeat of the French in India. Mir Qasim was heavily defeated in 1763, and in 1764, at the culminating Battle of Buxar (23 October), Sir Hector Munro and 7,000 men of the company army, including 1,500 British soldiers, defeated Mir Qasim and his allies, Shah Alam II, the Mughal Emperor, and Shuja-ud-dowla, the Nawab-Wazir of Oudh, who together fielded a force of 50,000 men. The company's conquest was attributed by contemporary Persian-language histories not to its military superiority, but to the factionalism and moral decline of the ruling Indian families of the region.[5]

Buxar was followed by the Treaty of Allahabad (1765), which recognized the British position in Bengal and Bihar, stabilizing the situation from the Indian as much as the British perspective. The Mughal Emperor conferred the right to collect revenue and conduct civil justice, the *diwan*, on the company. Shuja-ud-dowla accepted the settlement as a result of the company's invasion of Oudh, while Mir Qasim was left as an inconsequential exile. Bengal and Bihar were to provide a solid source of revenue and manpower, and to be the basis of British imperial power in Asia. The Madras and, to a greater extent, Bombay presidencies of the company lacked the resources of the Bengal Presidency, and neither, for a while, made great headway against local rivals, but Bengal enabled the company to act as an effective territorial power, not only in the Ganges valley, but elsewhere in India.

The defeat of the French left the British able to take initiatives elsewhere in India, successfully besieging Vellore in 1762 and Madurai in 1764, and in 1766 gaining the Northern Circars as the price of their alliance with the Nizam of Hyderabad. In contrast, the Peace of Paris of 1763 left France with only five bases in India – Pondicherry, Chandernagore, Yanaon, Karikal and Mahé – all of which were returned by Britain to France in 1765.

Pontiac's War

British victory in the Seven Years War had also altered the situation in North America. After the war the British failed to provide the customary presents that were seen by the Natives as compensation for the right to trade and travel, while British-American merchants acted in an arbitrary fashion and settlers moved into native lands, breaking agreements. Mounting tension led to Pontiac's War (1763–4), which involved a number of tribes, especially the Ottawa under Pontiac. However, the 'northern nations' were generally quiescent, and there was no unified effort among the Natives who rose, unsurprisingly so given the vast area at stake. Pontiac's influence was limited. Attempts at securing Native unity centred less on him than on Nativist religious revival leaders, such as Neolin, the Delaware prophet. This began a movement for unified resistance to Anglo-American expansion which continued until the war of 1812.

A series of attacks was launched by the Natives in May 1763. Settlers fled back over the Appalachians, and a number of lightly defended forts were captured or surrendered. The Natives were helped by the small size of the British army in North America and the vast area it had to cover. A series of Native victories in battle also prevented the British from relieving besieged forts, hit their communications, and lessened their confidence in their ability to move troops safely. Nevertheless, the major forts, with their sizeable garrisons and artillery, resisted siege. The Native Americans were least effective at siegecraft: they lacked cannon, and their ethos and method of warfare were not well suited to the lengthy, methodical, arduous and unheroic nature of the art. Denied the French support of the past, the Natives were also affected by shortages of supplies. By 1764, they were probably short of gunpowder, which had also been a problem for the Cherokee. The difficulty the Natives faced in sustaining long conflicts was an instance of the advantage that professional permanent forces had over societies in which conflict involved the bulk of the adult male population. The Natives did not launch attacks in 1764 possibly because they were satisfied by the 1763 Royal Proclamation establishing a line beyond which colonial settlement was prohibited. A threat to Native settlements in the Muskingum valley also encouraged the Natives to negotiate. A series of treaties ended the war. The Royal Proclamation – and the resumption of presents – suggests that the settlement was a compromise. The Natives returned all prisoners, but ceded no land.[6]

India, 1767–84

The initial stages of Pontiac's War indicate the danger of reading too much into Britain's success in the Seven Years War. So also in India did the war of 1767–9 with Haidar Ali of Mysore, an effective general whose forces were particularly strong in light cavalry. The British were unable to sustain an invasion of Mysore in 1768, whereas in 1769 Haidar's cavalry ravaged the Carnatic (thereby hitting the company's ability to raise taxes), advanced as far as Madras and dictated peace to the Council. A war with the Marathas in 1774–6 left an unsatisfactory peace and was followed, from 1778, by a fresh conflict in which, on 13 January 1779, a surrounded and battered British army advancing on Pune (Poona), the Maratha capital, was forced to sign a convention at Wadagaon that provided for the withdrawal of the army to Bombay. A fresh advance in 1781 also failed and led to a retreat with serious losses. The Marathas showed increasing effectiveness, emulating the infantry–artillery combinations of European armies while maintaining their superiority in cavalry. The British were also affected by problems of terrain and logistics, and by the need to fight Mysore at the same time. The Treaty of Salbai (May 1782) ended the war, with most British gains restored to the Marathas.

Further south, Anglo-Maratha hostilities gave Haidar an opportunity to attack. He had been angered by the British capture of the French base at Mahé, which Haidar saw as under his protection, an instance of the complex interaction of considerations of authority and power. On 10 September 1780 the Mysore army destroyed a British square at Perumbakam, killing or capturing the entire force of 3,720 men. Haidar pressed on to make gains in the Carnatic. The devastation spread by his cavalry hit British logistics, but Haidar was defeated by Eyre Coote at Porto Novo on 1 July 1781 and Madras was saved. In a repetition of Perumbakam another British force was defeated on 18 February 1782, when its ammunition ran out, but Haidar's successor, his son Tipu Sultan, suffered from the cessation of French support after they made peace with the British in 1783. Nevertheless, the cost of the war to the company led to pressure for its end, and in January 1784 the British garrison at Mangalore surrendered after a ten-month siege. The subsequent Treaty of Mangalore of 11 March 1784 was based on the *status quo ante bellum*. The British had been helped by the divided nature of their opponents in India, by the absence of any serious military challenge to Bengal, and by their ability to move troops from Bengal to the Carnatic.

South Asia

Elsewhere in Asia the Europeans were less successful. The Russians made no attempt to advance against Japan or China. In the Third Javanese War of Succession (1746–57) the Dutch suffered defeats in 1750 and 1755. The Dutch East India Company was far weaker than its British counterpart. Its profits fell in the 1730s and 1750s, ending the earlier programme of long-term expansion. The Dutch adopted a hesitant role in the Malay world, not least because of concern over the contrast between their weak defences in Malacca and the military strength of the expanding Bugis, although the Bugi siege of Malacca was to be repelled in 1784. Far from there being a tide of European advance, after a punitive expedition against Siak in 1761 there were no important Dutch operations in the Malay world until 1784.

Further west, in 1761–6, the Dutch faced a difficult war in Sri Lanka that indicated the limitations of the European military. Far from the war beginning with an act of European aggression, it was launched by Kirti Sri, ruler of the interior kingdom of Kandy. Exploiting discontent in the militarily weak Dutch coastal possessions, he overran much of the coast, although it proved far harder for the indigenous forces to capture fortified positions, and Dutch-held Negombo successfully resisted attack in 1761. Furthermore, the Dutch benefited from the ability of European powers to deploy troops from elsewhere in their imperial systems, in their case mainly from the East Indies.

Having regained the coastal regions by the end of 1763, the Dutch set out to take the interior in 1764. Six columns were sent against the capital, but they were as unsuccessful in this as the much earlier Portuguese expeditions into the interior in 1594, 1630 and 1638. There had been no improvement in European offensive military capability; the usual problems of operating in the tropics, particularly disease, difficult terrain and an absence of maps, were exacerbated by Kandyan resistance. Taking advantage of the jungle terrain, Kandyan sharpshooters harassed the Dutch, inflicting heavy casualties.

Learning from past mistakes was an important characteristic of successful European operations. In January 1765 the Dutch launched a new campaign, replacing swords and bayonets with less cumbersome machetes, providing a more practical uniform, and moving more rapidly. To begin with, the Dutch triumphed, capturing the deserted capital, but the Kandyans refused to engage in battle – always a sensible response to European firepower. As a result, Dutch energies were dissipated in seeking to control a country rendered intractable by disease and enemy raiders. Peace was made in 1766. Kandy would not be conquered until the British overran it in 1815.

Africa

Further west, the Europeans did not extend their power in the Persian Gulf, Southwest Asia and East Africa. A Portuguese attempt to regain Mombasa in 1769 failed. Having established a base at Fort Dauphin in 1748, the French did not conquer Madagascar until the 1890s. Elsewhere in Africa, Dutch advances from Cape Town only affected the local situation, as did operations along the North African coast, where Morocco captured Mazagan from the Portuguese in 1765, but was less successful against Spanish-held Melilla in 1774–5. The limitations of European naval and amphibious power were revealed in unsuccessful Spanish attacks on Algiers in 1775 and 1784.

Latin America

In Latin America Native resistance could only check, not reverse, the tide of advance. This was true of Araucanians in central Chile, of Caribs on St Vincent, of resistance to the Spaniards on the Mosquito coast of Nicaragua, and in the Guajiro peninsula in Colombia in the 1770s, and of the Muras in central Amazonia. Adept with their bows and arrows, and effective owing to their mobility and their avoidance of Portuguese firepower, the Muras harried Portuguese settlements and trade routes in the 1760s and 1770s.[7]

North America

Further north, the Spaniards found it difficult to consolidate their frontier to the north of Mexico. In 1751 the Pimas of Arizona rebelled, in the 1770s the Spaniards were hard pressed in the Santa Fe region, and in 1781 the successful Yuma rebellion thwarted Spanish plans for expansion through the Colorado valley and into central Arizona. The Spaniards faced what they, but not their opponents, saw as rebellion, and also pressure from tribes on the Great Plains moving south, especially the Comanche and the Utes. Well mounted and armed with French firearms, tribes such as the Apache were able to thwart the Spanish expeditions sent against them, for example in 1759 and 1775. In 1776 there were only 1,900 Spanish troops to defend the 1,800-mile frontier of Spanish North America. A successful Spanish attack on the Comanches in 1779 was followed by treaties with them in 1785–6: peace was now the Spanish goal, and they used goods and trade to lure the Native Americans.

At another end of North America the Aleuts of the Aleutian Isles had initially posed few problems for the Russians in their quest for furs. However, in 1761 effective resistance on the Fox Islands began. This was overcome in 1766 by an amphibious force deploying cannon. As earlier in Siberia, massacre and disease secured the Russian 'achievement'.

Many Native Americans supported the British during the American War of Independence (1775–83) and pressed hard on the frontier of European settlement, especially in New York and Pennsylvania in 1778. The Natives maintained the initiative at the close of the war, defeating the American Patriots in Kentucky in 1782. Expeditions by the Patriots, such as John Sullivan's campaign against the Iroquois in 1779, were often unsuccessful, in Sullivan's case in large part because of the logistical problems facing expeditions deep into the interior. However, despite the fighting quality of the Natives, the cumulative pressure of sustained conflict damaged their societies and disrupted their economies. In 1779 Sullivan destroyed many villages and 160,000 bushels of corn, causing much suffering.[8]

Russo-Turkish conflcits

With the benefit of more resources and a more fixed target, the Russians were more successful when war resumed against the Turks in 1768. Column formations using both firepower and bayonet charges helped bring success in battles such as Ryabaya Mogila, Larga and Kagul in 1770 and Kozludji in 1774. The Crimea was overrun in 1771, and the Ottoman fortress system on the Danube breached in 1770 and 1774. The Russians were increasingly expert in the deployment of their forces. The adoption of more flexible means of supply helped to reduce the cumbersome baggage trains, although logistics remained a serious problem until the development of railways in the nineteenth century, not least because of the primitive nature of the empire's administrative system. However, improvement permitted better strategic planning, including improved use of riverine and littoral communications. At sea the Russians heavily defeated the Turks at Cesmé in the Aegean in 1770. By the Treaty of Kutchuck-Kainardji of 1774, the Russians gained territory to the north of the Black Sea, including the coast as far as the Dniester.

The Russians were also successful against the Turks in their next conflict, in 1787–92. In 1787 the Russians defeated a Turkish attempt to regain the Crimea (gained by Russia in 1783), and in 1788 the Russians moved on to the offensive, taking the powerful fortress of Ochakov, which overlooked the entrance to the Bug and the Dnieper. In 1790 the Turkish forts in the Danube delta were captured. In the Black Sea the Turkish fleet was defeated at the Battles of the Dnieper (1788) and Tendra (1790).

Conclusions

Thus by 1790 there were important signs of European territorial advance, especially in India and to the north of the Black Sea. There were also advances elsewhere, for example by the Spaniards in California. However, it would be mistaken to exaggerate the extent of the gains in this period. It would also be mistaken to neglect European setbacks and defeats. Thus, in India, the British successes of 1757–65 should be considered alongside subsequent failures against the Marathas and Mysore. When war with Mysore resumed in 1790 the British were unsuccessful in their first year's campaign. Russian success against the Turks was not, initially, shared by the Austrians when they entered the war in 1788; an attack on Belgrade miscarried. The Native Americans were able to inflict defeats on the forces of the newly independent USA. The victory of the Miamis under

127

Little Turtle on the Maumee River in western Ohio (1790) was followed by the defeat of Arthur St Clair's army on the Wabash River in Ohio (1791).[9]

These setbacks are stressed in order to emphasize the importance to the European advance of the subsequent period, but, nevertheless, there were also aspects of European success in the years 1750–90 that are worth noting. The value of the 'global reach' provided by the flexibility of amphibious power was repeatedly demonstrated. Furthermore, although non-European powers could be successful, the military capability that the Europeans gained from warships, firepower and fortifications was formidable. The major centres of European power did not fall to non-European peoples. Spanish-ruled Manila fell to the British in 1762, not to a rising in the Philippines, nor to an attacking Asian power.

The importance of fortifications can be seen in a characteristic feature of the European presence: the desire, and the ability, to dig, and to do so in a planned fashion. European control was anchored by fortifications, for example those along the Bío Bío River in Chile, such as the fortress of Nacimiento, or the Spanish fortress at Pensacola in West Florida, founded in 1698, or that at Monterey, established in 1770 as the capital of New California. Similarly, in India the British developed powerful fortresses at Bombay, Calcutta and Madras. When George Paterson visited Bombay in 1770 he thought the square fort in which the British had sheltered against the Mughals in 1686 'by no means fit to sustain a modern attack', but noted more modern fortifications going up, including those on a hill overlooking the town. He was greatly impressed by the speed of the work:

> it must be fortified. Well this being agreed to, the fortifications were well planned and immediately carried into execution, and all the time they were employed about this, there were several thousands also constantly at work to take away the hill and blowing it up like fire and smoke. They both came on apace and very soon there will be no hill; but there will be fine fortifications . . . All these works put together may be very well defended by 10,000 men, an army sufficient to meet any power in the field that can attack this place.[10]

As with Spanish *presidios* and Russian lines of fortification, this was part of the process in which the European presence rested on the ability to dig. In 1788 Lord Cornwallis, the British commander in India, took an interest in the purchase of entrenching tools. Having already ordered '4,000 good iron shovels', he wanted '2,000 iron spades to be made immediately'.[11]

However, as ever, variety must be stressed. Due to a lack of interest and resources, many fortified positions were weak and poorly garrisoned. In 1710 the wood of the French fortress at Fort Louis (later Mobile), built in 1702, was so rotted by humidity and decay that it could not support the weight of the cannon. The garrison suffered from an absence of fresh meat, from an insufficient supply of swords, cartridge boxes, nails, guns and powder, from demoralization and desertion, and from the lack of a hospital.

Furthermore, the Europeans held no monopoly of fortifications. Eastern Native Americans had many palisaded villages in the seventeenth century, and with the introduction of firearms European-style bastions appeared to defend against cross-fire. There was at least one example of a masonry fort in New England. However, the Native Americans usually abandoned their forts when Europeans approached them, especially when the latter had cannon. They had learned that forts could be death traps.

The British encountered more formidable fortresses in India. Seringapatam fell in 1799, but in 1791 it had defied attack. Alyhgur fell in 1803, but in 1805 General Gerard Lake's force suffered over 2,000 casualties in four unsuccessful attempts to storm Bharatpur: Lake was unable both to neutralize the defensive fire and to blow the gates in, as he had done at Alyhgur. The frequency with which the British stormed fortresses in India is a reminder that firepower could only achieve so much. Most major fortifications erected by European forces survived native siege or attack if the assailants lacked the skills, resources and organization required for a lengthy siege. However, the possession of coastal fortresses did not bring control over the interior.

1790–1830

These four decades saw more territorial expansion by Europeans (and European-Americans) than over the previous four decades, although still far less than was to be the case in any forty-year period in the remainder of the nineteenth century. This expansion was not prevented by the serious conflicts between the European maritime powers that began in 1793, as the French Revolutionary Wars expanded, and lasted until 1815. Indeed, these conflicts encouraged European expansion, as fearful powers sought to block potential moves by opponents. Thus, British expansion in India owed much to concern about French plans, and Napoleon's expedition to Egypt in 1798 was designed to undermine the British position in South Asia.

Later, British sensitivity about the Persian Gulf was increased by the Franco-Persian alliance of May 1807 in which Napoleon promised to support Persia against Britain. This encouraged the British in November 1809 to sack the Wahabi base of Ras-ul-Khymah in the Persian Gulf from which the Wahabi pirates had attacked East Indiamen and British warships in the Arabian Gulf.

However, it would be misleading to ascribe European expansion largely to concern about other European powers. That was not the prime issue with the British in India in the early 1790s, nor with the (European-)Americans in North America in the same period, although the (European-)Americans were concerned about British intentions, and these did play a particular role in the 1810s. The Native position in the 'Old Northwest' was broken by Anthony Wayne's victory at the Battle of Fallen Timbers in 1794, a victory that allowed expansion into the region. In the battle, the natives were malnourished and, in part, taken by surprise, and they were also affected by a withdrawal of British support.

129

The American advance was consolidated by their victories in the 1810s over tribes with close ties to the British in Canada: the Shawnees at Tippecanoe in 1811 and at the Battle of the Thames (near London, Ontario) in 1813. Further south, the Creeks were attacked in 1813 and defeated at Tallasahatchee and Talladega. The following year Andrew Jackson attacked the centres of Creek power and stormed their fortified camp at Horseshoe Bend. The pace of expansion was pushed far more strongly and continuously by the newly independent United States than under the European powers, and was far more closely linked with the growing population and with a major extension of the cultivated area. There was also a powerful cultural and ideological component to American expansionism compounded of a strong belief in America's right and need to gain territory, as well as a love of adventure and glory.[12] The Americans also played a major role in influencing trade networks. In 1811 Astoria, an American post, was established at the mouth of the Columbia River.

A similar process can be seen in Australia, although the native population was not able to mount the opposition that was seen in North America. In both the demographic balance was against the locals. The situation was very different in South Asia and, albeit to a lesser extent, North Africa, while elsewhere in Africa the ecological situation was much harsher for Europeans than in Australasia or North America. Tropical diseases did not only devastate European forces in Africa; they were also a serious problem in the West Indies and parts of Asia. The British were thwarted in their 1803 war with the kingdom of Kandy by disease, as well as by inhospitable terrain, logistical problems and guerrilla attacks.

Nevertheless, the British were able to make major advances in South Asia, and their campaigns indicated what were to be some of the major themes of European transoceanic conflict in the nineteenth century, not least the primary importance of achieving the deployment of troops where they were initially required, and then moving them as needed in accordance with strategic plans. Logistics were transformed as part of an organizational–industrial–technological nexus that was inherent to the process of European change in this period.

India

The pace of British advance in India was formidable. In 1792 a successful advance on Seringapatam and the defeat of Tipu Sultan of Mysore outside his capital led Tipu to surrender and cede much of his territory. Two years later the British won the Second Rohilla War, and in 1799 in the Fourth Mysore War the British were both totally victorious and successful far more rapidly than in the Third War. Fearful of links between Tipu and the French, the British abandoned a planned expedition against Manila. In 1799 they successfully co-ordinated forces from Bombay and Madras and maintained the pace of their strategic offensive. Concentrating on position warfare, Tipu failed to display the necessary mobility. After a defeat at Malavelly, Tipu retreated into Seringapatam. The British artillery blew a breach in the ramparts which were successfully stormed under heavy fire.

The casualties included Tipu. The victorious forces pressed on to capture other forts, and the rest of Mysore rapidly surrendered. The British then restored the dynasty displaced by Haidar Ali, although important territories were annexed by the East India Company. Mysore was left landlocked, and the new ruler forbidden to maintain any army. Arthur Wellesley, later Duke of Wellington, was put in command of Mysore in 1800 and showed himself adept in pacification operations.

The next major challenge came from the Marathas. In response to the weapons and tactics introduced into India by the Europeans in the mid-eighteenth century Maratha armies became more professional, so that a strategy based on living off the land was less feasible. New infantry and artillery units proved expensive, leading to developments in revenue administration, banking and credit. These trends created political problems, while in addition the Marathas were greatly weakened by periods of civil war. There was a considerable shift in power from the centre to the peripheral Maratha states, and this made the British task easier because it hindered co-operation between their opponents.

When the Second Maratha War broke out in 1803 the British fielded 60,000 men on a number of fronts. The commander in the Deccan, Wellesley, showed himself a master of methodical yet rapid warfare. After war was declared on the two leading Maratha rulers, Dowlut Rao Sindhia, Maharaja of Gwalior, and Raguji Bhonsle II, Maharaja of Berar, Wellesley advanced, thus encouraging Britain's allies. At the Battle of Assaye (23 September), Wellesley, with 4,500 men, 17 cannon and 5,000 unreliable Indian cavalry, successfully confronted the combined army of Sindhia and Bhonsle, a force of 30,000 cavalry, 10,000 infantry trained by French officers and over 100 cannon. At Assaye, Wellesley demonstrated what he and other 'sepoy generals' believed essential for campaigning in India: speedy attack. This compensated for his numerical inferiority and for poor intelligence about the location of the Maratha forces. Wellesley's success in the battle owed much to bayonet charges, scarcely conforming to the standard image of Western armies gunning down masses of non-European troops relying on cold steel. Casualties accounted for over a quarter of the British force. The well-served Maratha artillery had been particularly deadly.

This artillery was also effective at Argaon (Argaum) on 29 November, although it could not prevent Wellesley from defeating Bhonsle. Wellesley's continued ability to take the initiative and to sustain the range and mobility of his force was instrumental in leading to a successful peace with Sindhia on 30 December: the Treaty of Surji-Anjangaon. The weak command structure and lack of money of the Marathas disrupted operations; the absence of regular pay destroyed discipline and control. In northern India,the British under Gerard Lake defeated Maratha armies, leading the Mughal Emperor to seek British protection. The following year, Lake defeated Jeswunt Rao Holkar, Maharaja of Indore, another major Maratha leader.

Supported by the resources of the fertile areas of India already under their control, the British thus showed themselves capable of defeating the most powerful of Indian forces. Bold leadership was also crucial, as was the high degree of military preparedness in the Revolutionary and Napoleonic period, and the extent to which the British were less willing than earlier conquerors to absorb Indian political and military values. However, the greater willingness to resort to force was costly. The commercial values of the East India Company were placed under great pressure and the company was nearly bankrupted by the campaigns of 1803–4. The cost of the war and the terms on which it ended were such that Maratha power was not crippled.

There was a renewed bout of British military activity in South Asia in 1814–18. War was declared against the Gurkhas of Nepal in 1814. Initial failures in 1814–15 owed much to poor British generalship, unfamiliarity with mountain warfare and the Gurkha combination of defensive positions, especially hill forts and stockades, with attacks on British detachments. British success was far from inevitable, but victories at Almora (1815), Malaun (1815) and Makwanpur (1816) eventually brought the conflict to a successful conclusion in March 1816. The victories owed much to the effective use of bayonet attacks, but also reflected luck, the skill of some commanders and the failure of the Gurkhas.[13] Further south, in 1815 the British conquered the kingdom of Kandy in the interior of Sri Lanka as a result of concerted operations by independently moving columns. The Marathas were rapidly crushed in 1817–18, thanks to victories at Kirkoe, Sitabaldi, Mahidpur, Koregaon and Satara. The subsequent treaties led to major acquisitions of territory, and the remaining Maratha leaders had to accept terms that brought them under British protection.

These victories brought to an end the challenge posed by one of the most dynamic elements in Indian society. The Marathas had successively resisted and supplanted the Mughals, but could not do the same to the British. Between 1799 and 1818 Mysore, Kandy, Nepal and the Marathas had all been humbled. There still remained other formidable powers in South Asia, especially Burma and the Sikhs. However, most of India was now under a greater degree of British power than hitherto, and this provided the British with a secure reservoir of soldiers, not least because they had come to dominate the market for military manpower.[14]

Successes brought fresh challenges. The Sikhs succeeded the Marathas as a threat to the British position in northern India, while Burmese expansion was seen as a challenge to Bengal. In the First Burmese War of 1824–6 Britain's amphibious power led to the capture of Rangoon and of Tenasserim in 1824. In 1825–6 the British advanced up the Irrawady to Mandalay, benefiting from the effective use of their river fleet and from the disciplined firepower of their infantry. In the subsequent peace Britain was ceded Arakan and Tenasserim.

Russian expansion

Russia and the newly independent United States of America were the other two 'European' powers that achieved most success. Having advanced south of the Danube in 1791, the Russians forced the Turks to accept terms the following year that left Russia firmly established on the Black Sea, a goal that had eluded Peter the Great. In the Caucasus the Russians captured Derbent in 1796 and annexed much of Georgia in 1801.

When war between Russia and Turkey resumed in 1806, the deficiencies of the Russian army, which included inadequately developed support services, did not prevent it from being an effective force. In 1806–12 the Russians occupied Moldavia and Wallachia, operated south of the Danube, and, as a result of Kutuzov's victory at Ruschuk (1811), gained Bessarabia at the Treaty of Bucharest.

In the Russo-Persian War of 1825–8 the Russians won the Battle of Ganja, captured Erivan and forced the Persians to sign the Treaty of Turkomanchi, which led to the Russian acquisition of the khanates of Erivan and Nakhichevan. In the Russo-Turkish War of 1828–9, the Russians again advanced into the Balkans. Tsar Nicholas I personally directed the successful siege of Varna (1828), and in 1829 Adrianople fell. To the east of the Black Sea, the Russians captured Anapa, Akshaltsikhe, Kars and Erzurum, and by the Treaty of Adrianople (1829) forced the Turks to abandon their position on the Circassian coast. To the east of the Caspian, the Russians annexed the lands of the Middle Kazak Horde in 1822, restructuring its organization and leadership, and introducing Russian administrative control based on a number of forts built in 1824–31. Further east, Russian naval raids and 'gunboat diplomacy' off Hokkaido and Sakhalin from the 1780s convinced some Japanese commentators that the country needed a navy and coastal artillery.[15]

North America

In the New World the Americans sought to impose their authority on the indigenous population in lands they had been ceded by European powers. The lessening of British support after American independence left Native Americans more vulnerable when the pace and pressure of settlement accelerated. The importance of foreign support was shown in 1786 when the Creeks of Alabama and Mississippi used arms supplied by Spanish governors to check the Americans' westward advance from Georgia. However, in 1795, Spain accepted the 31st parallel as the northern border of West Florida, opening the way for American penetration into the lands of the southeastern tribes. In the First Seminole War (1817–18) Andrew Jackson helped in his invasion by a force of Lower Creeks, increased American power in Florida, although the Second Seminole War of 1835–43 revealed the extent, to which Seminole power had not yet been crushed. Further west, the Russians established a base on the Californian coast, Fort Ross, in 1812. The Pomos who lived near by reacted violently, but disease and Russian firepower cut their numbers.

French imperialism

The expansion of Western powers was affected by the impact of conflict between them. In 1798 Napoleon had invaded Egypt, intending to make it a French base from which India could be threatened. After capturing Alexandria he defeated the Mamelukes, the de facto rulers of Egypt, at Shubra Khit and Embabeh, the Battle of the Pyramids, victories for defensive firepower over shock tactics. Cairo fell, but the French fleet was destroyed by the British under Horatio Nelson. This stranded the French, but Napoleon continued to consolidate his position, albeit in the face of a hostile population, which mounted an unsuccessful rising in Cairo. Napoleon pressed on to invade Palestine, but Acre successfully resisted. In the face of British naval power, the French were still isolated. Bonaparte abandoned his army and fled back to France by sea. The army left in Egypt was finally defeated by a British expeditionary force in 1801. This made it clear that Napoleon would not be able to project his power successfully along the Egypt–India axis. As a result, his victories in Egypt were of no lasting value in increasing French power projection.

Elsewhere, the French colonial presence shrivelled in the face of British pressure, although rebellion in Saint-Domingue and the sale of Louisiana to the USA in 1803 were also important. After the fall of Napoleon in 1815 it took several years before the French resumed the pace of expansion. They did not begin their second colonial empire until 1830, when they occupied Algiers with 37,000 troops. This had been intended to win popularity for the Bourbon Charles X, not to serve as the basis of a widespread empire.

After 1815

The Dutch, Portuguese and Spanish empires were also well hamstrung by the French Revolutionary and Napoleonic wars, although the first two had already lost their earlier dynamism. After the wars the Spaniards devoted their efforts to an unsuccessful attempt to retain their empire in Latin America, while Portugal was no longer able to maintain a successful imperial impetus.

The Dutch found it difficult to resume their earlier pace of expansion. Expeditions against Palembang in Sumatra were defeated in 1819 and initially in 1821, but they were eventually victorious that year. Also on Sumatra the Dutch only won the Padri War (1821–38) after defeats, including a serious one at Lintau in 1823. The Java War, which began in 1825, was only brought to a successful conclusion by the Dutch after five years of hard fighting. The conflict looked forward to the pattern of much imperial warfare over the following century. The Dutch were short of troops, but they benefited from Indonesian allies, including the Sultan of Yogyakarta. Initially, the Dutch were thwarted by the mobility and guerrilla tactics of their opponents, but they developed a network of fortified bases from which they sent out mobile columns that policed the local population, prevented the consolidation of rebel positions and attacked the rebels.

On the land frontiers of European powers, the Turks were affected by the success of insurrectionary movements in the Balkans. Risings there were not new, but they were now more successful. Greatly assisted by the Anglo-French–Russian naval victory over the Turks at Cape Navarino in 1827, the Greeks won their independence in 1830.

Reasons for European success

Nevertheless, compared with what was to come, the pace of Western expansion was still modest. Most of the world's population had never seen a European and in much of the eastern hemisphere the major conflicts did not involve Europeans. It was not until the technological transformations of the mid-nineteenth century – in communications, firepower and medicine – that the Western states would be able to seize control of much more of the world. Even then native co-operation was still important, especially in filling the ranks of imperial armies. Expansion in the late eighteenth and early nineteenth centuries, however, was important in creating the context for the subsequent core period of Western imperialism. A sense of superiority was encouraged. For example, the artistic account of Napoleon's invasion of Egypt in 1798 'laid the foundation for the cultural edifice of France's modern empire. Patrons, artists, and critics developed styles – ways of sponsoring, painting, and receiving accounts of the contemporary Orient, that rationalized and celebrated French intervention in the East.'[16]

More generally, territorial conquest became normative as the central facet of Western imperialism, and became intertwined with the role of imperial armies.[17] The focus was no longer so clearly on the power and rationale of trade, which had been much more central to the discourse of Europe's global role in the eighteenth century.

A reminder of the importance of the factors encouraging, or deterring, warfare and territorial conquest does not itself explain success. Instead, it is necessary to consider what helped the Europeans to offset the advantages enjoyed by their opponents' greater knowledge of, cultural identity with and administrative control over local territory and generally superior numbers locally. European success can be explained by a variety and varying combination of factors, including Europe's role as a major innovator of weapons and methods, and the different ambitions of European nations indicated, in part, by the failure of sophisticated East and South Asian states to develop oceanic naval power.

The way in which the combination held, or was held, together was in itself important: for example, the English East India Company was, despite its frequent internal disputes, a corporation of seamless continuity and was competing with personalized autocracies which were dependent on strong leadership and were vulnerable to recurrent succession crises. More generally, the Europeans benefited from the post-feudal, non-personalized nature of their military command systems and command philosophy, especially the application of reason and science to command problems. The same was equally true of weapons development and tactical theory, which, since the Renaissance, were far more highly developed in Europe. The number of manuals and speculative works on warfare seems to have been far greater there than elsewhere, and this helped change aspects of warfare that were hidebound, instinctive and traditional. Scientific developments were utilized. In addition European powers were able to use formidable quantities of munitions and other resources. In the relatively brief naval bombardment of Algiers in 1816 the British used 40,000 round shots and shells.[18]

The Europeans moved most towards a large-scale 'rationalization' of military units: they were to have uniform size, armaments, clothing, command strategies, and so on. Such developments made it easier to implement drill techniques that maximized firepower. They were not dependent on a particular political mechanism, for allied and subsidized units could be expected to fight in an identical fashion with 'national' units, a marked contrast to the situation in the Asiatic empires where there was a major difference between core and ancillary troops. The Europeans extended this model to India, training local units to fight as they did. This ensured that the Indian military labour market could be utilized to maximum effect.

It has been suggested that European-style use of firearms depended on types of drill that relied on patterns of constrained behaviour that in part reflected an ethic of self-constraint and a mechanistic aesthetic that were particularly developed in European culture.[19] Captain Robert Stuart, commander of a *sepoy* battalion in 1773, was convinced that only discipline, or rather a firepower-linked definition of it, would allow his unit to prevail. His instructions were shot through with assumptions about superiority, both functional and racial:

> As the superiority of English sepoys over their enemies, as likewise their own safety consist entirely in their steadiness, and attentiveness, to the commands of their officers, it is ordered, that no black officer or sepoy pretend to act, or quit his post without positive orders, he is to be put to death upon the spot . . . regularity and obedience to orders are our grand and only superiority.[20]

In 1776 the Scottish economist Adam Smith offered in his *Inquiry into the Nature and Causes of the Wealth of Nations* an analysis of the sociology of warfare, in which he contrasted nations of hunters, shepherds and husbandmen with the 'more advanced state of society', in which industry was important. These advanced societies were seen as providing a hierarchy of military organization and sophistication in which 'a well-regulated standing army' was vital to the defence of civilization. Firearms, Smith argued, were crucial in the onset of military modernity:

> Before the invention of fire-arms, that army was superior in which the soldiers had, each individually, the greatest skill in dexterity in the use of their arms . . . since the invention . . . strength and agility of body, or even extraordinary dexterity and skill in the use of arms, though they are far from being of no consequence, are, however, of less consequence . . . In modern war the great expence of fire-arms gives an evident advantage to the nation which can best afford that expence; and consequently, to an opulent and civilized, over a poor and barbarous nation. In ancient

times the opulent and civilized found it difficult to defend themselves against the poor and barbarous nations. In modern times the poor and barbarous find it difficult to defend themselves against the opulent and civilized.[21]

Smith exaggerated the military advantages of the 'opulent and civilized', but he captured an important shift. Those he termed 'civilized' were no longer on the defensive. This had been unclear in 1660–1750. Peter the Great had been defeated at the Pruth (1711), the Russians had been forced to abandon Persia (1732), and the Austrians to surrender Belgrade and northern Serbia to the Turks (1739). This process was not restricted to the Europeans. The Afghans overran Persia in 1722–3.

The nature of each of these episodes can be qualified, and the relationship between military development and civilization questioned; were, for example, the Turks less civilized than the Austrians, or the Persians than the Russians? Nevertheless, however defined, there is no doubting that a major shift occurred in Eurasia. By 1760 in East Asia and 1770 in Eastern Europe the land forces of China and the Europeans respectively were able to see off attacks by more primitively organized and less well-armed adversaries, and between 1750 and 1792 their land frontiers were pushed onward. Political and economic relations changed with this military shift. In the New World and Africa there was no comparable shift as in both the trends of the previous century were maintained: advancing frontiers of control and settlement in the New World, and no real changes in the situation between Europeans and non-Europeans in Africa.

In South Asia the situation was more complex. India was certainly an area of rapid changes in weaponry and military organizations. A volatile and pressurized international system was driving the pace of military adaptability. French experts taught Indians to cast cannon in the French style and also played a role in local fortification techniques. In hindsight Indian forces seemed obsolete, foredoomed to defeat by the British because of deficient weaponry and organization. When in the 1750s and 1760s many Indian mercenary troops came into the service of the British East India Company with their own weapons, the company officers considered them to be nearly worthless. Yet, it would be unwise to underrate the effectiveness of non-European forces in South Asia. The Sikhs were to be a formidable opponent for the British in the 1840s. There was no clear basis for any system of military ranking that put the Europeans foremost, and any suggestion of determinism in success has to be queried.

Accepting that, only European powers had to decide how best to organize, control and support transoceanic land and sea operations, and these became more important in the mid-eighteenth century as Britain and France developed *sepoy* forces in India that were larger, more effective and more dynamic than those of Portugal, and also sent appreciable numbers of regulars to North America. This led to a range of multiple military capability that no non-European power possessed, a range that was to be of great importance in helping to channel the products of nineteenth-century technological change and economic and demographic growth to European military and political advantage elsewhere in the world.

The unique European experience of creating a global network of empires and trade was based on an equally unique type of interaction between economy, technology and state formation. China and Japan were relatively centralized states. They knew how to build large ships and manufacture guns, their economies and levels of culture were not obviously below early modern European standards, and they wished to import little from Europe. However, there was hardly any interaction between these factors which might create development and change. In contrast, economic gain was a very important factor behind European maritime power projection: the possibility of profit acted as a powerful stimulus to technological development and improved organization for war, trade and colonization. These were to frame the nineteenth-century world.

9

THE TRANSFORMATION OF THE
EUROPEAN WORLD, 1775–1830

The revolutions that shook the European world from 1775 were of critical importance both in changing that world and in altering its relationship with non-European peoples. It is too easy to treat the two as in some fashion different, and to argue, in particular, that shifts in the power distribution within the European world did not alter its essentially exploitative relationship with the rest of the world and did not change the fundamental lineaments of capitalist economics, Christian and white supremacism, and imperialism by a multipolar state system (as opposed to a single empire). While the latter are all true, it was, nevertheless, the case that changes within the European system were important to the wider global position of this system.

The rise of the British empire

This chapter is concerned not with the struggle within Europe between the European powers, but rather with the position outside Europe, specifically the transformation of the colonial systems that focused on the loss of the American empires. Nevertheless, the struggle within Europe was important, for it helped to ensure that Britain, not France, became the leading European imperial state. This was crucial for the political culture that was to develop under imperial control. French-dominated colonies looked to Catholicism, civil law, French culture and language, and a different notion of representative government and politics to their British counterparts. The struggle between the European powers was central to the rise of the West, and to the question 'Which West?'

This was a struggle that was largely settled within Europe. Although it was very important that French colonies, and those of her allies, were captured by the British, this would have meant relatively little if Britain had succumbed to invasion, while, even if that had not occurred, a failure on the European continent of Britain's forces and alliance system could ensure that gains made overseas had to be returned. Thus, in the Peace of Aix-la-Chapelle of 1748 that ended the War of the Austrian Succession, the British returned Louisbourg, conquered in 1745, because the French had succeeded in overrunning the Austrian Netherlands (modern Belgium) and invading the United Provinces (modern Netherlands).

Similarly, in the Peace of Amiens of 1802 the British returned most of their colonial gains at the close of an unsuccessful conflict with Revolutionary France. In contrast, Napoleon's defeat on the European continent in 1814 and 1815 enabled Britain to keep those of its colonial conquests it wished to retain.

The Congress of Vienna of 1814–15 thus left Britain with Malta, Trinidad, Tobago, St Lucia, Guyana, Cape Colony, Mauritius, the Seychelles and the Dutch positions in Sri Lanka. Having crippled French, Danish, Dutch and Spanish naval power, Britain had been left free to execute amphibious attacks on their now-isolated colonies, as well as to make gains at the expense of non-European peoples. The route to India had been secured, and by 1815 Britain was the strongest power on the shores of the Atlantic and Indian oceans, as well as on the oceans themselves.

However, this was now a very different empire to the situation in 1775. Then, the majority of British subjects outside Britain were white (although the population of the West Indian colonies were predominantly black slaves), Christian, of British (or at least European) origin, and ruled with an element of local self-government. By 1815 none of this was true. This was partly due to British expansion, especially a growing focus on Asia, which predated the loss of the Thirteen Colonies, but also to the loss of those colonies, which were to provide the core of the United States of America.[1] Furthermore, this process was not restricted to the British. By 1815 most of the transoceanic European world outside the western hemisphere was British. By 1830, thanks to the Latin American Wars of Liberation, this was true of the vast majority of all European possessions abroad.

The situation was not to last; indeed, 1830 was the year of the French occupation of Algiers, the basis of their subsequent North African empire, and French intervention there had been suggested to Napoleon in 1802 by Jeanbon Saint André. Had Napoleon been more successful in Egypt, then the rest of the Mediterranean littoral of Africa might have followed. Nevertheless, the unique imperial oceanic position that Britain occupied in the Revolutionary and, even more, Napoleonic and post-Napoleonic periods was to be of importance to European imperialism, as well as to the subsequent history of Britain. France was to become a great imperial power again, Portugal and the Dutch were to make gains, and Germany, Italy, Belgium and the United States were to become imperial powers, but for none of these was empire as important and as central a feature of public culture as it was for Britain. Edmund Burke had told the Commons that Robert Clive, the victor of Plassey, 'has laid open such a world of commerce; he has laid open so valuable an Empire, both from our present possessions and our future operations; he has laid open additional manufactures and revenues . . . The Orient sun never laid more glorious expectations before us.'

Furthermore, British hegemony ensured that on the global scale there was no effective limit by other European powers to the expansion of British territorial control. The consequences of this were readily apparent in South Asia and Australasia.

The American Revolution

This was not an inevitable development. Indeed, the American Revolution had suggested that the British empire might collapse, or at least lose the hegemonic position it had attained thanks to victory in the Seven Years War. Such a decline seemed entirely probable, given contemporary belief in the cyclical character of power and also the experience of the earlier (relative) decline of European hegemonic powers: Portugal, Spain, the Dutch and France.

The rejection of the authority of a monarch by a part of his dominions and the willingness to defend such a rejection with the use of force was scarcely unprecedented when hostilities broke out in New England in 1775. The history of Catalonia or Hungary over the previous 150 years was ample demonstration of the precarious nature of authority in the territorial accumulations that constituted most of the states of the period. The American Revolution was significant because, very unusually, it was successful, and led to a new state; because it challenged the logic of colonialism; and because of the future importance of the United States.

The Declaration of Independence of 1776 represented a modification, if not rejection, of much of the *ancien régime*. Slavery and an inegalitarian socio-economic structure were accepted in the new state, but the political institutions and practices that characterized the newly independent society, ranging from republicanism to relative freedom of religion and speech, reflected the political vitality of aspirations that were not restricted to America. As a result, the American Revolution, which Britain accepted in 1783 after a bitter struggle that witnessed humiliating defeats at Saratoga (1777) and Yorktown (1781), has been frequently linked to a series of rebellions and revolutions in late eighteenth-century Europe that has been collectively referred to as the Atlantic Revolution.

It is sometimes overlooked that these revolutions usually arose as a result of political contingencies and that their aspirations and demands were rejected by large numbers of those they claimed to speak for. The causes of the American Revolution can be found more in an unwilling and hesitant response to the confused tergiversations of British policy, as remedies for the fiscal burden of imperial defence were sought in the context of heavy national indebtedness after the Seven Years War, than in any general desire for liberty. A lack of understanding of colonial society and aspirations on the part of the British government played major roles in the developing crisis. It was exacerbated in 1774 by the view that concessions would be seen as weakness, leading to fresh demands; earlier, in the 1760s, the unwillingness to resort to coercion had contributed to serious indecision in the handling of the situation by the British government. A similar lack of understanding can be seen among the reformist Spanish officials who helped to cause tension in Latin America, including the Quito uprising of 1765.[2]

The American Revolution looked back to seventeenth-century British traditions of resistance to unreasonable royal demands as much as to contemporary European intellectual debates. In some respects it was a second version of the

English Civil War, one in which the principal source of support for royal authority (from within the colonies) again came from Anglican loyalists.[3] It is also important to appreciate the tensions caused by developments within the colonies, not least the disruptive consequences of rapid population growth, and of the Great Awakening in religious consciousness, and the challenges to established patterns and practices of authority and social influence.[4]

This crisis in imperial relations was part of a more general collapse in European control in the New World in the century from 1775. Yet, rather than suggesting any inevitable clash, it is necessary to explain why the process of reaching and endlessly redefining a consensus that underlay and often constituted government in this period broke down. In the Seven Years War Anglo-Americans resisted efforts by the commanders to treat them as subjects, rather than as the allies they believed themselves to be. After the war many resisted Parliament's efforts to project its sovereign authority across the Atlantic. The debate over the terms of empire that grew out of the war evolved into an effort to limit the exercise of state power by defining the natural and constitutional rights of individuals and groups within the body politic.[5]

Disagreements over the colonial bond cut to the core of the nature of the British empire, which was that of a reciprocal profitability controlled by the British state, as expressed through the sovereignty of Parliament. This system, enshrined in the Navigation Acts, was publicly condemned in the American colonies, with attacks on the consumption of tea, and thus on the profitability of the East India Company. From 1770 the Sons of Liberty sought to prevent the drinking of British tea. When the North ministry passed a Tea Act in 1773, allowing the company to sell its tea directly to consignees in America, a measure designed to cut the cost of tea in America, this was condemned by Patriot activists unwilling to accept Parliament's right to affect American taxation. Ten thousand pounds' worth of tea was seized from three ships in Boston Harbour by Sons of Liberty led by Samuel Adams and thrown into the water.

Yet, before drawing a straight line from such clashes to the outbreak of the Revolution, and then the loss of the colonies, it is necessary to note the resilience of the empire in areas where there could still be serious clashes over the pretensions and policies of the crown.[6] This was true of Britain's Caribbean colonies:

> Despite the political impasses experienced by most islands, the British West Indies contributed significantly to their own defence during the American War . . . Even at their most fractious, the assemblies vied with one another in protestations of loyalty.[7]

This is significant because political consciousness was well developed among the colonists. This was seen not only with the assemblies but also with the development of the press. Thus, newspapers began on Jamaica with the *Weekly Jamaica Courant* (1718), and this was followed by the *St Jago Intelligencer* (1756), and the *Cornwall Chronicle* from Montego Bay (1773). Elsewhere, the *Barbados*

Gazette (1738) was followed by the *St Christopher Gazette* (1747), the *Antigua Gazette* (1748) and the *Royal Grenada Gazette* (1765).[8] In contrast, the first vernacular newspaper in Calcutta was not established until 1818.

When the Americans invaded Canada in 1775–6 they found very little support, and, instead, a rallying to the crown. Initial American success was turned into failure when British reinforcements arrived by sea. When France joined the war in 1778 no attempt was made to invade or reconquer Canada. As a result, the rebellion of the Thirteen Colonies led to the sundering of the British North American world. Canada became more firmly a part of the empire as a result of the immigration of many loyalists from the Thirteen Colonies, and this was to play a major role in the successful resistance there to American attack in 1812–14. Conversely, despite continuing links and influence, the politics, society, economy and culture of the United States moved apart from Britain, in large part due to the rapidity of change under the early republic, although it is necessary to note that diversity had begun from the founding of British North America.[9]

More generally, the same process of division can also be seen with the collapse of the New World empires. Spain lost its land possessions, but not its Caribbean islands, Cuba and Puerto Rico. The Latin Wars of Independence, however, very much affected the links between these islands and the former colonies on the mainland.

Alongside any sense of the process of collapse as in some way inevitable has come an understanding of the role of particular circumstances. The role of other European powers in helping undermine the empires of their rivals was important. There was no united opposition to decolonization, no more than there was to be after 1945, indeed even less so than then. Instead, European states saw opportunities in the difficulties of their rivals, and were prepared to help revolution. This was despite the fact that it would lead to new independent states, rather than to the transfer of colonial control that had hitherto been the case with transoceanic conflict between European powers. Thus, in the American War of Independence France, Spain and the United Provinces all fought against the British, and the French gave important military assistance to the revolutionaries before they entered the war in 1778. The Spaniards were more wary, as they were worried about the impact of the example of revolution on their own colonies, and came to fear America's trans-Appalachian ambitions, but they entered the war in 1779.[10]

Revolution on Saint-Domingue

The international context was also important with the successful slave rebellion that occurred on the French colony of Saint-Domingue in August 1791. Hostility between revolutionaries in Paris and conservative whites in the colony helped destabilize the situation and provide opportunities for the rebels. Troops were sent from France in 1792 and slavery was abolished in the colony in 1793 (and in all the French colonies the following year), but, greatly assisted by the impact of yellow fever on French troops, the determination of the black population not to remain under French rule ultimately prevailed. In 1793 Spain went to war with France and provided aid to the rebels. British troops also intervened, only to withdraw, leaving the colony divided between black forces under Toussaint L'Ouverture and mulattoes under André Rigaud. Toussaint defeated Rigaud in 1800 and overran neighbouring Spanish Santo Domingo in 1801.

Peace with Britain in 1802 gave Napoleon an opportunity to counter-attack. He sent 20,000 troops under his brother-in-law Charles Leclerc, and Toussaint was treacherously seized during negotiations in 1802 (he died in prison in 1803). Napoleon hoped that Saint-Domingue would be part of a French empire in the West that would include Louisiana, Florida, Cayenne, Martinique and Guadeloupe. However, resistance continued, and in 1803 the resumption of war with Britain led to a blockade of Saint-Domingue's ports. Hit by yellow fever and with their food supplies cut, the French lost the initiative and were repulsed.

Driven back to Le Cap, the French force agreed a truce with Toussaint's successor, Jean-Jacques Dessalines, and in November 1803 was transported by British warships to Jamaica. The surviving white settlers fled to Cuba. The independence of Haiti, the second independent state in the New World, was proclaimed on 1 January 1804. The black Jacobins who had set out to create a new society, as well as to destroy the old, had succeeded.[11]

Latin American Wars of Independence

French failure on Saint-Domingue owed much to the intractability of the task, although the impact of the hostility of Britain, the world's leading naval power, was significant, as it was also to be in the Latin American Wars of Independence. The latter were important not only in causing (and reflecting) a major lasting transformation of European power, but also because they led not to one or two hegemonic powers in Latin America capable of matching the USA, but rather to a number of states.

Political factors provided a crucial context for the Latin American wars, and these conflicts deserve considerable attention because the collapse of Spanish (and to a lesser extent Portuguese) power on the mainland was a major shift in global power that led to a permanent change in the character of European colonialism. The long-established colonial societies of Latin America (up to three centuries old at the time of their demise) were of formative importance in the New World, and also displayed a measure of syncretism that is of wider interest.

The Spaniards were weakened more by political than by military problems. The weaknesses of Spain itself were significant: alongside the political and economic disruption caused by the Peninsular War of 1808–13, there was serious post-Napoleonic disruption. Napoleon's seizure of power in Spain in 1808 had led to a breakdown of structures of authority and practices of power in the empire and to a struggle for control. With the exception of Peru, governing *juntas* in 1809 and 1810 assumed authority in Spanish America in the name of the imprisoned

Ferdinand VII. However, the *juntas* found their authority contested, and the situation was made more difficult in 1814 when Ferdinand VII, having returned to power, chose to use force in order to restore royal authority in Spanish America. As a consequence, the royal authorities there suppressed the autonomy movements, although not that in the distant Plate estuary.[12]

However, the cause of Ferdinand VII faced many difficulties. The royalists (Spanish supporters) in Latin America were badly divided, and their divisions interacted with contradictions within Spain's incoherent policies. Civil and military authorities clashed frequently, as did metropolitan and provincial administrations. For example, in New Granada (now Colombia), the viceroy and the commander-in-chief were bitter rivals. Furthermore, financial shortages forced the royalist army to rely on the seizure of local supplies and on forced loans, which proved a heavy burden on the population and antagonized them from Spanish rule. The royalist forces sent from Spain were also hit by disease, especially yellow fever and dysentery, and were forced to recruit locally, leading to fresh political problems. New Granada had largely welcomed the royal army from Spain under Pablo Morillo at first in 1815, but by 1819 there was widespread support for an independent Colombia.[13]

Spain did not possess any technological advantages akin to those enjoyed by the conquistadores in the early sixteenth century. Indeed, she was regarded as militarily backward by other European powers. The insurgents, for their part, were partly supplied by arms dealers in the USA. Spanish governments sent relatively few weapons to their troops in the Americas. Most of the weapons used by the royalists were acquired locally. If anything, the insurgents had a slight advantage in weaponry.[14]

Nevertheless, the course of the conflict was not foreordained. As in other wars of liberation, the colonial power enjoyed more success than is frequently appreciated. This was true both of the degree of local support for the Spaniards and of conflict in the field. Victories at Huaqui (1811) and Sipe Sipe (1815) led to Spanish reconquests of Upper Peru (Bolivia), and that of Rancagua (1814) led to the reconquest of Chile. In 1806 and 1812 the Spaniards suppressed rebellions in Venezuela led by Francisco Miranda. The Spaniards were helped by the limited support enjoyed by the revolutionaries and by their lack of funds. Although there was revolutionary enthusiasm among the rebel officers, the same was not true of the bulk of the peasant conscripts. Furthermore, there was no compensation in the shape of reliable payment. Venezuelan revolutionary forces were also poorly supplied and armed, and inadequately trained.

The conflict swayed back and forth. Simon Bolívar, who had fought under Miranda, escaped to New Granada, raised a volunteer force and invaded Venezuela in 1813. He won a number of battles, but the Venezuelan republic lacked widespread support, and its forces were short of funds and arms. Having fled to Jamaica, Bolívar returned again to Venezuela, but his expedition, mounted from Haiti in 1816, failed to win support and was abandoned. Another expedition was defeated in 1818. There were also Spanish victories elsewhere. At Cancha-Rayada in Chile in 1818 a Spanish army under Mariano Osorio defeated José de San Martin; while at Bombino in Ecuador in 1822 royalist forces were able to delay Bolivár's invasion of Ecuador.

However, the Spaniards suffered from the debilitating impact of weaknesses in Spain, and from the willingness of independence forces in South America to travel great distances in order to affect the struggle elsewhere. After Argentina had gained independence in 1816, forces under San Martin and Bernard O'Higgins crossed the Andes and defeated the royalists in Chile at the Battles of Chacabuco (1817) and Maipo (1818), before moving north into Peru, which was invaded in 1820. Lima was captured in 1821, but the Spaniards were not crushed. Further north, Bolivár invaded New Granada from Venezuela in the summer of 1819, crossing the Andes via the allegedly impassable Pisba Pass, a bold move made necessary by difficult conditions in Venezuela. Losses on the crossing were high. Bolivár then outmanoeuvred and defeated the Spaniards at Boyacá; victory enabled him to seize Bogotá and create a republic. As President, Bolivár, the following year, moved on to found the state of the Republic of Greater Colombia, comprising what is now Colombia, Venezuela and Ecuador, although much still remained in Spanish hands.

The Spanish effort was weakened by revolution in Spain in 1820, which led to the cancellation of a 20,000-strong expeditionary force, the first major reinforcement for the royalists in Latin America since 1815, and one that was much needed. In addition, Morillo was ordered to negotiate a truce, which gave Bolivár breathing space and made Spain appear weak. Furthermore, the new liberal political system in Spain failed to fulfil Latin American expectations. The Spanish majority in the Cortes rejected the idea of home rule.

When war resumed the demoralized royalists in Venezuela were defeated in 1821. Bolivár and Antonio José de Sucre pressed on to 'free' Ecuador in 1822, especially thanks to Sucre's victory at Pichincha, before advancing into Peru in 1823. In 1824 a pro-Spanish/royalist rising in Peru was supported by the dispatch of Spanish troops. However, Bolivár defeated the Spaniards in the Peruvian Andes at Junín, and Sucre followed suit at Ayacucho. Royalist morale had been low from the beginning, but sank lower when the war appeared lost.[15] The following year Sucre overran Upper Peru, which was renamed Bolivia. In 1826 the fortress of Ancud on the island of Chiloé off south Chile, the last Spanish stronghold in South America, surrendered.

Further north, in Central America, rebellion against Spanish rule began in 1810. Led by Father Miguel Hidalgo, this was defeated by General Calleja, outside Mexico City (1811) and at the Battle of the Bridge of Calderón (1812). The royalists used local militias against the rebels. They were helped by the ethnic character of the rising. Largely *mestizo*, it was seen as a threat to the creoles as well as to Spanish authority. More generally, the ethnic complexities of Latin America restricted the appeal of radical ideologies and movements, for, just as many creoles resented control from Europe, others were concerned about the possibility of risings by the mixed-blood and native populations. This was less true of the River Plate

146

region than of Mexico and the Andean chain, as the creole population was preponderantly more important in the former. Peru was a centre of creole conservatism, while Bolívar himself had little sympathy with the idea of multiracial majority rule.

Insurgents who had captured Texas in 1812–13 were overthrown later in 1813. In Mexico the rebellion was continued by Father José María Morelos, a *mestizo*, but he was defeated in 1815 by Calleja, now Viceroy of New Spain, and executed. Guerrilla action continued, led by Vicente Guerrero. The strengths and limitations of such action were amply illustrated. For example, in the Papantla region near Veracruz, which had rebelled in 1812, the royalist reconquest of the towns by 1818 did not end the rebellion. Instead, it changed it into a guerrilla war, with royalist garrisons in the towns unable to control rural hinterlands. In the summer of 1820 a change of strategy under a new royalist commander, José Rincón, altered the tempo of the war. Whereas previously the rainy season had served as a break in campaigning, providing the rebels with an opportunity to recover, Rincón planned no such break. In a campaign against the rebel stronghold of Coyusquihui, he circled the area with forts and kept campaigning. This hit the rebels, but the royalists were badly affected by disease. Both sides agreed to a settlement in December 1820.[16]

This conflict is a reminder of the extent to which the defeat of Morelos in 1815 did not lead to an end of the insurgency, but rather to more fighting. However, affected by the regionalism that made it difficult to establish a common front, the insurgency fragmented, as indeed did the army as units engaged in counter-insurgency operations with little central supervision, while their commanders tried to build up local power bases. By 1820, helped by numerous pardons, the guerrilla war was nearly over.[17]

Rebellion in Mexico had been largely overcome, but Spanish rule collapsed, because the liberal constitutional revolution in Spain of 1820 was not welcome to those who wielded power in Mexico and to the strong creole conservatism of many. In November 1820 the viceroy had ordered Augustín de Iturbide to destroy what was left of the rebellion, but in early 1821 he agreed with the rebels on a declaration of independence. As this was widely acceptable, the new regime gained power with very little fighting, and none at all in the provinces from California to Texas: a situation very different to that in much of Spanish South America. The new *junta* was dominated by army officers. Liberalism in Spain thus encouraged conservatives in Mexico to support independence. Iturbide declared himself Emperor Augustin I in 1822, but he was forced to abdicate in 1823 after the army turned against him.[18] Spanish forces seeking to regain Mexico were defeated by Santa Anna at Tampico in 1829.

In Brazil the Regent, Dom Pedro, rebelled against his father, King John of Portugal, in 1822. However, the northern provinces and the coastal cities south of Rio remained loyal and had to be conquered. This was done in large part thanks to the successful use of naval force: the Brazilians hired British officers and men. In 1823 the Portuguese were forced to leave Sálvador da Bahia and the Brazilian squadron also captured Maranhão (São Luis), Belém do Pará and Montevideo. In the case of the last the squadron supported the blockade of the city by Brazilian forces. The garrison, which had already held out against the land blockade for many months, quickly surrendered. The following year a rising in the province of Pernambuco was suppressed after Recife had been blockaded into surrender. Other risings in the north were also suppressed. As a consequence, Brazil (Portuguese Latin America) retained a coherence that Spanish Latin America lacked and was never to regain. By 1826 there were nine independent states in Latin America: Mexico, Central America, Colombia, Peru, Bolivia, Chile, Brazil, Paraguay and the Argentine Confederation.

The violent beginnings of nationhood in Latin America had a traumatic impact on society, and also helped colour the nature of political culture. The need that both the revolutionaries and the royalists faced to create new armies put a premium on overcoming problems in recruitment and in resisting desertion. Remedies were often brutal. Recruitment was enforced with violence and the threat of violence, desertion punished savagely, frequently with executions, and supplies raised through force. There was much burning and destruction – of crops, haciendas, towns – both in order to deny resources and to punish.

Transformation in the Western world

The revolutions in the New World led to a situation in which relations with the indigenous peoples were to be pursued very differently to during the colonial period. Then, ministers of Europe and royal officials in the colonies, who were not answerable to local opinion, had sought to direct relations as part of the process by which they ruled the colonies. After independence the situation changed radically, and indigenous peoples were put under greater pressure. This was largely within the areas where the new states had clear sovereignty, but there was also some extension of their sway into the Pacific, beginning in 1832 when Ecuador annexed the Galapagos Islands, by then a base for whaling. European culture and the European economy remained very important to the newly independent states; least so to Haiti. However, the terms of the relationship had altered, while, due to developments in Europe, the range of models of European political and social organization had expanded.

This range contributed to a sense of flux in what should now be seen as a Western rather than a European world, one that centred on the French Revolution and its defiance of the *ancien régime*. Looked at differently, this sense of flux was part of a widespread chaos. Lester Langley has recently argued that chaos was crucial to understanding the revolutions in the New World: 'What explained their triumphs was the creativity made possible by chaos. What explained their failure was the inability to contain that chaos.'[19]

This chaos also affected the European empires outside the New World. Indeed, it would be actively misleading to imply that, apart from the revolutions in the principal settlement colonies, the European presence outside Europe was essentially a matter of more of the same, in short of a process that can be discussed in terms of the expansion of territorial control.

An expansion of European imperial control in the eastern hemisphere can indeed be seen in 1775–1830, especially for the British, but also for the Russians, although the Portuguese and Spaniards could not compensate for their losses in the New World. This expansion was important, but there were also significant transformations within the imperial world, including shifts in European racism.

Race and emancipation

There was a benign side to this process, one that focused on emancipation, but was not confined to that. In 1787 a very different settlement to that which characterized European expansion was established at what was symbolically termed Freetown in West Africa. The settlers came from London's blacks. Although some had come to England in the course of their working life, individually as seamen or as servants, the great majority of those who became involved in the Sierra Leone expedition were loyalists from the American War of Independence, discharged in England after the end of the war. Most were poor, in their twenties, and lived in the East End. Since there were relatively few women among them, or among the previous black community in England, a significant number took white wives. The great majority of newspaper items covering the Sierra Leone expedition were sympathetic in tone. Combined with intermarriage and the good public response to the appeal for money to help poor blacks, this suggests that racial hostility may have been less common than has often been assumed. The Committee for the Relief of the Black Poor and key government members appear to have been motivated by humanitarianism springing from Christian convictions, gratitude towards loyalist blacks and abolitionist sympathies. Freetown was long to remain a symbol of this idealism,[20] although the settlement encountered many difficulties. The Sierra Leone settlement explicitly forbade slavery.

The French Revolution led to an emphasis on another current of idealism, one that was secular rather than evangelical. Already, in February 1788, the Société des Amis des Noirs had been founded. It pressed for the abolition of the slave trade and, eventually and without compensation, of slavery. One of its founders, Jacques-Pierre Brissot, argued that blacks had the same capacities as whites. The society attracted much interest from reforming clergy.[21]

The French Revolution led to a Utopian idealism in which the liberties affirmed by the revolutionaries were believed to be inherent in humanity and thus of global applicability. On 19 November 1792, in response to appeals for help from radicals in Zweibrücken and Mainz, the National Convention passed a decree declaring that the French people would extend fraternity and assistance to all peoples seeking to regain their liberty. As a general principle, this was subversive of all international order; it was also unrealistic and was revoked by the National Convention on 14 April 1793, Danton pointing out that it would oblige the French to assist a revolution in China.

Idealistic sentiments were essentially directed to European audiences, but they are also seen as more widely applicable. In January 1792 the attention of the National Assembly was directed by its Colonial Committee towards Madagascar. Instead of territorial expansion, there was a call

> not to invade a country or subjugate several savage nations, but to form a solid alliance, to establish friendly and mutually beneficial links with a new people . . . today it is neither with the cross nor with the sword that we establish ourselves with new people. It is by respect for their rights and views that we will gain their heart; it is not by reducing them to slavery . . . this will be a new form of conquest.

In October 1794 the National Convention was told that France would gain influence in India if it stood for justice and influence.[22]

Initially, however, the slave trade was not banned by France; indeed, it reached its peak during the years 1789–91.[23] This reflected the value of the West Indies to the French economy. It was also argued that slaves were not French, and, therefore, that slavery and the revolution were compatible. The major rising in Saint-Domingue in 1791 altered the situation, leading to a complex conflict in which, in 1793, the Civil Commissioner, Léger Sonthonax, freed the slaves in the Northern Province in order to win their support. The following year the National Convention abolished slavery in all French colonies.[24]

This idealism did not protect the French position in Saint-Domingue and also fell victim to the reaction and consolidation associated with Napoleon. Nevertheless, there was a wider current of idealism, much of which drew on Protestant evangelism. The slave trade was abolished by Denmark in 1802 by government decree (without an abolitionist campaign), and anti-slavery ideology developed in the United Provinces, but developments in Britain were more important, both because of her imperial power and due to her potential influence on other states. Christian assumptions about the unity of mankind and the need to gather Africans to Christ played a major role in influencing British opinion, although, to supporters of slavery, an acceptance of blacks as fully human did not preclude slavery, and they were presented as degraded by their social and environmental backgrounds. The ruling in the Somerset case of 1772 that West Indian slave owners could not forcibly take their slaves from England ended slavery in the British Isles. In 1787 the Society for the Abolition of the Slave Trade, a national lobbying group, was established. Its pressure helped lead to the Dolben Act of 1788 by which conditions on the slave ships were regulated. However, pressure to abolish the trade was hindered by the importance of the West Indies to the British economy, as well as by the opposition of George III and the House of Lords, and the conservative response to reform agitation that followed the French Revolution.[25]

Nevertheless, there was an upsurge in abolitionism from the 1800s. This was a popular cause, and one in which women played a prominent role.[26] In 1805

William Pitt the Younger, the Prime Minister, issued orders-in-council which banned the import of slaves into newly captured territories after 1807 and in the meantime limited the introduction of slaves to 30 per cent of the number already there. This legislation was taken much further by the next government, the Ministry of all the Talents, which in 1806 supported the Foreign Slave Trade Act that ended the supply of slaves to conquered territories and foreign colonies. The Abolition Act of 1807 banned slave-trading by British subjects and the import of slaves into the older colonies. In 1811 participation in the slave trade was made a felony, although on Mauritius, which was captured in 1810, the now illegal slave trade continued with the connivance of the first two British governors. Sugar production there considerably expanded after 1825.[27] With effect from 1808, the slave trade was also banished by America.

Britain also used her international strength to put pressure on other states to abolish or limit the slave trade. Not only did it now seem morally wrong, but it was also seen as giving an advantage to rival plantation economies. In 1810 pressure was exerted on Portugal, then very much a dependent ally, to restrict the slave trade as a preparation for abolition. In 1815 the returned Bourbon regime in France was persuaded to ban the slave trade and, under British pressure, the Congress of Vienna issued a declaration against the trade. In 1817 an Anglo-Portuguese treaty limited the slave trade in Brazil to south of the Equator, and an Anglo-Spanish treaty contained similar provisions. The British navy was used to enforce such provisions.

These moves can be presented in a benign light, and can be seen as an important shift in Europe's relationship with the rest of the world. However, such an account has to be qualified by three significant points. First, much of the slave trade continued, while slavery itself had not been abolished. Second, abolition *can* be presented as a response to economic developments, rather than as the product of ideological pressures. Third, racism remained strong, and was brutally displayed in the colonies, for example in the murderous treatment of the Aborigines of Tasmania.[28]

As far as the slave trade was concerned, it continued, not least because slavery had not been abolished. Although demand for labour was in large part met from the children of existing slaves, the continuation of slavery ensured that even where the slave trade had been abolished smuggling continued, although it was not very extensive in the British Caribbean. More particularly, the slave trade to the leading market, Brazil, was not effectively ended until 1850, and that to the second market, Cuba, until the 1860s. Slavery itself was not ended in the British colonies until the Emancipation Act of 1833, in the French colonies until 1848, in the Dutch colonies until 1863, in the United States until 1865, in Cuba until 1886 and in Brazil until 1888. Thus, the hardship, exploitation, misery and cruelty that focused on slavery and on the slave trade continued after the 1810s.

The end of the slave trade and of slavery has been ascribed by some commentators to a lack of profitability, caused by a developing economy, rather than to humanitarianism.[29] This view, however, is simplistic and underplays the multiplicity of factors that played a role. As far as profitability was concerned, there are indications that slave plantations in the West Indies remained profitable;[30] as they also did in Brazil and Cuba. Furthermore, the plantation economy represented an important asset base and the limited convertibility of assets did not encourage disinvestment from slavery. Too much money was tied up in mortgages and annuities that were difficult to liquidate in a hurry.

Instead of problems within the slave economy, it is more appropriate to look at the pressures towards abolition from outside. In the British empire, and especially in Britain itself, these included and contributed to a marginalization of groups that had encouraged and profited from European demand for tropical goods.[31] Furthermore, the reforming, liberal middle-class culture that became so important in much of the European world, especially in Britain and parts of the United States, regarded slavery as abhorrent, anachronistic and associated with everything it deplored. Thus, the ministry that pushed through the Great Reform Act of 1832 that revised the electoral franchise to the benefit of the middle class also ended slavery in Britain's colonies. Many Whig candidates included an anti-slavery platform in their electoral addresses.[32] Anti-slavery was less important and popular in most of continental Europe, whether in Catholic France or the Protestant Netherlands.[33]

It is also appropriate to note that control over labour continued, as did labour flows. In place of slaves the British West Indies and other colonies received cheap Indian indentured labour, although sugar production declined.[34] Similarly, in the 1750s Native slavery was abolished by the Portuguese in Amazonia, but they developed a system of forced government service.

The end of the slave trade and subsequently slavery did not mark the close of the powerful racism of the period. This drew on notions of an inherent racial hierarchy that was based on ideas of sharply distinguished races and on supposed differences between the races that could be classified in a hierarchical fashion and whose genesis was traced back to the sons of Adam. Race was seen in physical attributes, particularly skin colour. The argument that bile was responsible for the colour of human skin, advanced as a scientific fact by ancient writers, was repeated without experimental support by eminent eighteenth-century scientists, including Buffon, Feijoo, Holbach and La Mettrie. This error was linked to false explanations, such as that of Marcello Malpighi (1628–94), Professor of Medicine in Bologna and the founder of microscopic anatomy, who believed that all men were originally white, but that the sinners had become black. An Italian scientist, Bernardo Albinus, proved to his own satisfaction in 1737 that Negro bile was black, and in 1741 a French doctor, Pierre Barrère, published experiments demonstrating both this and that the bile alone caused the black pigment in Negro skin. This inaccurate theory won widespread acclaim, in part thanks to an extensive review in the *Journal des Savants* in 1742, and played a major role in the prevalent mid-century belief that blacks were another species of man without the ordinary human organs, tissues, heart and soul. In 1765 the chief doctor in the leading hospital in Rouen, Claude Nicolas Le Cat, demonstrated that Barrère's theory was wrong, but he was generally ignored and Barrère's arguments continued to be cited favourably.[35]

Influential writers argued in favour of polygenism – the different creation of types of humans. This led to suggestions that blacks were not only a different species, but also related to great apes, such as orang-utans. This was related to the argument that although blacks were inherently inferior, they were particularly adapted to living in the tropics. Their ability to cope better than whites with diseases there was held to exemplify an inherent difference that was linked to a closeness to animals that lived there. This was held to justify slavery.[36]

By the end of the century most advanced opinion no longer regarded blacks as a different species of man, but as a distinct variety. This interpretation, monogenesis – the descent of all races from a single original group – was advanced by Johann Friedrich Blumenbach, a teacher of medicine at the University of Göttingen, who in 1776 published *De Generis Humani Varietate*, an influential work of racial classification. Blumenbach was a key figure in the development of anthropology and his book went through several editions.

Race was also linked to alleged moral and intellectual characteristics, and to stages in sociological development. This encouraged a sense of fixed identity as part of a compartmentalized view of mankind, rather than an acceptance of an inherent unity and of shared characteristics. This compartmentalism encouraged classification, although the factors that were supposed central to the diversity of human groups, and thus to their classification, varied. Religious and biological explanations of apparent differences between races, with blacks as the children of the cursed Ham, were important. They were linked to the idea that species of animals had been separately created by God.[37]

There was also an interest in environmental influences, especially climate, which were regarded as explaining apparently fundamental contrasts in behaviour. Montesquieu and Buffon explained colour as due to exposure to the tropical sun. There was also interest in the display of similar characteristics by widely dispersed peoples, and this suggested to some commentators that human society should be seen in terms of common responses to circumstances; rather than with an emphasis on a common biblical source, with changes arising as a result of subsequent dispersion.[38]

Aside from the assessment of the inherent characteristics of non-Europeans, a belief in progress, and in the association of reason with European culture, necessarily encouraged a hierarchy dominated by the Europeans, and thus a treatment of others as inferior. Thus, although monogenesis can be seen as a benign theory that could contribute to a concept of the inherent brotherhood of man that was voiced during the Enlightenment and especially in the Revolutionary period, it was also inherently discriminatory. Blumenbach assumed the original ancestral group to be white and that climate, diet, disease and mode of life were responsible for the developments that led to the creation of different races.

Characteristics and developments were understood in terms of the suppositions of European culture, and this led to, and supported, the hierarchization already referred to.[39] This was also true of the developing idea of cultural relativism seen, for example, in Johann Gottfried von Herder's *Auch eine Philosophie der Geschichte* (1774).

Among 'advanced' thinkers, notions of brotherhood were subordinated to a sense that Enlightenment and Revolutionary ideas and movements originated within the Western world. Irrespective of the nobility of outsiders, their societies appeared deficient and defective, and thus inferior. This can be seen in writing on history and sociology, for example William Robertson's influential *History of America* (1777), in which the conquering Europeans were seen as more advanced economically and socially, while Natives were presented as debilitated and concerned with self-gratification,[40] not a practice that recommended itself to theorists of the period.

Attitudes to empire 1775–1830

The transformation of the Western world thus led to a very contained egalitarianism. Knowledge was employed to reformulate Western superiority, rather than to sap it. This process was not restricted to human races. Instead, the quest for knowledge, the determination to know, was directed at the entire non-Western world. Furthermore, the process was much more insistent in 1775–1830 than hitherto. The pace of exploration was stepped up, particularly in Africa, North America and Australasia. Mapping became both more widespread and more detailed.[41]

The natural world was actively pursued. The collection of new species of plants and animals was a major interest. Charles III, who founded a Royal Botanical Garden in Madrid, also sent a scientific expedition to Spanish America in 1785 in order to discover plants with medicinal properties. The botanist Joseph Banks (1743–1820) sailed round the world with Cook and also collected plants on expeditions to Newfoundland and Iceland. Succeeding George III's favourite, John, 3rd Earl of Bute, as Director of the new Royal Botanic Gardens at Kew in 1772, Banks helped to make them a centre for botanical research based on holdings from around the world.[42] The role of this research in helping schemes for the 'improvement' of agriculture in Britain, Africa, India and the West Indies, an imperial cross-pollination to complement that of established trades, in other words providing a rationale for empire, was important:

> A sacred theory of agriculture comforted those who imposed themselves on India, Australasia, and Africa. The rational use of Nature replaced piety as the foundation of imperial Providence, government became the Demiurge [creator], and universal progress, measured by material abundance, its promised land.[43]

Thus colonization was good for all, both colonizers and the colonized, because it permitted the improving use of knowledge. Reason was at the forefront of such an ideology, not Christianity; although the two were not seen as opposites: indeed, reason was also presented as a way to demonstrate the truths of religion.

The role of ideas in providing a guide to Europe's relations with the outside world, and also an explanation for imperialism, has been ably probed in a number of works, including Christopher Bayly's *Imperial Meridian. The British Empire and the World 1780–1830* (Harlow, 1989) and Richard Drayton's *Nature's Government. Science, Imperial Britain, and the 'Improvement' of the World* (New Haven, 2000). In another valuable piece Drayton has argued that

> the Enlightenment . . . contributed a fundamental element to the ideology which sustained the Second British Empire: the faith that Empire might be an instrument of cosmopolitan progress, and could benefit the imperialized as well as the imperializers. The liberal imperialism of the nineteenth and twentieth centuries may be seen as driven by this secular species of evangelical fervour.[44]

This approach has great value. It helps explain why the European states and their publics gave support to imperial expansion in the nineteenth century, far more so than by, say, the 1930s, or, even more so, the 1960s. As a consequence, it is necessary to understand the ideas circulating in the early nineteenth century, especially in the leading imperial power, Britain.

These ideas were given visual expression in 1830 in Edward Quin's influential *Historical Atlas in a Series of Maps of the World, as Known at Different Periods*. This offered a diffusionist model of culture in which the centres of civilization that comprised Europe impacted on the world. Colour was used to depict civilization. What was 'unknown' by Europeans (and the classical civilizations they acknowledged as roots) was enveloped in darkness – black and grey clouds. Quin explained that 'China and America were as much in existence in the days of Cyrus as they are now, although unknown to the great mass of civilized human beings'. In addition,

> there has always been, in every age of the world, parts of the earth, not unknown to the geographer or the historian, but classed, by their want of civilization, of regular government, and of known and recognized limits, under the general description of *barbarous countries*. Such was Scythia through all antiquity, and such is the interior of Africa at the present moment . . . tribes having no settled form of government, or political existence, or known territorial limits. These tracts of country, therefore, we have covered alike in all the periods, with a flat olive shading; which the eye of the student will observe on the skirts of all the maps, and which designates throughout the work, those barbarous and uncivilized countries to which we have adverted.[45]

Such an approach accorded with the teleology and Eurocentrism of European thought.

The 'interior of Africa' was still proving intractable to European explorers in 1830. This was especially so in the vast tract between Sudan and southern Africa. In 1816 a British expedition sought to penetrate up the Congo River in order to discover if it was the outlet of the Niger. Led by Commander James Tuckey, this was a failure that at once showed the growing capability of European society and the limitations of expansionism. Tuckey was in command of the *Congo*, the first steamship on an African river, but the boat did not operate correctly, the expedition was blocked by difficult cataracts on the river, and Tuckey and many of his men died of disease. No further progress was to be made until 1877, when Stanley completed the first descent of the Congo. Tuckey's very career showed the range of British activity. Born in 1776, he worked on a merchantman in the Caribbean, before serving in the navy off Sri Lanka (1795) and in the East Indies and the Red Sea (1800), and going to New South Wales to establish a colony at Port Phillip (1802–4), where he made a survey of the nearby coastline. As with many travellers, Tuckey published a travelogue: *Account of a Voyage to Establish a Colony at Port Phillip* (1805).

It is necessary to be cautious before arguing that a totally new attitude to the outside world and to European expansion developed in 1775–1830. In the age of the projectors at the end of the seventeenth and beginning of the eighteenth century there had been similar attitudes, specifically a commodification of the rest of the world, linked to a belief that the Europeans had the rightful knowledge to exploit and understand it. This, for example, had been the language associated with John Law's Mississippi Scheme, the attempt in the late 1710s to exploit Louisiana for the benefit of French public finances and the French economy. Similar arguments had been deployed by the political economists of the period, such as Charles Davenant, and had been seen in the hopes surrounding the commercial projects of the period, especially the East India Companies.

Irrespective of the earlier history of particular ideas and attitudes, it is also appropriate to query how far these ideas and attitudes were responsible for the expansion of European power, commerce and settlement in 1775–1830. In particular, if an emphasis is placed on the decisions of men on the spot, rather than metropolitan authorities, and associated circles of opinion, then it is unclear how far coherent sets of ideas affected imperialism and acted as enablers of European power. For example, it is possible to be sceptical about the role of imperial ideology for those who initially exploited the flax, timber, seals and whales on and near New Zealand, although the missionaries who arrived from 1814 can more readily be discussed in terms of a European sense of mission.[46] A very different mission led to the creation of a penal colony in Australia in 1788; one that was fully under state direction.

Once established, this colony was increasingly affected by the same economic pressures that operated within the European world, specifically the search for markets and materials. Thus, industries in Europe sought raw material for the textile industries required to clothe the growing population. Cotton came from India, but it became economic to bring fine wool from Australia. This led to major developments in the 1820s as the expansion of grazing land was encouraged, and helped provide a dynamic behind British expansion in southeast Australia and Tasmania. This process led to conflict with local peoples. In Tasmania the spread of sheep ranching clashed with Aboriginal migration paths, leading to the Black War of the 1820s.

More generally, the dynamic of economic change in response to a Europe-centred globalism led to significant economic and social disruption both within European colonies and in areas that were not under territorial control. Existing practices were made less profitable, if not redundant, and in colonies there was a related desire to control in order to improve economic possibilities. Thus, there was a preference for settled agriculture and communities, rather than for more nomadic activities and lifestyles. In many areas this led to a decline of tribal peoples and others who could, or did, not respond to new cash crops.

It would be mistaken to imagine that economic pressures were coterminous with European colonialism. Instead, areas in the New World that had thrown off European colonial control were greatly affected by economic developments and demands that spanned the Atlantic world. Thus, in the USA pressure for transport improvements reflected the desire to open new markets and production areas both for the American economy and for export. The Western Inland Lock Navigation Company, incorporated in 1792 to open navigation between the Hudson River and the Ontario and Seneca lakes, led to the Erie Canal, completed in 1825.

More generally, the dynamics of the Western-dominated commercial system extended well beyond colonial bounds and, indeed, included societies that had resisted and rejected Western control. Thus, in Haiti the plantation economy producing for European markets survived black independence. Slavery had gone, but the black elite who ran the state used forced labour in order to protect their plantations from the preference of people to live as peasant proprietors. Thus, the attractions of the global economy triumphed over the potential consequences of independence; a triumph that rested on pressure and force, not free choice, and that offered nothing to help social progress.[47] In addition, Haiti was affected by competition from the products of those Caribbean islands that remained colonies.

The first American circumnavigation of the world was intimately linked with trading with societies that did not want Western control. Captain Robert Gray obtained furs on the northwest coast of North America, sold them in Canton, and bought tea which he sold in Boston. This first circumnavigation by an American ship, made in 1787-90, was organised by Boston merchants, and it was followed by a second in which Gray entered the Columbia River in 1790. Fifty fur-trade voyages to the northwest coast were made by Americans between 1795 and 1804. This process was not free from tension. In 1792, Gray clashed with the Kwakiuts in Queen Charlotte Sound, while the Russians regarded the Americans as interlopers.[48]

Western commercial activity also had a demographic impact. The whalers who travelled to Hawaii brought diarrhoea, influenza, measles, smallpox, tuberculosis, venereal disease and whooping cough, hitting the population very hard. Local sexual mores ensured that syphilis was particularly devastating.[49]

New systems of economic activity were often environmentally harmful. Thus, whereas native whaling in the northern Pacific does not appear to have depleted whale stocks, the situation was very different when European and Northern American whalers arrived. Without any interest in conservationist methods or ethos, they embraced inefficient methods that killed many whales but failed to bring in large numbers of those they had harpooned: instead, many died and fell to the ocean floor.[50] The Russian sea-otter and sealing catch off North America fell dramatically by the 1820s as animals were hunted to near extinction, while bay whaling of whales that came inshore to breed and sealing had been so devastating off Australia and New Zealand by the 1840s that there were few left to hunt.

Improved communications helped foster demand for such products. It also made colonial officials more readily answerable to instructions from Europe, as part of a greater integration of empire, although it was not until after this period that telegraphs, regular steamship services and railways secured such an integration. Within colonies, better communications also helped erode the regionalism that had been such a pronounced feature of empire in the seventeenth and eighteenth centuries, as settlement and other European activities had then spread without any equivalent deepening of centripetal links.

Clearly it would be foolish to neglect the role of the state in British expansion in 1775–1830,[51] but equally it is necessary to note the important and independent role of people on the spot. This was more the case at and beyond the frontier of empire, as in New Zealand, and less the position within settlement colonies. In the latter the views of government were important. Alongside the impact of metropolitan and other ideas favouring a new interpretation of imperialism in the period 1775–1830, it is appropriate to note the role of institutional and other continuities. In India, for example, the East India Company continued to play a central role until the Indian Mutiny of 1857; in 1858 the crown assumed full sovereignty over India. Similarly, over much of Canada, the Hudson's Bay Company continued to dominate life, even more so after 1821, when it merged with the North-West Company.[52] Such bodies adapted to changing imperial ideologies, but also presented a powerful continuity.

The impact of autonomous agencies and independent individuals can also be seen in the case of other empires. Thus, within the Russian system, in 1766 Ivan Solovief, a merchant from Okhotsk, organized a fleet that successfully attacked the eastern Aleutian Islands. In 1815 an independent initiative by George Sheffer, an employee of the Russian-American Company chartered in 1799, nearly led to the acquisition of Hawaii.[53]

The transformation of the European world is open to investigation from a number of directions. Alongside a territorial emphasis that would focus on the loss of control over much (although far from all) of the New World, and the increasingly Old World (indeed Asiatic) character of European empire in the period 1775–1830, there is a stress on changes, or at least fresh definitions, in attitudes towards non-Europeans. These provided a new focus for the racism that was more important in the European empires after the loss of most of the New World settlement colonies. The way was clear for the imperial ideology and colonial expansion of the remainder of the nineteenth century.

10

CONCLUSIONS

In all your conferences with the Ottoman ministers you cannot too strongly impress upon their minds the dangerous tendency of the avowed principles of the present French government if the most absolute anarchy can be so called, where the miserable people, deluded by the specious pretence of liberty, groan under the most despotic tyranny. Your Excellency will explain to them that those principles aim at nothing less than the subversion of all the established religious and forms of government in the whole world, by means the most atrocious which the mind of man will ever conceive . . . without the shadow of justice, and in a manner unexampled in the history of the most barbarous and savage nations.[1]

The instructions sent in 1794 to Robert Liston, British envoy in Constantinople, asserting that barbarism within Europe had been reinvented with the French Revolution, were in a tradition of seeking the alliance of non-Westerners against other Western powers. Such a policy had long focused on the Turks, although it had also ranged to include other polities, not least North American tribes and Indian rulers. Furthermore, such a practice was to continue during the heyday of Western imperialism. The Ethiopians who crushed an Italian invasion in 1896 benefited from French and Russian arms.

This is a reminder at the outset of this chapter of the cross-currents that characterized Europe's relations with the wider world. To recap, the discussions of exploration, commerce, the slave trade and the composition of the transoceanic forces of European states have all emphasized the importance of co-operation by native societies. The same point emerges, more generally, in the discussion of imperial rule. Apparently ironically, this co-operation proved most fragile in the case of the European settlement colonies in the New World, although, looked at differently, they found it easiest to win the support, or at least acceptance, of other European powers.

Alongside this pattern of continued co-operation with native societies, there was another of change, specifically growth: in the number of Europeans travelling and settling abroad, in the volume of trade, in other aspects of integration within empires, as well as in the extent of European knowledge about, and control over, the outside world. These processes interacted, contributing to a stronger European imprint elsewhere. Furthermore, the European presence in the world became both more far-flung and better integrated. Thus, before the widespread industrialization of the century after our period closes, the Europeans had already created a dominant position. Analyses of this dominance and of its causes vary, but it is clearly necessary to discuss it in relative terms. In particular it is important to look at the extent to which Asian systems failed to maintain their economic momentum, a process that has been blamed on the oppressive pressures of caste societies and heavy government regulation,[2] although it is also possible to focus on more political factors.

The European presence also literally speeded up. Although, by 1830, the railway had yet to make an impact outside Europe, the British had already used a steamship in the First Burmese War. Furthermore, even more conventional technology had become more effective. For example, partly in response to the erosion of the British East India Company's monopoly, a greater emphasis on speed characterized trade with the Far East. In 1817 the fully laden China fleet sailed from Canton River to the Channel in 109 days. The European maritime impact was helped by success against scurvy, the deadly product of vitamin C deficiency. In 1795 the British Admiralty introduced a winning remedy: a daily issue of lemon juice concentrate to all hands.

Migration played a major role in increasing European impact. China had a far greater population than Europe, but although inland 'colonies' were created, as the Chinese consolidated their successes against the Dzhungars of Xinjiang from the 1690s to the 1750s, the Chinese lacked overseas settlement colonies other than Taiwan, where Chinese rule was followed by a settlement that limited the Native population. European powers took care, sometimes brutally so, to prevent the Chinese in ports such as Batavia and Manila from gaining power. The major movement of Chinese to other continents in the nineteenth and twentieth centuries came within a system of state sovereignty and governmental regulation established by European imperial powers and their successors.

Thanks to the colonies, it was possible for part of the general European population increase that began in the 1740s to move outside Europe. This was not restricted to the subjects of the imperial powers. Of the approximately half a million people who emigrated from southwest Germany and Switzerland in the eighteenth century, about 40 per cent went to North America, the rest to Hungary, Prussia and Russia. Similarly, Rhineland emigration was shared by North America, Hungary, Prussia, Russia and Galicia (southern Poland). Between 1760 and 1775, at least 12,000 German immigrants entered the port of Philadelphia. American independence ended the residual powers of the British crown over migration, and the importance of this independence for migration was increased as America expanded, particularly with the Louisiana Purchase.

American independence altered demographic patterns within the English-language world. In 1815–30 the majority of emigrants from the British Isles went to Canada (including Newfoundland), while most migrants there came from the British Isles. In part due to the migration of Loyalists from the Thirteen Colonies,[3] the population of Upper Canada rose from 6,000 in 1785, to 25,000 by 1796, 60,000 by 1811 and 150,000 by 1824.[4] Such numbers had a major impact.

The same was true of Australia, although numbers were smaller. The first settlement in New South Wales in 1788 was a penal colony, and others followed, especially Van Diemen's Land (Tasmania) from 1803. Free immigrants also came to New South Wales from 1793, and their scope was enlarged in 1829 when Britain annexed Western Australia and established there its first settlement as the centre of a free colony.

Migration strengthened links between colonies and homeland, and also encouraged the replication of the culture and institutional structures of Europe. Thus, in the British colonies the press developed further with the launching of papers in colonies that had hitherto lacked them – the *Bermuda Gazette* (1784), and the *Honduras Gazette and Commercial Advertiser* (1826) in Belize – as well as more titles in colonies that already had a newspaper, for example Grenada, the Bahamas and Bermuda.

Emigration also had an impact on the societies from which the migrants came, and thus has to be understood as a complex process stemming from pressures and hopes within these societies. In large part emigration arose from those who were under pressure from changes within Europe, for example changes in tenurial arrangements.[5]

The importance of continued migration was captured by David Quinn in a thoughtful counterfactual passage in which he highlighted the importance of Europe's industrial dynamics, by asking what would have happened had this growth ceased in the mid-eighteenth century. His speculation is worth quoting at some length as the piece is not well known, and as the idea offers an instructive corrective to assumptions about inevitable expansion and, moreover, one that might throw light on contemporary concerns:

> all the intrusive settlement patterns in Asia – and such as there were in Africa as well – might well have faded out as a result of indigenous attrition had it not been for the industrializing powerhouse into which Europe turned from the later eighteenth century . . . probable that the settlement patterns already established in Mexico, Peru, probably the Plate and a few other regions could have sustained themselves without the addition of capital sustenance or anything more than residual trade with Europe . . . Virginia might not have the internal resources or will to carry her people across the mountain chain . . . When we come to Pennsylvania, New York, and above all Massachusetts . . . the tradition of an expanding self-reliance and of the balance of urban and rural interests together with the differentiation of skills in their population and the habit of capital-accumulation, could quite probably have enabled them, strengthened by their own merchant marine, to become the heirs

of a great part of the east central part of North America, perhaps to the Mississippi. The biggest question mark would lie over the capacity of the indigenes to stage something of a come-back once European settlements had ceased to be bolstered by officials and soldiers and by increasing numbers of emigrants . . . even in eastern North America it was by no means certain that before 1750 the Iroquois might not have before them an expanding and constructive future gained at the expense of the Europeans.[6]

This thesis is more than a passing curiosity. It is a reminder that the past is a matter of steps rather than a smooth process, and also that the strength and nature of the transoceanic European presence were primarily the products of developments within Europe. Alongside the deployment of military power and the exercise of political authority, demographic and economic movements provided the dynamism that ensured that the multifarious links between Europe and its outer world remained potent.

These movements, the deployment and the exercise, were all subject to unexpected developments within Europe. The extent to which this led to uncertainty about the future of Europe's position in the world is unclear. In his *Decline and Fall of the Roman Empire* (1776–88), Edward Gibbon argued that it was unlikely that Europe would again be overcome by barbarian invaders: 'Cannon and fortifications now form an impregnable barrier against the Tartar horse; and Europe is secure from any future irruption of Barbarians; since, before they can conquer, they must cease to be barbarous' (IV, pp. 166–7).

Europe's imperial expansion was now seen as a possible safeguard of the civilization's future. Gibbon (IV, p. 166) argued that in what was seen as the unlikely event of civilization collapsing in Europe before new barbarian inroads

> Europe would revive and flourish in the American world, which is already filled with her colonies and institutions . . . America now contains about six millions of European blood and descent; and their numbers, at least in the North, are continually increasing. Whatever may be the changes of their political situation, they must preserve the manners of Europe.

Europe's place in the world was in part a reflection of developments within non-European societies and states. Aside from the obvious point of their variety, it would be foolish to exaggerate the limitations of non-European societies and the deficiencies of their governments. More generally, it is necessary to be cautious in developing views of the 'East' (where most non-Europeans lived) as backward, and in presenting its institutions and cultures as static and as hostile to modernization and capitalism.[7] The same is also true of other non-Western societies. In the late seventeenth century Ottoman Turkey, Mughal India and Manchu China all ruled populations that were larger than any European state, and each state had been able to cope with serious problems in mid-century and then to revive in strength.

It is all too easy to minimize the dynamism of systems categorized as conservative.

Yet, while true of this period, this dynamism was less apparent a century later, although, as a recent study of elite politics and military society in Egypt has indicated,[8] it is important not to ignore signs of significant change. Alongside their failures, Turkey, Persia and the Barbary States of North Africa were each able to achieve defensive successes, but they failed to regenerate their domestic structures and political processes. Whereas in the sixteenth and seventeenth centuries the Ottomans, Safavids and Mughals had been generally successful in linking their frontier areas with their imperial objectives and also in controlling interregional trade routes, in the eighteenth century they were to suffer at the hands of Afghan, Arab, Persian and Türkmen tribes.[9] The imperial Islamic states were challenged by other Islamic states, and in Persia the Safavids were replaced.

Although the successor states in Persia and Afghanistan deployed considerable power in the eighteenth century, patrimonial autocracy – the style of government in much of Asia – seemed increasingly unable to produce a scale and regularity of resources sufficient to sustain military competitiveness in the context of mounting European pressure; such pressure was of increasing importance in India from the 1750s. It was also more serious for the Turks from 1683 and for Persia from 1722, although the process of increasing pressure was not continuous. Furthermore, it was of limited importance for China, Burma, Siam and Indo-China until the nineteenth century. Nevertheless, the relationship between structures of command and longer-term developments affecting resource mobilization were no longer so favourable to non-European societies. In addition, to simplify often complex gaps in military capability, the armed forces of the non-European imperial forces lacked the degree of standardization, order and training that the Europeans increasingly achieved.

Christopher Bayly has argued that the years 1780–1820 witnessed a 'world crisis' and that

> the European 'Age of Revolutions' was only one part of a general crisis affecting the Asian and Islamic world and the colonies of European settlement . . . when the long-term political conflicts unleashed by the decline of the great hegemonies of the Ottomans, Iran, the Mughals and the monarchies of the Far East and southeast Asia came to a head.[10]

It is unclear whether the crisis described by Bayly was as widespread as he claims – the description is inappropriate for China and Japan, while earlier peaks of crisis can be given for Persia, Burma and Siam – but his argument directs attention to common problems encountered by the Asian empires.

A reminder of the state of flux outside the European world does not help us assess the reasons why, in the nineteenth century, this was to be increasingly dominated by European powers. Clearly, there were long-term reasons and also those that were more specific to the period 1830–1900, both in so far as European strength and non-European weakness were concerned. With regard to the long term, the greater relative effectiveness of European states owed much to more insistent practices of governmental intervention and also to the development of a culture in which planning and the measurement, understanding and control of time and space played greater roles. These cultural and psychological attitudes and procedures enabled the Europeans to take particular advantage of technological changes, and also ensured that they were better able to analyse and systematize military practices, to discuss new options, and to consider war in its political and social contexts. As long as the European powers were busy with what was in effect the long European civil war of 1792–1815, their armed forces responding to the challenge of French power and its use, and subsequently with political disorder that peaked in 1848, the resulting global military capability of the European states was restricted in its consequences. However, this situation was to change later in the century and the Europeans were rapidly to come to dominate Africa and much of Asia.

The contrast that had characterized European expansion before 1775 – between settlement colonies and those that were non-settlement (either commercial positions or lands with a majority of non-Europeans) – continued. New acquisitions followed one or other path, as can be seen with the contrasting British treatment of two islands: Australia and Sri Lanka. The choice of path was the product of the decisions of individual projectors, entrepreneurs and (large numbers of) migrants, as much as of government. The common pattern was the belief that European control fulfilled a wider purpose. This was differently constituted and expressed. Notions of divine providence, geopolitical determinism, racial purpose and secular progression all played parts in what was a complex and shifting mental picture that it is misleading to dissect and classify too precisely. In terms of collective psychology, ideological drive, demographic growth, economic resources, systematized and applied knowledge, technological capability and military potential the Western powers were ready to take over the world.

NOTES

All books published in London unless otherwise stated.

INTRODUCTION

1 J.-P. Rubiés, *Travel and Ethnology in the Renaissance: South India through European Eyes, 1250–1625* (Cambridge, 2000), p. 393. See also S.B. Schwartz (ed.), *Implicit Understandings: Observing, Reporting and Reflecting on the Encounters between Europeans and other Peoples in the Early Modern Era* (Cambridge, 1994).
2 P.J. Marshall, 'The Great Map of Mankind. The British Encounter with India', in A. Frost and J. Samson (eds), *Pacific Empires: Essays in Honour of Glyndwr Williams* (Carlton South, 1999), p. 244.
3 G. Obeyesekere, *The Apotheosis of Captain Cook: European Myth-making in the Pacific* (Princeton, 1992); M. Sahlins, *How 'Natives' Think: About Captain Cook, For Example* (Chicago, 1995).
4 R. Blackburn, *The Making of New-World Slavery* (London, 1998).

2 EXPLORATION

1 For example, *Atlas Istorii*, pp. 39–40, 71. See, more recently, G. Barratt, *Russia in Pacific Waters, 1715–1825* (Vancouver, 1981) and *Russia and the South Pacific, 1696–1840, I: The Russians and Australia* (Vancouver, 1988), *II, Southern and Eastern Polynesia* (Vancouver, 1988) and *Melanesia and the Western Polynesian Fringe* (Vancouver, 1990).
2 J. Jackson, *Flags along the Texas Coast. Charting the Gulf of Mexico, 1519–1759: A Reappraisal* (Austin, 1995).
3 W.A.R. Richardson, 'Mercator's Southern Continent: Its Origins, Influence and Gradual Demise', *Terrae Incognitae*, 25 (1993), pp. 67–98.
4 D. Faussett, *Writing the New World. Imaginary Voyages and Utopia of the Great Southern Land* (Syracuse, 1993) and (ed.), *The Southern Land, Known* by Gabriel de Foigny (Syracuse, 1993).
5 G. Williams, 'The Inexhaustible Fountain of Gold: English Projects and Ventures in the South Seas, 1670–1750', in J.E. Flint and Williams (eds), *Perspectives of Empires: Essays Presented to Gerald S. Graham* (London, 1973), pp. 27–53; D. Reinhartz, 'Shared Vision: Hermann Moll and His Circle and the Great South Sea', *Terrae Incognitae*, 19 (London, 1987), pp. 1–10.
6 B. Hooker, 'Identifying "Davis's Land" in Maps', *Terrae Incognitae*, 21 (London, 1989), pp. 55–61.

7 G. Williams, *The Great South Sea: English Voyages and Encounters, 1570–1750* (New Haven, 1997); A. Sharp, *The Journal of Jacob Roggeveen* (Oxford, 1970).

8 Benjamin Keene, envoy in Spain, to Duke of Bedford, Secretary of State, 21 May 1749, PRO. SP. 94/135 fols 265–8.

9 R.H. Fisher, *Bering's Voyages: Whither and Why* (Seattle, 1977).

10 G. Williams, *The British Search for the Northwest Passage in the Eighteenth Century* (1962); W. Barr and G. Williams (eds), *Voyages to Hudson Bay in Search of a Northwest Passage 1741–1747, I: The Voyage of Christopher Middleton 1741–1742, II: The Voyage of William Moor and Francis Smith 1746–1747* (London, 1995).

11 J.C. Beaglehole, *The Exploration of the Pacific* (3rd edn, Stanford, 1966); O.H.K. Spate, *Paradise Found and Lost. The Pacific since Magellan. III* (London, 1988).

12 D.A. Baugh, 'Seapower and Science: The Motives for Pacific Exploration', in D. Howse (ed.), *Background to Discovery. Pacific Exploration from Dampier to Cook* (Berkeley, 1990), pp. 32–42.

13 J.E. Martin-Allanic, *Bougainville Navigateur et les découvertes de son temps* (Paris, 1964).

14 For a good modern edition, Bougainville, *Voyage autour du monde*, edited by J. Proust (Paris, 1982).

15 F.E. Cuppage, *James Cook and the Conquest of Scurvy* (Westport, Conn., 1994).

16 J.C. Beaglehole, *The Life of Captain James Cook* (London, 1974).

17 R.A. Skelton (ed.), *The Journals of Captain James Cook: Charts and Views* (1969); A. David (ed.), *The Charts and Coastal Views of Captain Cook's Voyages: The Voyage of the 'Endeavour' 1768–1771* (London, 1988).

18 I. Jones and J. Jones, *Oceanography in the Days of Sail* (Sydney, 1992).

19 M.R. de Brossard, *Kerguelen: le decouvreur et ses îles* (Paris, 1970–1).

20 C. Gaziello, *L'Expédition de Lapérouse 1785–1788* (Paris, 1984).

21 H.M. Majors, 'The Hezeta–Bodega Voyage of 1775', *Northwest Discovery*, 1 (1980), pp. 208–52.

22 H.R. Wagner, 'The Last Spanish Exploration of the Northwest Coast and the Attempt to Colonize Bodega Bay', *California Historical Society Quarterly*, 10 (1931), pp. 311–45.

23 D.C. Cutter, *Malaspina and Galiano: Spanish Voyages to the Northwest Coast, 1791 and 1792* (Seattle, 1991) and *California in 1792: A Spanish Naval Visit* (Norman, Okla., 1990); R. Inglis (ed.), *Spain and the North Pacific Coast: Essays in Recognition of the Bicentennial of the Malaspina Expedition, 1791–1792* (Vancouver, 1992).

24 D. Mackay, *In the Wake of Cook. Exploration, Science, and Empire, 1780–1801* (London, 1985); B. Anderson, *Surveyor of the Sea* (Seattle, 1960); W.K. Lamb (ed.), *The Voyage of George Vancouver, 1791–1795* (London, 1984); R. Fisher and H. Johnston (eds), *From Maps to Metaphors. The Pacific World of George Vancouver* (Vancouver, 1993).

25 F. Horner, *The French Reconnaissance: Baudin in Australia 1801–1802* (Melbourne, 1987).

26 Barratt, *Russia and the South Pacific 1696–1840, I* (Vancouver, 1988), *Melanesia and the Western Polynesian Fringe* (Vancouver, 1990).

27 J.H. Parry, *Trade and Dominion. The European Overseas Empires in the Eighteenth Century* (London, 1971), pp. 208–9.

28 E.J. Goodman, 'The Exploration and Mapping of the Arctic Coast of North America', *Terrae Incognitae*, 18 (1986), pp. 55–72; A. Savours, *The Search for the North West Passage* (London, 1999).

29 A.V. Postnikov, 'The Search for a Sea Passage from the Atlantic Ocean to the Pacific via North America's Coast: On the History of a Scientific Competition', *Terrae Incognita*, 32 (2000), pp. 31–52.

30 J.Vercoutter, *A la Recherche de l'Egypt oubliée* (Paris, 1986), pp. 31–7.

31 J. Gascoigne, *Science in the Service of Empire. Joseph Banks, the British State and the Uses of Science in the Age of Revolution* (Cambridge, 1998), pp. 179–80.

32 R. Hallett, *The Penetration of Africa to 1815* (London, 1965).

33 R.S. Weddle, *The French Thorn: Rival Explorers in the Spanish Sea, 1682–1762* (College Station, Tex., 1991); W.C. Foster (ed.), *The La Salle Expedition to Texas: The Journal of Henri Joutel, 1684–1687* (Austin, 1998).

34 E.J. Burrus, *Kino and the Cartography of Northwestern New Spain* (Tuscan, 1965).

35 F. Bergon (ed.), *The Journals of Lewis and Clark* (London, 1989).

36 D.L. Flores (ed.), *Jefferson and Southwestern Exploration. The Freeman and Custis Accounts of the Red River Expedition of 1806* (Norman, Okla., 1984).

37 Y. Jones, *Chinese and Japanese Maps. An Exhibition Organized by the British Library* (London, 1974), pp. 774–7; T.N. Foss, 'A Western Interpretation of China: Jesuit Cartography', in C.E. Ronan and B. Oh (eds), *East Meets West: The Jesuits in China, 1582–1773* (Chicago, 1988), pp. 235–6.

3 KNOWLEDGE

1 For the geographical background, M. Bowen, *Empiricism and Geographical Thought from Francis Bacon to Alexander von Humboldt* (Cambridge, 1981).

2 E. Kajdański, 'The Authenticity of Maurice Benyowsky's Account of His Voyage through the Bering Sea: The Earliest Description and the Earliest Drawings of St Lawrence Island', *Terrae Incognitae*, 23 (1991), pp. 51–80.

3 J.E.D. Williams, *From Sails to Satellites: The Origin and Development of Navigational Science* (Oxford, 1992).

4 A popular introduction is offered by D. Sobel, *Longitude* (1996). Other works include E.S. Whittle, *The Inventor of the Marine Chronometer: John Harrison of Foulby* (Wakefield, 1984).

5 E.A. Reitan, 'Expanding Horizons: Maps in the *Gentleman's Magazine*, 1731–1754', *Imago Mundi*, 37 (1985), pp. 54–62.

6 V. Valerio, 'Late Eighteenth- and Early-nineteenth-century Italian Atlases', in J.A. Wolter and R.E. Crim (eds), *Images of the World. The Atlas through History* (Washington, 1997), p. 263.

7 K. Zandvliet, *Mapping for Money. Maps, Plans and Topographic Paintings and Their Role in Dutch Overseas Expansion during the 16th and 17th Centuries* (Amsterdam, 1998), quote p. 209.

8 R.A. Abou-El-Haj, 'The Formal Closure of the Ottoman Frontier in Europe, 1699–1703', *Journal of the American Oriental Society*, 89 (1969).

9 G. Jewsbury, *The Russian Annexation of Bessarabia, 1774–1828* (Boulder, 1976); M. Atkin, *Russia and Iran, 1780–1828* (Minneapolis, 1980).

10 J.D. Black (ed.), *The Blathwayt Atlas* (2 vols, Providence, 1970–5), I, 49–55; P. Barber, 'Necessary and Ornamental: Map Use in England under the Later Stuarts, 1660–1714', *Eighteenth-Century Life*, 14 (1990), p. 19.

11 R.I. Ruggles, *A Country so Interesting: The Hudson's Bay Company and Two Centuries of Mapping, 1670–1870* (Montréal, 1991).

12 D. Hopkins, 'Jens Michelsen Beck's Map of a Danish West Indian Sugar-plantation Island: Eighteenth-century Colonial Cartography, Land Administration, Speculation, and Fraud', *Terrae Incognitae*, 25 (1993), pp. 99–114, quote p. 107.

13 M. Pelletier, 'La Martinique et La Guadeloupe au lendemain du Traité de Paris (10 février 1763) l'oeuvre des ingénieurs génieurs géographes', *Chronique d'Histoire Maritime*, 9 (1984), pp. 22–30. For the use of maps for British colonial administration, P.A. Penfold (ed.), *Maps and Plans in the Public Record Office, II: America and West Indies* (2 vols, 1974).

14 M.H. Edney, *Mapping an Empire. The Geographical Construction of British India, 1765–1843* (Chicago, 1997), quote p. 340.

15 Ibid.

16 B. Belyea, 'Inland Journeys, Native Maps', in G.M. Lewis (ed.), *Cartographic Encounters. Perspectives on Native American Mapmaking and Map Use* (Chicago, 1998), p. 142.

17 P. Galloway, 'Debriefing Explorers: Amerindian Information in the Delisles' Mapping of the Southeast', in Lewis (ed.), *Cartographic Encounters*, p. 231. See also G.M. Lewis, 'Frontier Encounters in the Field: 1511–1925', in Lewis (ed.), *Cartographic Encounters*, pp. 9–32, and L. De Vosey Jr, 'American Indians and the Early Mapping of the Southeast', in W.P. Cumming (ed.), *The Southeast in Early Maps* (3rd edn, Chapel Hill, 1998), pp. 65–7, 94–5.

18 J.B. Harley, 'Maps, Knowledge and Power', in D. Cosgrove and S. Daniels (eds), *The Iconography of Landscape* (Cambridge, 1988), pp. 277–312, 'Silences and Secrecy: The Hidden Agenda of Cartography in Early Modern Europe', *Imago Mundi*, 40 (1988), pp. 111–30, 'Cartography, Ethics and Social Theory', *Cartographica*, 27/2 (1990), pp. 4–6, and 'Power and Legitimation in the English Geographical Atlases of the Eighteenth Century', in J.A. Wolter and R.E. Crim (eds), *Images of the World. The Atlas through History* (Washington, 1997), pp. 161–204, esp. 181–92.

19 I.C. Taylor, 'Official Geography and the Creation of "Canada"', *Cartographica*, 31/4 (1994), pp. 1–15.

20 G.J. Alder, 'Standing Alone: William Moorcroft Plays the Great Game, 1808–1825', *International History Review*, 2 (1980), pp. 172–215.

21 D. Howse and N.J.W. Thrower, *A Buccaneer's Atlas. Basil Ringrose's South Sea Waggoner* (Berkeley, 1992).

22 M.H. Edney, 'Cartographic Confusion and Nationalism: The Washington Meridian in the Early Nineteenth Century', *Mapline*, 69–70 (1993), p. 48.

23 P.J. Marshall and G. Williams, *The Great Map of Mankind. British Perceptions of the World in the Age of Enlightenment* (1982), p. 303.

24 G.J. Goodman and C.A. Lawson (eds), *Retracing Major Stephen H. Long's 1820 Expedition: The Itinerary and the Botany* (Norman, Okla., 1995).

25 J.F. Henry, *Early Maritime Artists of the Pacific Northwest Coast, 1741–1841* (Seattle, 1984).

26 F. Horner, *The French Reconnaissance: Baudin in Australia 1801–1803* (Melbourne, 1987).

27 J. Browne, *The Secular Art* (New Haven, 1983).

28 See, for example, P.E.H. Hair, A. Jones and R. Law (eds), *Barbot on Guinea: The Writings of Jean Barbot on West Africa 1678–1712* (1992).

29 L. Wolff, *Inventing Eastern Europe: The Map of Civilization on the Mind of the Enlightenment* (Stanford, 1994).

30 B. Dolan, *Exploring European Frontiers. British Travellers in the Age of Enlightenment* (2000).

31 J.R. Knowlson, 'George Psalmanaazar: The Fake Formosan', *History Today*, 15 (1965), pp. 871–6; D. Eilon, 'Gulliver's Fellow-traveller Psalmanaazar', *British Journal for Eighteenth-Century Studies*, 8 (1985), pp. 172–8.

32 P.G. Adams, *Travellers and Travel Liars 1660–1800* (Berkeley, 1962).

33 J.M. Lafont, 'Politics and Architecture in the French Settlements', K. Jain, 'French Settlements in India', P. Pichard, 'City Planning and Architecture in Pondicherry', and K.T. Ravindran, 'Colonial Urbanism: A Cross-cultural Perspective on Pondicherry', in *Reminiscences. The French in India* (New Delhi, 1997), pp. 26–8, 91–140. For a focus on the 'hybrid' city that resulted from colonialism, J. Parker, *Making the Town: Ga State and Society in Early Colonial Accra* (2000).

34 J.S. McLennan, *Louisbourg from its Foundation to its Fall, 1713–1758* (Sydney, 1957); F.J. Thorpe, *Rémparts Lointains: La politique française des travaux publics à Terre Neuve et à l'île Royale, 1695–1758* (Ottawa, 1980).

35 M.W. Lewis and K.E. Wigen, *The Myth of Continents: A Critique of Metageography* (Berkeley, 1997).
36 K.M. Adams, 'Distant Encounters: Travel Literature and the Shifting Images of the Toraja of Sulawesi, Indonesia' *Terrae Incognitae*, 23 (1991), p. 92.

4 ATTITUDES

1   A. Pagden, *Lords of all the World: Ideologies of Empire in Spain, Britain and France, c.1500–1800* (New Haven, 1995).
2   D. Goffman, *Britons in the Ottoman Empire, 1642–1660* (Seattle, 1998). See also, N. Matar, *Turks, Moors, and Englishmen in the Age of Discovery* (New York, 1999).
3   W.R. Ward, *The Protestant Evangelical Awakening* (Cambridge, 1992).
4   B.S. Schlenther, 'Religious Faith and Commercial Empire', in P.J. Marshall, *The Oxford History of the British Empire, II: The Eighteenth Century* (Oxford, 1998), p. 131.
5   S. Neill, *A History of Christianity in India 1707–1858* (Cambridge, 1985).
6   M. Kelly, *Early Missionaries' Impact on Hawaiians and their Culture* (Honolulu, 1988).
7   E.R. Hambye, *History of Christianity in India, III: The Eighteenth Century* (Bangalore, 1997).
8   J. Alden, *The Making of an Enterprise: The Society of Jesus in Portugal, its Empire, and beyond 1540–1750* (Stanford, 1996).
9   P. Caraman, *The Lost Paradise: An Account of the Jesuits in Paraguay 1607–1768* (1975).
10 B. Guy, *The French Image of China, before and after Voltaire* (Geneva, 1963).
11 A.C. Ross, *A Vision Betrayed. The Jesuits in Japan and China, 1541–1741* (Edinburgh, 1994); R. Po-Chia Hsia, *The World of Catholic Renewal 1540–1770* (Cambridge, 1998), pp. 186–93. For Jesuit syncretism in India, I.G. Zupanov, *Disputed Mission: Jesuit Experiments and Brahminical Knowledge in Seventeenth-century India*, (New Delhi, 2000).
12 P.A. Goddard, 'Christianization and Civilization in Seventeenth-century French Colonial Thought' (D.Phil., Oxford, 1990), pp. 262, 364; G.D. Jones, *The Conquest of the Last Maya Kingdom* (Stanford, 1998), pp. 300–2, 318–21, 329–35.
13 H.W. Crosby, *Antiqua California. Mission and Colony on the Peninsular Frontier, 1697–1768* (Albuquerque, 1994), pp. 29–39.
14 Arthur Dobbs to the 3rd Earl of Bute, 2 June 1762, Mount Stuart, papers of the 3rd Earl, 2/74.
15 D.F. Allen, 'Charles II, Louis XIV and the Order of Malta', *European History Quarterly*, 20 (1990), pp. 324–5.
16 H.L.A. Dunthorne, '"The Generous Turk": Some Eighteenth-century Attitudes', *The Historian*, 68 (2000), pp. 18–22; A. Thomson, *Barbary and Enlightenment. European Attitudes towards the Maghreb in the Eighteenth Century* (Leiden, 1987).
17 A. Gunny, 'Images of Islam in Some French Writings of the First Half of the Eighteenth Century', *British Journal for Eighteenth-Century Studies*, 14 (1991), p. 200.
18 J. Harris, 'Introduction', in J. Harris and M. Snodin (eds), *Sir William Chambers. Architect to George III* (New Haven, 1996), p. 4.
19 M. Degros, 'Les Consulats de France sous la Révolution. Les états barbaresques', *Revue d'Histoire Diplomatique*, 105 (1991), p. 117.
20 G. Sale (ed.), *The Koran* (1734), dedication, iv.
21 B. Smith, *European Vision and the South Pacific, 1768–1850* (Oxford, 1960); B. Smith and R. Joppien, *The Art of Captain Cook's Voyages* (New Haven, 1988); B. Smith, *Imaging the Pacific: In the Wake of Cook's Voyages* (New Haven, 1992).
22 P.J. Marshall, 'The Great Map of Mankind', in A. Frost and J. Samson (eds), *Pacific Empires: Essays in Honour of Glyndwr Williams* (Carlton South, 1999), pp.

239–41; T.B. Clark, *Omai: The First Polynesian Ambassador to England* (San Francisco, 1941).

23 K.L. Nero and N. Thomas (eds), *An Account of the Pellew Islands* (2001).

24 A.W. Crosby, *Ecological Expansion. The Biological Expansion of Europe, 900–1900* (Cambridge, 1986), pp. 228–30, 234.

25 A. Pagden, *The Fall of Natural Man. The American Indian and the Origins of Comparative Ethnology* (2nd edn, Cambridge, 1986), and *European Encounters with the New World* (New Haven, 1993).

26 H. Laurens, *Aux Sources de l'Orientalisme. La Bibliothèque orientale de Barthélemi d'Herbelot* (Paris, 1978); D.F. Lach and E.J. Van Kley, *Asia in the Making of Europe. A Century of Advance* (Chicago, 1993).

27 J.M. Lafont, *Indika. Essays in Indo-French Relations 1630–1976* (Delhi, 2000), p. 34.

28 A. Gunny, *Images of Islam in Eighteenth-century Writing* (1996).

29 M. Byrd, 'Monuments to the People: The Napoleonic Scholars and Daily Life in Ancient Egypt', *Consortium on Revolutionary Europe. Selected Papers, 1997*, p. 247.

30 See, more generally, J. MacKenzie, *Orientalism. History, Theory and the Arts* (Manchester, 1995); P. Godrej and P. Rohatgi, *Scenic Splendors. India through the Printed Image* (1989).

31 P.J. Marshall and G. Williams, *The Great Map of Mankind. British Perceptions of the World in the Age of Enlightenment* (1982), pp. 67–164; S. Murr, *L'Inde philosophique entre Bossuet et Voltaire* (2 vols, Paris, 1987); P.J. Marshall, *The British Discovery of Hinduism in the Eighteenth Century* (Cambridge, 1970), 'The Founding Fathers of the Asiatic Society', *Journal of the Asiatic Society*, 27 (1985), pp. 63–77, and 'Taming the Exotic: The British and India in the Seventeenth and Eighteenth Centuries', in G.S. Rousseau and R. Porter (eds), *Exoticism in the Enlightenment* (Manchester, 1990), pp. 46–65; G. Cannon and K.R. Brine (eds), *Objects of Enquiry: The Life, Contributions, and Influences of Sir William Jones, 1746–1794* (New York, 1995); M. Priestman, *Romantic Atheism. Poetry and Freethought 1780–1830* (Cambridge, 1999).

32 B. Guy, 'Rousseau and China', *Revue de Littérature Comparée*, 30 (1956), pp. 531–6; H. Cohen, 'Diderot and China', *Studies on Voltaire*, 242 (1986), pp. 219–32; J.J. Clarke, *Oriental Enlightenment: The Encounter between Asian and Western Thought* (1997).

33 J.P. Greene, *Pursuits of Happiness. The Social Development of Early Modern British Colonies and the Formation of American Culture* (Chapel Hill, 1988) and *The Intellectual Construction of America. Exceptionalism and Identity from 1492 to 1800* (Chapel Hill, 1993); K.O. Kupperman (ed.), *America in European Consciousness 1493–1750* (Chapel Hill, 1995).

34 R. Atwood, *The Hessians. The Mercenaries from Hessen-Kassel in the American Revolution* (Cambridge, 1980).

35 H. Dippel, *Germany and the American Revolution, 1770–1800: A Sociohistorical Investigation of Late Eighteenth-century Political Thinking* (Chapel Hill, 1977).

36 F. Felsenstein (ed.), *English Trader, Indian Maid: Representing Gender, Race, and Slavery in the New World. An Inkle and Yarico Reader* (Baltimore, 1999).

37 H.J. Lüsebrink and M. Tietz (eds), *Lectures de Raynal. L'Histoire des deux Indes en Europe et en Amérique au XVIIIe siècle* (Oxford, 1991).

38 R.E. Close, 'Toleration and its Limits in the Late Hanoverian Empire: The Cape Colony 1795–1828', in S. Taylor, R. Connors and C. Jones (eds), *Hanoverian Britain and Empire* (Woodbridge, 1998), p. 303.

39 P.S. Onuf, *Jefferson's Empire. The Language of American Nationhood* (Charlottesville, 2000), pp. 18–52, quote p. 51.

40 J. Roach, 'Body of Law. The Sun King and the *Code Noir*', in S.F. Melzer and K. Norberg (eds), *From the Royal to the Republican Body. Incorporating the Political in Seventeenth and Eighteenth-century France* (Berkeley, 1998), pp. 113–30.

41 C.R. Boxer, *The Portuguese Seaborne Empire, 1415–1825* (1969).

42 T.M. Curley, *Sir Robert Chambers: Law, Literature and Empire in the Age of Johnson* (Madison, Wis. 1998). More generally, see K. Teltscher, *India Inscribed: European and British Writing on India 1600–1800* (New Delhi, 1995).

43 N. Bhattacharyya-Panda, 'The English East India Company and the Hindu Laws of Property in Bengal, 1765–1801: Appropriation and Invention of Tradition' (D.Phil., Oxford, 1996).

44 A.F.C. Wallace, *Jefferson and the Indians: The Tragic Fate of the First Americans* (Cambridge, Mass., 1999).

5 TRADE

1 S. Chaudhury and M. Morineau (eds), *Merchants, Companies and Trade. Europe and Asia in the Early Modern Era* (Cambridge, 1999), especially N. Steensgaard, 'The route through Quandahar: The Significance of the Overland Trade from India to the West in the Seventeenth Century', pp. 55–73; R.P. Matthee, *The Politics of Trade in Safavid Iran. Silk for Silver, 1600–1730* (Cambridge, 1999), esp. pp. 238–9.

2 M. Postlethwayt, *Great-Britain's True System* (1757), pp. 264–5.

3 J.I. Israel, *Dutch Primacy in World Trade, 1585–1740* (Oxford, 1989); P. Emmer, *The Dutch in the Atlantic Economy, 1580–1880: Trade, Slavery, and Emancipation* (Aldershot, 1998).

4 J. Delumeau, *Le Mouvement du port de Saint Malo 1681–1720* (Rennes, 1966).

5 C. Manning, *Fortunes à faire. The French in Asian Trade, 1719–48* (Aldershot, 1996); A. Sinha, 'French Trade in India in the Eighteenth Century', in *Indo-French Relations: History and Perspectives* (New Delhi, 1990), pp. 37–50.

6 Joseph de Bauffremont, *Journal de campagne dans les pays barbaresques, 1766*, edited by M. Chirac (Paris, 1981).

7 J.R. Bruijn, *The Dutch Navy of the Seventeenth and Eighteenth Centuries* (Columbia, SC, 1993), pp. 150–1, 155.

8 M. Duffy, *Soldiers, Sugar and Seapower: The British Expeditions to the West Indies and the War against Revolutionary France* (Oxford, 1987), p. 7.

9 J.V. Beckett, *Coal and Tobacco: The Lowthers and the Economic Development of West Cumberland 1660–1760* (Cambridge, 1981).

10 J.R. Bruijn, F.S. Gaastra and I. Schöffer (eds), *Dutch–Asiatic Shipping in the Seventeenth and Eighteenth Centuries* (3 vols, The Hague, 1979–87); P. Lawson, *The East India Company: A History* (Harlow, 1993).

11 O. Prakash, *European Commercial Enterprise in Pre-colonial India* (Cambridge, 1998), pp. 255–6; P. Haudrère, 'The Compagnie des Indes Orientales', in R. Vincent (ed.), *The French in India* (Bombay, 1990), p. 37.

12 C. Koninckx, *The First and Second Charters of the Swedish India Company (1731–1766): A Contribution to the Maritime, Economic and Social History of North-western Europe in its Relationships with the Far East* (Courtrai, 1980). See also, O. Feldbaek, *India Trade under the Danish Flag, 1772–1808* (Copenhagen, 1969).

13 E. Fauré, *La Banqueroute de Law* (Paris, 1977).

14 C.R. Boxer, *From Lisbon to Goa, 1500 to 1750: Studies in Portuguese Maritime Expansion* (1984).

15 R. Gaston, 'La France et la politique commerciale de l'Espagne au XVIIIe siècle', *Revue d'Histoire Moderne et Contemporaine*, 6 (1959), p. 287.

16 AE. CP. Esp. 537 fol. 258.

17 N. Zahedieh, 'The Merchants of Port Royal, Jamaica, and the Spanish Contraband Trade, 1655–92', *William and Mary Quarterly*, 3rd series, 43 (1986), pp. 570–93.

18 H.E.S. Fisher, *The Portugal Trade: A Study of Anglo-Portuguese Commerce 1700–1770* (1971).

19 D.M. Ladd, *The Making of a Strike: The Mexican Silver Workers' Struggles in Real Del Monte 1766–1775* (Lincoln, Nebr., 1988).

20 G.J. Walker, *Spanish Politics and Imperial Trade 1700–1789* (1979).

21 F.C. Spooner, *Risks at Sea: Amsterdam Insurance and Maritime Europe, 1766–1780* (Cambridge, 1983).

22 P. Butel, *Les Négociants bordelais, l'Europe et les Îles au XVIIIe siècle* (Paris, 1974); D. Miquelon, *Dugard of Rouen: French Trade to Canada and the West Indies, 1729–1770* (Montréal, 1978).

23 J.J. McCusker and R.R. Menard, *The Economy of British America 1607–1789* (Chapel Hill, 1991).

24 P.P. Hill, *French Perceptions of the Early American Republic, 1783–1793* (Philadelphia, 1988).

25 F. Charles-Roux, *Les Origines de l'expédition d'Egypte* (Paris, 1910).

26 F.L. Nussbaum, 'The Formation of the New East India Company of Calonne', *American Historical Review*, 38 (1933), pp. 475–97.

27 G. Taboulet, *La Geste française en Indochine* (2 vols, Paris, 1955–6), I, pp. 161–279.

28 J.M. Price, *France and the Chesapeake. A History of the French Tobacco Monopoly, 1674–1791, and of its Relationship to the British and American Tobacco Trades* (Ann Arbor, 1973), p. 242.

29 P. Lawson, *The East India Company: A History* (1993).

30 H. Bowen, *Revenue and Reform: The Indian Problem in British Politics 1757–1773* (Cambridge, 1991); H. Mui and L. Mui, *The Management of Monopoly. A Study of the East India Company's Conduct of its Tea Trade, 1784–1833* (Vancouver, 1984).

31 E.H. Pritchard, *The Crucial Years of Early Anglo-Chinese Relations 1750–1800* (Pullman, Wash., 1936), pp. 236–311.

32 O. Prakash, *European Commercial Enterprise in Pre-colonial India* (Cambridge, 1998), p. 79. See, more generally, P. Haudrère, *La Compagnie française des Indes au XVIIIe siècle, 1719–1795* (Paris, 1989).

33 P.H. Boulle, 'French Mercantilism, Commercial Companies and Colonial Profitability', in L. Blussé and F. Gaastra (eds), *Companies and Trade* (The Hague, 1981), pp. 97–117; O. Petré-Grenouilleau, 'Dynamique Sociale et croissance. À propos du prétendu retard du capitalisme maritime français', *Annales*, 52 (1997), pp. 1263–74.

34 T.J. Schaeper, *The French Council of Commerce* (Columbus, Ohio, 1983); Haudrère, 'Un Aspect des relations entre le pouvoir royal et le grand commerce maritime au XVIIIe siècle: Les Commissaires du Roi auprès de la Compagnie française des Indes, 1720–1770', *L'Information Historique* (December 1976), pp. 221–5.

35 M. Giraud, *Les Métis canadien: Son rôle dans l'histoire des provinces de l'Ouest* (Paris, 1945); H.A. Innis, *The Fur Trade in Canada* (2nd edn, Toronto, 1956); W.J. Eccles, *Canada under Louis XIV, 1663–1701* (Toronto, 1964); J. Brown (ed.), *The Fur Trade Revisited* (Lansing, 1994).

36 J.G. Clark, *New Orleans, 1718–1812: An Economic History* (Baton Rouge, 1970); J.F. Bosher, 'Government and Private Interests in New France', *Canadian Public Administration*, 10 (1967), pp. 110, 124; D.R. Farrell, 'Private Profit and Public Interest: Individual Gain, State Policy and French Colonial Expansion', *Proceedings of the Western Society for French History*, 14 (1987), pp. 70–7.

37 L. Joré, *Les Établissements français sur la côte occidentale d'Afrique de 1758 à 1809* (Paris, 1965), pp. 114–17.

38 H. Bowen, *Revenue and Reform. The Indian Problem in British Politics 1757–1773* (Cambridge, 1991).

39 C. Roure, 'La Réglementation du commerce français au Levant sous l'ambassade du marquis de Villeneuve, 1728–41', in J.P. Filippini (ed.), *Dossiers sur le commerce français en Méditerranée orientale au XVIIIe siècle* (Paris, 1976), pp. 34, 37–76, 89.

40 H.A. Innis, *The Cod Fisheries: The History of an International Economy* (2nd edn, Toronto, 1954).

41 A.J. Ray, *Indians in the Fur Trade, 1660–1870* (Toronto, 1974).

42 R. Fisher, *Contact and Conflict* (Vancouver, 1977); J.R. Gibson, *Otter Skins, Boston Ships, and China Goods. The Maritime Fur Trade of the Northwest Coast, 1785–1841* (Montréal, 1992).

43 J.M.R. Owens, 'New Zealand before Annexation', in G.W. Rice (ed.), *The Oxford History of New Zealand* (2nd edn, Auckland, 1992), pp. 28–53.

44 A. Griffin, 'London, Bengal, the China Trade and the Unfrequented Extremities of Asia: The East India Company's Settlement in New Guinea, 1793–95', *British Library Journal*, 16 (1990), pp. 151–73.

45 R. Barnett, *North India between Empires: Awadh, the Mughals and the British 1720–1801* (Berkeley, 1980); C.A. Bayly, *Rulers, Townsmen and Bazaars: North Indian Society in the Age of British Expansion, 1770–1870* (Cambridge, 1983) and *Indian Society and the Making of the British Empire* (Cambridge, 1988).

46 M.A. Ali, 'Recent Theories of Eighteenth-century India', *Indian Historical Review*, 13 (1987), pp. 101–10; H. Hossain, *The Company Weavers of Bengal: The East India Company and the Organization of Textile Production in Bengal, 1750–1813* (Delhi, 1988); S. Chaudhuri, *From Prosperity to Decline: Eighteenth-century Bengal* (New Delhi, 1995). The debate is reviewed with characteristic skill in P.J. Marshall, 'Reappraisal: The Rise of British Power in Eighteenth-century India', *South Asia*, new series, 19 (1996), pp. 71–6.

47 S. Sen, *Empire of Free Trade. The East India Company and the Making of the Colonial Marketplace* (Philadelphia, 1998).

48 M.H. Fisher (ed.), *The Travels of Dean Mahomet. An Eighteenth-century Journey through India* (Berkeley, 1997), p. 58.

49 M.C. Ricklefs, *A History of Modern Indonesia since c. 1730* (2nd edn, 1993), pp. 90–1; G. Knaap, *Shallow Waters, Rising Tide: Shipping and Trade in Java around 1775* (Leiden, 1996).

50 R. Connors, 'Opium and Imperial Expansion: The East India Company in Eighteenth-century Asia', in S. Taylor, R. Connors and C. Jones (eds), *Hanoverian Britain and Empire* (Woodbridge, 1998), pp. 248–66.

51 J. Walvin, *Fruits of Empire. Exotic Produce and British Taste, 1660–1800* (1997), p. 16; P. Lawson, 'Tea, Vice and the English State, 1660–1784', in Lawson, *A Taste for Empire and Glory. Studies in British Overseas Expansion, 1660–1800* (Aldershot, 1997), pp. 1–21.

52 S.B. Schwartz, *Sugar Plantations in the Formation of Brazilian Society: Bahia, 1550–1835* (Cambridge, 1985).

53 A.L. Butler, 'Europe's Indian Nectar: The Transatlantic Cacao and Chocolate Trade in the Seventeenth Century' (M.Litt., Oxford, 1993).

54 R. Stein, 'The French Sugar Business in the Eighteenth Century: A Quantitative Study', *Business History*, 22 (1980), pp. 6, 10, 12.

55 AN. AM. B7 375, 5, 26 Jan. 1750.

56 J. Tarrade, *Le Commerce colonial de la France à la fin de l'Ancien Régime: L'Évolution du régime de 'l'Exclusif' de 1763 à 1789* (2 vols, Paris, 1972), II, p. 759.

57 C.D. Edwards, *Eighteenth Century Furniture* (Manchester, 1996).

58 J. Clark, *La Rochelle and the Atlantic Economy during the Eighteenth Century* (1982).

6 MIGRATION, SETTLEMENT, SLAVERY AND COLONIES

1 K.G. Davies, 'The Living and the Dead: White Mortality in West Africa, 1684–1732', in S.L. Engerman and E.D. Genovese (eds), *Race and Slavery in the Western Hemisphere: Qualitative Studies* (Princeton, 1975), pp. 88–93.

2 G. Martin (ed.), *The Founding of Australia* (Sydney, 1978); A. Frost, *Botany Bay Mirages: Illusions of Australia's Convict Beginnings* (Melbourne, 1994).

3 G. Williams, 'The First Fleet and after: Expectation and Reality', in T. Delamothe and C. Bridge (eds), *Interpreting Australia* (1988), pp. 24–40.

4 G.J. Ames, 'Colbert's Grand Indian Ocean Fleet of 1670', *Mariner's Mirror*, 76 (1990), pp. 230–1, 236–9.

5 I.K. Steele, *The English Atlantic, 1675–1740: An Exploration of Communication and Community* (Oxford, 1986).

6 P. Bakewell, 'Spanish America: Empire and its Outcome', in J.H. Elliott (ed.), *The Hispanic World* (1991), pp. 74–5.

7 N. Canny (ed.), *Europeans on the Move: Studies on European Migration, 1500–1800* (Oxford, 1994).

8 R.C. Harris (ed.), *Historical Atlas of Canada* (Toronto, 1987), I, plates 48, 53.

9 C.J. Ekberg, *French Roots in the Illinois Country. The Mississippi Frontier in Colonial Times* (Champaign, Ill., 2000), p. 177.

10 J.F. Bosher, *Business and Religion in the Age of New France, 1600–1760* (Toronto, 1994).

11 P.A. Goddard, 'Christianization and Civilization in Seventeenth-century French Colonial Thought' (D.Phil., Oxford, 1990), pp. 278, 304; J.F. Bosher, 'The Imperial Environment of French Trade with Canada, 1660–1685', *English Historical Review*, 108 (1993), p. 778, and 'The Gaigneur Clan in the Seventeenth-century Canada Trade', in O.U. Janzen (ed.), *Merchant Organization and Maritime Trade in the North Atlantic, 1660–1815* (St John's, Newfoundland, 1998), pp. 31, 35.

12 R.V. Wells, *The Population of the British Colonies in America before 1776: A Survey of Census Data* (Princeton, 1975); A. Fogleman, 'Migrations to the Thirteen British North American Colonies, 1700–1775: New Estimates', *Journal of Interdisciplinary History*, 22 (1992), pp. 691–709.

13 T. Burnard, '"The Countrie Continues Sicklie": White Mortality in Jamaica, 1655–1780', *Social History of Medicine*, 12 (1999), pp. 45–72.

14 A.L. Karras, *Sojourners in the Sun: Scottish Migrants in Jamaica and the Chesapeake, 1740–1800* (Ithaca, 1993). See, more generally, B. Bailyn, *The Peopling of British North America: An Introduction* (1987) and *Voyagers to the West: A Passage in the Peopling of America on the Eve of the Revolution* (New York, 1986).

15 D.W. Galenson, *White Servitude in Colonial America: An Economic Analysis* (Cambridge, 1981); M.S. Quintanilla, 'Late Seventeenth-century Indentured Servants in Barbados', *Journal of Caribbean History*, 27 (1993); D.M. Hockedy, 'Bound for a New World: Emigration of Indentured Servants via Liverpool to America and the West Indies, 1697–1707', *Transactions of the Historic Society of Lancashire and Cheshire*, 144 (1995), pp. 121–2.

16 M.S. Wokeck, *Trade in Strangers: The Beginnings of Mass Migration to North America* (University Park, Penn., 1999).

17 J.M. Johnson, *Militiamen, Rangers, and Redcoats. The Military in Georgia, 1754–1776* (Macon, Ga., 1992), p. 75.

18 C.A. Brasseaux, 'The Image of Louisiana and the Failure of Voluntary French Emigration, 1683–1731', and G.R. Conrad, 'Immigration Forcé: A French Attempt to Populate Louisiana, 1717–1720', both in *Proceedings of the Fourth Annual Meeting of the French Colonial Historical Society* (1979).

19 J.N. Biraben, 'Le Peuplement du Canada français', *Annales de Démographie Historique* (Paris, 1966), pp. 104–39; J. Dupâquier (ed.), *Histoire de la population française, II: De la Renaissance à 1789* (Paris, 1988), pp. 125–7.

20 P.N. Moogk, 'Reluctant Exiles: The Problems of Colonisation in French North America', *William and Mary Quarterly*, 46 (1989), pp. 463–505.

21 J. Michel, *La Guyane sous l'Ancien Régime* (Paris, 1989).

22 G.M. Hall, *Africans in Colonial Louisiana: The Development of Afro-Creole Culture in the Eighteenth Century* (Baton Rouge, 1992).

23 D. Turley, *Slavery* (Oxford, 2000). See, for example, K.M. Adams, 'Distant Encounters: Travel Literature and the Shifting Images of the Toraja of Sulawesi, Indonesia', *Terrae Incognitae*, 23 (1991), pp. 83, 85.

24 P.W. Bamford, *Fighting Ships and Prisons: The Mediterranean Galleys of France in the Age of Louis XIV* (Minneapolis, 1973).

25 A.R. Ekirch, *Bound for America: The Transportation of British Convicts to the Colonies, 1718–1775* (Oxford, 1987); W. Oldham, *Britain's Convicts to the Colonies* (1990).

26 Bailyn, *Voyagers to the West*, pp. 463–4.

27 C.A. Palmer (ed.), *The Worlds of Unfree Labour: From Indentured Servitude to Slavery* (Aldershot, 1998).

28 D. Sweet, 'Native Resistance in Eighteenth-century Amazonia: The "Abominable Muras" in War and Peace', *Radical History Review*, 53 (1992), p. 58.

29 For wide-ranging works, among the extensive literature on the subject, B. Solow (ed.), *Slavery and the Rise of the Atlantic System* (Cambridge, 1991) and J.E. Inikori and S.L. Engerman (eds), *The Atlantic Slave Trade: Effects on Economies, Societies, and Peoples in Africa, the Americas, and Europe* (Durham, NC, 1992).

30 G. Debien, *Les Esclaves aux Antilles Française: XVII–XVIII siècle* (Basse-Terre, Guadeloupe, 1974); R.L. Stein, *The French Slave Trade in the Eighteenth Century: An Old Regime Business* (Madison, Wis., 1979); J. Tarrade, *Le Commerce colonial de la France à la fin de l'Ancien Régime* (Paris, 1972), II, p. 759. See, more generally, W.B. Cohen, *The French Encounter with Africans: White Response to Blacks, 1530–1880* (Bloomington, 1980) and E. Saugéra, *Bordeaux port négrier. XVIIIe–XIXe siècles. Chronologie, économie, idéologie* (Paris, 1995); J. Dupâquier (ed.), *Histoire*, p. 127.

31 British Library, Additional Manuscripts vol. 36797 fol.1.

32 Dupâquier (ed.), *Histoire*, p. 128.

33 D. Richardson, 'The British Empire and the Atlantic Slave Trade, 1660–1807', in P.J. Marshall (ed.), *The Oxford History of the British Empire, II: The Eighteenth Century* (Oxford, 1998), pp. 442, 446.

34 C.A. Palmer, *Human Cargoes: The British Slave Trade to Spanish America, 1700–1739* (1981).

35 D. Richardson and M.M. Schofield, 'Whitehaven and the Eighteenth-century British Slave Trade', *Transactions of the Cumberland and Westmorland Antiquarian and Archaeological Society*, 102 (1992), pp. 183–204.

36 N. Tattersfield, *The Forgotten Trade, Comprising the Log of the Daniel and Henry of 1700 and Accounts of the Slave Trade from the Minor Ports of England 1698–1725* (1991).

37 M. Elder, *The Slave Trade and the Economic Development of Eighteenth-Century Lancaster* (Preston, 1992).

38 C. Fick, *The Making of Haiti: The Saint-Domingue Revolution from Below* (Knoxville, 1991), p. 27; W.C. Johnson, *Soul by Soul: Life Inside the Antebellum Slave Market* (Cambridge, Mass., 2001).

39 D.H. Akenson, *If the Irish Ran the World: Montserrat, 1630–1730* (Montréal, 1997); H. Beckles and A. Downes, 'The Economics of Transition to the Black Labor System in Barbados, 1630–1680', *Journal of Interdisciplinary History*, 18 (1987).

40 A.E. Smith, *Colonists in Bondage: White Servitude and Convict Labor in America, 1607–1776* (Chapel Hill, 1947).

41 B.W. Higman, *Slave Populations of the British Caribbean 1807–1834* (Baltimore, 1984).

42 R. Law, *The Oyo Empire c.1600–c.1836: A West African Imperialism in the Era of the Atlantic Slave Trade* (Oxford, 1977).

43 J.F. Searing, *West African Slavery and Atlantic Commerce. The Senegal River Valley, 1700–1860* (Cambridge, 1993); D.R. Wright, *The World and a Very Small Place in Africa* (Armonk, 1997).

44 R. Law, 'King Agaja of Dahomey, the Slave Trade, and the Question of West African Plantations: The Mission of Bulfinch Lambe and Adomo Tomo to England, 1726–32', *Journal of Imperial and Commonwealth History*, 19 (1991), pp. 138–63; P.E. Hair and R. Law, 'The English in Western Africa to 1700', in N. Canny (ed.), *The Oxford History of the British Empire, I: The Origins of Empire* (Oxford, 1998), p. 261.

45 J. Thornton, *Africa and Africans in the Making of the Atlantic World, 1400–1800* (2nd edn, Cambridge, 1998).

46 C.A. Palmer, 'From Africa to the Americas: Ethnicity in the Early Black Communities of the Americas', *Journal of World History*, 6 (1995), p. 236.

47 P.D. Morgan, *Slave Counterpoint: Black Culture in the Eighteenth-century Chesapeake and Lowcountry* (Chapel Hill, 1998).

48 T. Burnard, 'European Migration to Jamaica, 1655–1780', *William and Mary Quarterly*, 3rd series, 53 (1996), pp. 791, 793.

49 P.H. Wood, *Black Majority: Negroes in Colonial South Carolina from 1670 through the Stono Rebellion* (New York, 1974), pp. 314–23.

50 J. Sidbury, *Ploughshares into Swords: Race, Rebellion, and Identity in Gabriel's Virginia, 1730–1810* (Cambridge, 1997).

51 R.R. Rea, 'Urban Problems and Responses in British Pensacola', *Gulf Coast Historical Review*, 3 (1987), p. 56.

52 G. Metcalf, *Royal Government and Political Conflict in Jamaica 1729–1783* (1965), pp. 33–79; O. Patterson, 'Slavery and Slave Revolts: A Socio-historical Analysis of the First Maroon War – Jamaica, 1655–1740', *Social and Economic Studies*, 19 (1970); M. Craton, *Testing the Chains. Resistance to Slavery in the British West Indies* (1982), pp. 61–96; M. Campbell, *The Maroons of Jamaica, 1655–1796: A History of Resistance, Collaboration and Betrayal* (Trenton, NJ, 1990).

53 D. Eltis, *The Rise of African Slavery in the Americas* (Cambridge, 2000), p. 136.

54 J.C. Miller, *Way of Death: Merchant Capitalism and the Angolan Slave Trade, 1730–1830* (Madison, Wis., 1988) and, quote, 'World's Apart: Africans' Encounters and Africa's Encounters with the Atlantic in Angola, before 1800', *Actas do Seminário Encontro de Povos e Culturas em Angola*, Luanda, 1995, no page numbers in original.

55 J.E. Chaplin, *An Anxious Pursuit. Agricultural Innovation and Modernity in the Lower South, 1730–1815* (Chapel Hill, 1993).

56 A. Pagden, 'Europe and the Wider World', in J. Bergin (ed.), *The Seventeenth Century* (Oxford, 2001), pp. 207–9.

57 Voltaire, *Candide* (1759), ch. 19. See J.M. Postma, *The Dutch in the Atlantic Slave Trade, 1600–1815* (1990).

58 P. Manning, *Slavery and African Life: Occidental, Oriental, and African Slave Trades* (Cambridge, 1990).

59 M. Giraud, *A History of French Louisiana, V: The Company of the Indies, 1723–1731* (Baton Rouge, 1991), p. 317.

60 L. Campbell, 'Recent Research on Andean Peasant Revolutions, 1750–1820', *Latin American Research Review*, 14 (1979), pp. 3–50; J.R. Fisher, A.J. Kuethe and A. McFarlane (eds), *Reform and Insurrection in Bourbon New Granada and Peru* (Baton Rouge, 1990); O. Cornblit, *Power and Violence in a Colonial City: Oruro*

from the Mining Renaissance to the Rebellion of Túpac Amaru, 1740–1782 (Cambridge, 1995).

61 W.E. Washburn, 'The Moral and Legal Justifications for Dispossessing the Indians', in J.M. Smith (ed.), *Seventeenth Century America: Essays in Colonial History* (Chapel Hill, 1959), pp. 24–32.

62 A. Frost, 'New South Wales as Terra Nullius: The British Denial of Aboriginal Land Rights', *Historical Studies*, 19 (1981), pp. 513–23.

63 A.W. Crosby, *Ecological Imperialism. The Biological Expansion of Europe, 900–1900* (Cambridge, 1993).

64 D.H. Akenson, *If the Irish Ran the World: Montserrat, 1630–1730* (Montréal, 1997).

65 W. Holton, *Forced Founders: Indians, Debtors, Slaves, and the Making of the American Revolution in Virginia* (Chapel Hill, 1999).

66 R. Bliss, *Revolution and Empire. English Politics and the American Colonies in the Seventeenth Century* (Manchester, 1993).

67 W.E. Washburn, *The Governor and the Rebel: A History of Bacon's Rebellion in Virginia* (Chapel Hill, 1957); S.S. Webb, *1676: The End of American Independence* (New York, 1984).

68 N. Canny and A. Pagden (eds), *Colonial Identity in the Atlantic World 1500–1800* (Princeton, 1987).

69 L. Vorsey, *The Indian Boundary in the Southern Colonies, 1763–1775* (Chapel Hill, 1966), pp. 162–4.

70 R.Bonney, *Kedah 1771–1821. The Search for Security and Independence* (Oxford, 1971), VI, pp. 52–101, 110; D.K. Bassett, *British Trade and Policy in Indonesia and Malaysia in the Late Eighteenth Century* (Hull, 1971), pp. 73–96.

71 P. Nightingale, *Trade and Empire in Western India, 1784–1806* (Cambridge, 1970), IX, pp. 240–2.

72 P. Lawson, *The Imperial Challenge: Quebec and Britain in the Age of the American Revolution* (Montréal, 1989).

73 R.H. Balmer, *A Perfect Babel of Confusion: Dutch Religion and English Culture in the Middle Colonies* (Oxford, 1989).

74 E. Wolf II, *The Book Culture of a Colonist American City. Philadelphia Books, Bookmen, and Booksellers* (Oxford, 1988).

75 J. Horn, *Adapting to a New World. English Society in the Seventeenth-century Chesapeake* (Chapel Hill, 1994); A. Kulikoff, *Tobacco and Slaves: The Development of Southern Cultures in the Chesapeake, 1680–1800* (Chapel Hill, 1986).

76 C. Bridenbaugh and R. Bridenbaugh, *No Peace beyond the Line* (1972); R.C. Ritchie, *Captain Kidd and the War against the Pirates* (1987); M. Rediker, *Between the Devil and the Deep Blue Sea: Merchant Seamen, Pirates, and the Anglo-American Maritime World, 1700–1750* (Cambridge, 1987); P. Linebaugh and M. Rediker, *The Many-Headed Hydra: Sailors, Slaves, Commoners, and the Hidden History of the Revolutionary Atlantic* (London, 2000).

77 C.E. Clark, *The Public Prints: The Newspaper in Anglo-American Culture* (Oxford, 1994).

78 A. Wood (ed.), *The History of Siberia, From Russian Conquest to Revolution* (London, 1991).

79 A. Ortiz, *Eighteenth-century Reforms in the Caribbean. Miguel de Muesas, Governor of Puerto Rico, 1769–76* (1983).

80 M.P. McKinley, *Pre-revolutionary Caracas: Politics, Economy and Society 1777–1811* (Cambridge, 1985).

81 C.I. Archer, *The Army in Bourbon Mexico 1760–1810* (Albuquerque, 1979).

82 K. Maxwell, *Pombal. Paradox of the Enlightenment* (Cambridge, 1995).

83 C.A. Bayly, *Rulers, Townsmen and Bazaars: North Indian Society in the Age of British*

Expansion, 1770–1870 (Cambridge, 1983) and *Indian Society and the Making of the British Empire* (Cambridge, 1988).

84 M.H. Fisher, *Indirect Rule in India: Residents and the Residency System, 1764–1858* (1991).

85 H.V. Bowen, *Revenue and Reform: The Indian Problem in British Politics 1757–1773* (Cambridge, 1991).

86 J.P. Greene, *Peripheries and Center. Constitutional Development in the Extended Polities of the British Empire and the United States 1607–1788* (1990).

87 A.C. Metcalf, *Family and Frontier in Colonial Brazil. Santa de Parnaiba 1580–1822* (Berkeley, 1992).

88 D.H. Usner, *Indians, Settlers and Slaves in a Frontier Exchange Economy. The Lower Mississippi Valley before 1783* (Chapel Hill, 1992).

89 E.A.H. John, *Storms Brewed in Other Men's Worlds: The Confrontation of Indians, Spanish and French in the Southwest, 1540–1795* (College Station, Tex., 1975).

90 See, for example, T.J. Barfield, *The Perilous Frontier: Nomadic Empires and China, 221 BC to AD 1757* (Oxford, 1989) and B.L.Walker, *The Conquest of Ainu Lands. Ecology and Culture in Japanese Expansion, 1590–1800* (Berkeley, 2001).

91 R. White, *The Middle Ground: Indians, Empires and Republics in the Great Lakes Region, 1651–1815* (Cambridge, 1991). See also C.G. Calloway, *Crown and Calumat: British-Indian Relations, 1783–1815* (Norman, Okla., 1971).

92 E. Hinderaker, *Elusive Empires. Constructing Colonialism in the Ohio Valley, 1673–1800* (Cambridge, 1997), p. xi. See also R.A. Williams, *Linking Arms Together. American Indian Treaty Visions of Law and Peace, 1600–1800* (1999), esp. pp. 135–6.

93 J.D. Drake, *King Philip's War. Civil War in New England 1675–1676* (Amherst, Mass., 1999), p. 198.

94 K.Y. Daaku, *Trade and Politics on the Gold Coast, 1600–1720* (Oxford, 1970), pp. 96–114.

95 P.D. Morgan, 'Encounters between British and "indigenous" peoples, c.1500–c.1800', in M. Daunton and R. Halpern (eds), *Empire and Others. British Encounters with Indigenous Peoples 1600–1850* (1999), p. 64.

96 P. Gerhard, *The Southeast Frontier of New Spain* (Princeton, 1979).

97 D.J. Weber, *The Spanish Frontier in North America* (New Haven, 1992), pp. 204–12; J. Jackson (ed.), *Imaginary Kingdom: Texas as Seen by the Rivera and Rubí Military Expeditions, 1729 and 1767* (Austin, 1995).

7 WARFARE WITH NON-EUROPEANS, 1650–1750

1 N. Thompson, *Earl Bathurst and the British Empire* (Barnsley, 1999), pp. 167–8.

2 C.R. Boxer, 'The Siege of Fort Zeelandia and the Capture of Formosa from the Dutch, 1661–21', *Transactions and Proceedings of the Japan Society of London*, 24 (1926–7), pp. 16–47.

3 M. Bassin, 'Expansion and Colonialism on the Eastern Frontier: Views of Siberia and the Far East in Pre-Petrine Russia', *Journal of Historical Geography*, 14 (1988), pp. 3–8.

4 G.A. Lantzeff and R.A. Pierce, *Eastward to Empire. Exploration and Conquest on the Russian Open Frontier, to 1750* (Montréal, 1973), p. 175.

5 D. Van der Cruyse, *Louis XIV et le Siam* (Paris, 1991), pp. 406–7; M. Jacq-Hergoualceh, 'La France et le Siam de 1680 à 1685: Histoire d'un échec', *Revue Française d'Histoire d'Outre-Mer* (1995), pp. 257–75; R.S. Love, 'Monarchs, Merchants, and Missionaries in Early Modern Asia: The Missions Étrangères in Siam, 1662–1684', *International History Review*, 21 (1999), pp. 1–27.

6 E. Winius, 'Portugal's "Shadowy Empire in the Bay of Bengal"', *Camoes Center Quarterly*, 3/1 and 2 (1991), pp. 40–l.

7   B.P. Lenman, 'The East India Company and the Emperor Aurangazeb', *History Today*, 33 (1982), pp. 36–42.

8   R.P. Matthee, *The Politics of Trade in Safavid Iran. Silk for Silver 1600–1730* (Cambridge, 1999), pp. 185–8.

9   R.D. Bathurst, 'Maritime Trade and Imamate Government: Two Principal Themes in the History of Oman to 1728', in D. Hopwood (ed.), *The Arabian Peninsula. Society and Politics* (1972), pp. 99–103.

10 C.R. Boxer and C. de Azevedo, *Fort Jesus and the Portuguese in Mombasa 1593–1729* (1960); J. Kirkman, *Fort Jesus* (Oxford, 1974).

11 J. Thornton, 'The Art of War in Angola, 1575–1680', *Comparative Studies in Society and History*, 30 (1988), pp. 360–78, and *The Kingdom of Kongo: Civil War and Transition, 1642–1718* (Madison, Wis., 1983).

12 W.J. Eccles, *Frontenac: The Courtier Governor* (Toronto, 1959), pp. 157–72.

13 P.M. Malone, *The Skulking Way of War. Technology and Tactics among the New England Indians* (Baltimore, 1993).

14 J.A. Sainsbury, 'Indian Labor in Early Rhode Island', *New England Quarterly*, 48 (1975), pp. 378–93.

15 G.D. Jones, *The Conquest of the Last Maya Kingdom* (Stanford, 1998).

16 A. Arkayin, 'The Second Siege of Vienna (1683) and its Consequences', *Revue Internationale d'Histoire Militaire*, 46 (1980), pp. 114–15.

17 M.C. Ricklefs, *War, Culture and Economy in Java, 1677–1726* (The Hague, 1990), and *A History of Modern Indonesia since c. 1300* (2nd edn, Basingstoke, 1993), pp. 85–97.

18 A. Deshpande, 'Limitations of Military Technology: Naval Warfare on the West Coast, 1650–1800', *Economic and Political Weekly*, 25 (1992), pp. 902–3.

19 A. Delcourt, *La France et les établissements français au Sénégal entre 1713 et 1763* (Dakar, 1952); J.F. Searing, *West African Slavery and Atlantic Commerce, 1700–1860* (Cambridge, 1993).

20 Delaval to Lord Dartmouth, Secretary of State, 15 Ap. 1713, PRO. SP. 89/22; M.S. Anderson, 'Great Britain and the Barbary States in the Eighteenth Century', *Bulletin of the Institute of Historical Research*, 29 (1956), pp. 87–107.

21 B.H. Sumner, *Peter the Great and the Ottoman Empire* (Oxford, 1949), pp. 39–42; L.R. Lewitter, 'Jean-Nicole Moreau de Brassey's Letter on the Moldavian Campaign of Peter I', *Jahrbücher Geschichte Osteuropas*, 40 (1992), pp. 5, 17–29.

22 E.V. Anisimov, *The Reforms of Peter the Great: Progress through Coercion in Russia* (Moscow, 1993), pp. 255–61.

23 A.S. Donnelly, *The Russian Conquest of Bashkiria, 1552–1740* (New Haven, 1968); M. Khodarkovsky, *Where Two Worlds Met: The Russian State and the Kalmyk Nomads 1600–1771* (Ithaca, 1992).

24 J.C. Rule, 'Jerome Phélypeaux, Comte de Pontchartrain and the Establishment of Louisiana', in J.F. McDermott (ed.), *Frenchmen and French Ways in the Mississippi Valley* (Urbana, 1969), pp. 179–97; N.M. Belting, *Kaskaskia under the French Regime* (Urbana, 1948).

25 R.D. Edmunds and J.L. Peyser, *The Fox Wars. The Mesquakie Challenge to New France* (Norman, Okla., 1993).

26 P.D. Woods, 'The French and the Natchez Indians in Louisiana, 1700–1731', *Louisiana History*, 19 (1978), pp. 413–35; M. Giraud, *A History of French Louisiana, V: The Company of the Indies, 1723–1731* (Baton Rouge, 1991).

27 Woods, *French–Indian Relations on the Southern Frontier, 1699–1762* (Ann Arbor, 1980), pp. 111–46; M.S. Arnold, *Colonial Arkansas, 1686–1804* (Fayetteville, 1991), pp. 31, 99–106.

28 J. Hemming, *Red Gold: The Conquest of the Brazilian Indians, 1500–1760* (2nd edn, 1995).

8 WARFARE WITH NON-EUROPEANS, 1750–1830

1 G.B. Malleson, *History of the French in India* (1886), pp. 231–82; H.H. Dodwell, *Dupleix and Clive* (1920); V.G. Hatalkar, *Relations between the French and the Marathas, 1668–1815* (Bombay, 1958), pp. 87, 274; G. Bodinier, 'Les Officiers français en Inde de 1750 à 1793', in *Trois Siècles de présence française en Inde* (Paris, 1995), pp. 69–89; G.J. Bryant, 'The Military Imperative in Early British Expansion in India, 1750–1785', *Indo-British Journal* (1996), p. 20.

2 L.H. Gipson, *Zones of International Friction: North America, South of the Great Lakes Region, 1748–1754* (New York, 1939).

3 W. Eccles, 'The Fur Trade and Eighteenth-century Imperialism', *William and Mary Quarterly*, 3rd series, 40 (1983), pp. 341–62; R. White, *The Middle Ground: Indians, Empires, and Republics in the Great Lakes Region, 1650–1815* (Cambridge, 1991).

4 R.L. Meriwether, *The Expansion of South Carolina, 1729–1765* (Kingsport, Tenn., 1940), pp. 213–40; D.H. Corkran, *The Cherokee Frontier: Conflict and Survival, 1740–1762* (Norman, Okla., 1962); T. Hatley, *The Dividing Paths: Cherokees and South Carolinians through the Era of Revolution* (New York, 1993).

5 M.H. Fisher (ed.), *The Travels of Dean Mahomet. An Eighteenth-century Journey through India* (Berkeley, 1997), p. 8.

6 H.H. Peckham, *Pontiac and the Indian Uprising* (Princeton, 1947); J.M. Sosin, *Whitehall and the Wilderness* (Lincoln, Neb., 1961); G.E. Dowd, *A Spirited Resistance: The North American Struggle for Indian Unity 1745–1815* (Baltimore, 1992).

7 D. Sweet, 'Native Resistance in Eighteenth-century Amazonia: The "Abominable Muras" in War and Peace', *Radical History Review*, 53 (1992), pp. 49–82.

8 J.R. Fischer, *A Well-executed Failure: The Sullivan Campaign against the Iroquois, July–September 1779* (Columbia, SC, 1997).

9 W. Sword, *President Washington's Indian War: The Struggle for the Old Northwest, 1790–1795* (Norman, Okla., 1985).

10 Diary of George Paterson, May 1770, BL. India Office, Mss. Eur. E379/1, p. 184.

11 Cornwallis Papers, PRO, London.

12 F.L. Owsley Jr and G.A. Smith, *Filibusters and Expansionists: Jeffersonian Manifest Destiny, 1800–1821* (Tuscaloosa, 1997).

13 J. Pemble, *The Invasion of Nepal. John Company at War* (Oxford, 1971).

14 D.H.A. Kolff, *Naukar, Rajput and Sepoy: The Ethnohistory of the Military Labour Market in Hindustan, 1450–1850* (Cambridge, 1990).

15 C. Totman, *Early Modern Japan* (Berkeley, 1993), pp. 482–93.

16 T. Porterfield, *The Allure of Empire. Art in the Service of French Imperialism 1798–1836* (Princeton, 1998), p. 7.

17 D. Peers, *Between Mars and Mammon. Colonial Armies and the Garrison State in India, 1819–1835* (1995); C.A. Bayly, 'The First Age of Global Imperialism, c. 1760–1830', *Journal of Imperial and Commonwealth History*, 26/2 (1998), pp. 28–47.

18 C.N. Parkinson, *Edward Pellew, Viscount Exmouth, Admiral of the Red* (1934), pp. 419–72.

19 H. Kleinschmidt, 'Using the Gun: Manual Drill and the Proliferation of Portable Firearms', *Journal of Military History*, 63 (1999), pp. 601–29.

20 Stuart, orders, BL. Add. 29198 fols. 120, 123.

21 Adam Smith, *Inquiry into the Nature and Causes of the Wealth of Nations*, edited by R. Campbell (2 vols, Oxford 1976), II, pp. 699, 708.

9 THE TRANSFORMATION OF THE EUROPEAN WORLD, 1775–1830

1 F. Madden with D. Fieldhouse, *Imperial Reconstruction, 1763–1840: The Evolution of Alternative Systems of Colonial Government* (Westport, Conn., 1987).

2   J.R. Fisher, A.J. Kuethe and A. McFarlane (eds), *Reform and Insurrection in Bourbon New Granada and Peru* (Baton Rouge, 1990).

3   B. Bailyn, *The Ideological Origins of the American Revolution* (Cambridge, Mass., 1967); J.C.D. Clark, *The Language of Liberty, 1660–1832. Political Discourse and Social Dynamics in the Anglo-American World* (Cambridge, 1993).

4   For a specific area, G.H. Nobles, *Divisions throughout the Whole: Politics and Society in Hampshire County, Massachusetts, 1740–1775* (Cambridge, 1983).

5   F. Anderson, *Crucible of War. The Seven Years' War and the Fate of Empire in British North America, 1754–1766* (New York, 2000).

6   J.P. Greene, 'The Jamaica Privilege Controversy, 1764–66: An Episode in the Process of Constitutional Definition in the Early Modern British Empire', *Journal of Imperial and Commonwealth History*, 22 (1994).

7   A.J. O'Shaughnessy, *An Empire Divided. The American Revolution and the British Caribbean* (Philadelphia, 2000), pp. 196, 200.

8   R. Cave, 'Early Printing and the Book Trade in the West Indies', *Library Quarterly*, 48 (1978), pp. 163–92.

9   R.A. Burchell (ed.), *The End of Anglo-America: Historical Essays in the Study of Cultural Divergence* (Manchester, 1991); D. Hancock, 'Transatlantic Trade in the Era of the American Revolution', in F.M. Leventhal and R. Quinault (eds), *Anglo-American Attitudes. From Revolution to Partnership* (Aldershot, 2000), p. 65.

10 J.R. Dull, *A Diplomatic History of the American Revolution* (New Haven, 1985); L.T. Cummins, *Spanish Observers and the American Revolution 1775–1783* (Baton Rouge, 1991).

11 C.L.R. James, *The Black Jacobins: Toussaint L'Ouverture and the San Domingo Revolution* (1980); D.P. Geggus, 'The Haitian Revolution', in F.W. Knight and C.A. Palmer (eds), *The Modern Caribbean* (Chapel Hill, 1989), pp. 21–50.

12 Amid the massive literature on the subject, it is worth noting S. Clissold, *Benjamin O'Higgins and the Independence of Chile* (1968); J. Lynch, *The Spanish American Revolutions, 1808–1826* (New York, 1986); S.P. Mackenzie, *Revolutionary Armies in the Modern Era. A Revisionist Approach* (1997), pp. 51–67.

13 J.E. Rodríguez O., 'The Emancipation of America', *American Historical Review*, 105 (2000), p. 145.

14 M.P. Costeloe, *Response to Revolution: Imperial Spain and the Spanish American Revolutions, 1810–1840* (Cambridge, 1986).

15 M.L. Woodward, 'The Spanish Army and the Loss of America, 1810–1824', *Hispanic American Historical Review*, 48 (1968), pp. 586–607.

16 M.T. Ducey, 'Village, Nation, and Constitution: Insurgent Politics in Papantla, Veracruz, 1810–1821', *Hispanic American Historical Review*, 79 (1999), pp. 471–2, 476.

17 C.I. Archer, 'The Army of New Spain and the Wars of Independence, 1790–1821', *Hispanic American Historical Review*, 61 (1981), pp. 705–14, and 'Insurrection–Reaction–Revolution–Fragmentation: Reconstructing the Choreography of Meltdown in New Spain during the Independence Era', *Mexican Studies*, 10 (1994), pp. 63–98; B. Hamnett, 'Royalist Counterinsurgency and the Continuity of Rebellion: Guanajuato and Michoacán, 1813–1820', *Hispanic American Historical Review*, 62 (1982); V. Guedea, 'The Process of Mexican Independence', *American Historical Review*, 105 (2000), pp. 119–20.

18 T. Anna, *The Fall of the Royal Government in Mexico City* (Lincoln, Neb., 1978); J.E. Rodríguez O. (ed.), *Mexico in the Age of Democratic Revolutions* (Boulder, n.d.), pp. 97–132.

19 L.D. Langley, *The Americas in the Age of Revolution 1750–1850* (New Haven, 1996), p. 286.

20 S.J. Braidwood, *Black Poor and White Philanthropists. London's Blacks and the Foundation*

of the Sierra Leone Settlement 1786–1791 (Liverpool, 1994). For a jaundiced contemporary response, A.M. Falconbridge, *Narrative of Two Voyages to the River Sierra Leone* (1794) edited in D. Coleman, *Maiden Voyages and Infant Colonies. Two Women's Travel Narratives of the 1790s* (1998).

21 D.P. Resnick, 'The Société des Amis Noirs and the Abolition of Slavery', *French Historical Studies* (1972), p. 560.

22 *Archives parlementaires de 1790 à 1860: Recueil complet des débats législatifs et politiques des chambres françaises* (127 vols, Paris, 1879–1913), XXXVII, p. 152; S.P. Sen, *The French in India, 1763–1816* (Calcutta, 1958), p. 530.

23 D. Geggus, 'Racial Equality, Slavery and Colonial Secession during the Constituent Assembly', *American Historical Review* (1989), p. 1296.

24 J.J. Pierce, 'The Struggle for Black Liberty: Revolution and Emancipation in Saint-Domingue', *Consortium on Revolutionary Europe. Selected Papers, 1997*, pp. 168–79.

25 D.B. Davis, *The Problem of Slavery in the Age of Revolution, 1770–1823* (Ithaca, 1975); D. Turley, *The Culture of English Antislavery, 1780–1860* (1991); J.R. Oldfield, *Popular Politics and British Anti-slavery* (Manchester, 1995); J. Jennings, *The Business of Abolishing the British Slave Trade, 1783–1807* (1997).

26 C. Midgley, *Women against Slavery: The British Campaigns, 1780–1870* (1992); C. Sussman *Consuming Anxieties: Consumer Protest, Gender and British Slavery, 1713–1833* (Stanford, 2000).

27 R. Anstey, *The Atlantic Slave Trade and British Abolition, 1760–1810* (1975); A.J. Barker, *Slavery and Antislavery in Mauritius, 1810–33: The Conflict between Economic Expansion and Humanitarian Reform under British Rule* (1996).

28 L. Ryan, *The Aboriginal Tasmanians* (Brisbane, 1981).

29 For a classic statement, E. Williams, *Capitalism and Slavery* (Chapel Hill, 1944).

30 S. Drescher, *Econocide: British Slavery in the Era of Abolition* (1977).

31 C. Shammas, 'The Revolutionary Impact of European Demand for Tropical Goods', in J.J. McCusker and K. Morgan (eds), *The Early Modern Atlantic Economy* (Cambridge, 2000), p. 183.

32 J.R. Ward, *British West Indian Slavery, 1750–1834: The Process of Amelioration* (1988).

33 S. Drescher, *From Slavery to Freedom: Comparative Studies in the Rise and Fall of Atlantic Slavery* (New York, 1999).

34 M. Kale, *Fragments of Empire: Capital, Slavery and Indian Indentured Labor in the British Caribbean* (Philadelphia, 1998).

35 G.S. Rousseau, 'Le Cat and the Physiology of Negroes', *Studies in Eighteenth-Century Culture* (1973). For another aspect of skin colour, D. Dabydeen, 'References to Blacks in William Hogarth's Analysis of Beauty', *British Journal for Eighteenth-Century Studies*, 5 (1982).

36 P.D. Curtin, *The Image of Africa: British Ideas and Actions, 1750–1850* (Madison, Wis., 1964); K. Jacoby, 'Slaves by Nature? Domestic Animals and Human Slaves', *Slavery and Abolition*, 15 (1994), pp. 89–97; R. Wokler, 'Apes and Races in the Scottish Enlightenment: Monboddo and Kames on the Nature of Man', in P. Jones (ed.), *Philosophy and Science in the Scottish Enlightenment* (Edinburgh, 1988), pp. 152–6.

37 M.T. Hodgen, *Early Anthropology in the Sixteenth and Seventeenth Centuries* (Philadelphia, 1964).

38 H. West, 'The Limits of Enlightenment Anthropology: Georg Forster and the Tahitians', *History of European Ideas*, 20 (1989), pp. 147–60; R. Wokler, 'Anthropology and Conjectural History in the Enlightenment', in C. Fox, R. Porter and R. Wokler (eds), *Inventing Human Science: Eighteenth-century Domains* (Berkeley, 1995), pp. 31–52.

39 T. Bendyshe (ed.), *The Anthropological Treatises of Johann Friedrich Blumenbach* (1865); M. Banton, *Racial Theories* (Cambridge, 1987).

40   K. O'Brien, 'Between Enlightenment and Stadial History: William Robertson on the History of Europe', *British Journal for Eighteenth-Century Studies*, 16 (1993), pp. 58, 60–1.

41   A.V. Postnikov, *The Mapping of Russian America* (Milwaukee, 1995).

42   J. Gascoigne, *Joseph Banks and the English Enlightenment: Useful Knowledge and Polite Culture* (Cambridge, 1994).

43   R. Drayton, *Nature's Government. Science, Imperial Britain, and the 'Improvement' of the World* (New Haven, 2000), p. 80.

44   R. Drayton, 'Knowledge and Empire', in P.J. Marshall (ed.), *The Oxford History of the British Empire, II: The Eighteenth Century* (Oxford, 1998), p. 250.

45   E. Quin, *Historical Atlas in a Series of Maps of the World, as Known at Different Periods* (1830).

46   A. Salmond, *Between Worlds: Early Exchanges between Maori and Europeans, 1773–1815* (Honolulu, 1997).

47   A. Dupuy, *Haiti in the World Economy: Class, Race, and Under-development since 1700* (Boulder, 1989).

48   J. Scofield, *Hail Columbia, Robert Gray, John Kendrick and the Pacific Fur Trade* (Portland, Oreg., 1993).

49   D. Stannard, *Before the Horror* (Honolulu, 1989).

50   R.L. Webb, *On the Northwest: Commercial Whaling in the Pacific Northwest 1790–1967* (Vancouver, 1980).

51   A. Frost, *Convicts and Empire: A Naval Question 1776–1811* (Melbourne, 1980); M. Steven, *Trade, Tactics and Territory: Britain in the Pacific, 1783–1823* (Melbourne, 1983); D.M. Mackay, *A Place of Exile: The European Settlement of New South Wales* (Melbourne, 1985) and *In the Wake of Cook: Exploration, Science and Empire, 1780–1801* (Wellington, 1985).

52   A.S. Morton, *A History of the Canadian West to 1870–71* (Toronto, 1939).

53   R.A. Pierce, *Russia's Hawaiian Adventure 1815–1817* (Berkeley, 1965).

10 CONCLUSIONS

1   Additional instructions for Robert Liston, 26 Feb. 1794, PRO. FO. 78/15 fols 46–7.

2   A.K. Smith, *Creating a World Economy: Merchant Capital, Colonialism, and World Trade, 1400–1825* (Boulder, 1991).

3   C. Moore, *The Loyalists: Revolution, Exile, Settlement* (Toronto, 1984).

4   H.I. Cowan, *British Immigration to British North America: The First Hundred Years* (Toronto, 1961).

5   J.W. Bumsted, *The People's Clearance: Highland Emigration to British North America 1770–1815* (Edinburgh, 1982).

6   D.B. Quinn, *European Approaches to North America, 1450–1640* (Aldershot, 1998), pp. 329–31.

7   F. Fernández-Armesto, *Millennium* (London, 1995); J. Goody, *The East in the West* (Cambridge, 1996).

8   J. Hathaway, *The Politics of Households in Ottoman Egypt. The Rise of the Qazdaglis* (Cambridge, 1997).

9   J.J.L. Gommans, *The Rise of the Indo-Afghan Empire c. 1710–1780* (Leiden, 1995), p. 3.

10 C.A. Bayly, *Imperial Meridian. The British Empire and the World 1780–1830* (Harlow, 1989), pp. 164–92, esp. pp. 164–5.

SELECTED
FURTHER READING

It scarcely needs pointing out that such a section could easily run to several volumes, and anyway dates very rapidly. Given the constraints of space, I have adopted the following rules. First, I concentrate on works published from 1990 on the grounds that earlier studies can be tracked down through their bibliographies and notes. Second, given the likely linguistic skills of most readers, I have only cited works published in English. Obviously there is much of great value published in other languages. As many books span the topics covered in individual chapters, I provide an undifferentiated list. Those who wish to keep up with the subject are encouraged to read the articles and reviews in the specialist journals such as the *Hispanic American Historical Review*, the *Journal of Imperial and Commonwealth History*, the *Proceedings of the Annual Meeting of the French Colonial Historical Society*, *Terrae Incognitae*, and the *William and Mary Quarterly*.

G.J. Ames, *Colbert, Mercantilism and the French Quest for Asian Trade* (Dekalb, 1996).

R. Anstey, *The Atlantic Slave Trade and British Abolition 1760–1810* (London, 1975).

M. Archer, *India and British Portraiture, 1770–1825* (London, 1979).

B. Bailyn and P. Morgan (eds), *Strangers within the Realm: Cultural Margins of the First British Empire* (Chapel Hill, 1991).

C.A. Bayly, *Imperial Meridian. The British Empire and the World 1780–1830* (Harlow, 1989).

J.C. Beaglehole, *The Exploration of the Pacific* (3rd edn, Stanford, 1966).

J.F. Bosher, *Business and Religion in the Age of New France, 1600–1760* (Toronto, 1994).

H. Bowen, *Elites, Enterprise and the Making of the British Overseas Empire, 1688–1775* (London, 1996).

C.R. Boxer, *The Portuguese Seaborne Empire, 1415–1825* (London, 1969).

D. Brading, *Haciendas and Ranchos in the Mexican Bajió: Leon, 1700–1860* (Cambridge, 1978).

——, *Miners and Merchants in Bourbon Mexico, 1763–1810* (Cambridge, 1978).

R.A. Burchell (ed.), *The End of Anglo-America: Historical Essays in the Study of Cultural Divergence* (Manchester, 1991).

K.M. Butler, *The Economics of Emancipation: Jamaica and Barbados, 1823–1843* (Chapel Hill, 1995).

P.J. Cain and A.G. Hopkins, *British Imperialism: Innovation and Expansion, 1688–1914* (London, 1993).

D.M. Cantor, *Pre-revolutionary Caracas: Politics, Economy, and Society, 1777–1811* (Cambridge, 1985).

N. Canny (ed.), *Europeans on the Move. Studies on European Migration, 1500–1800* (Oxford, 1994).

—— (ed.), *The Oxford History of the British Empire, I: The Origins of Empire* (Oxford, 1998).

K.N. Chaudhuri, *The Trading World of Asia and the English East-India Company 1660–1760* (Cambridge, 1978).

P.A. Coclanis, *The Shadow of a Dream: Economic Life and Death in the South Carolina Low Country, 1670–1820* (Oxford, 1989).

W.B. Cohen, *The French Encounter with Africans: White Response to Blacks, 1530–1880* (Bloomington, 1980).

P.D. Curtin, *The Image of Africa: British Ideas and Actions, 1750–1850* (Madison, Wis., 1964).

——, *The Rise and Fall of the Plantation Complex: Essays in Atlantic History* (Cambridge, 1990).

K.G. Davies, *The Royal African Company* (London, 1957).

R. Davis, *The Rise of the Atlantic Economies* (London, 1973).

T.M. Devine, *The Tobacco Lords: A Study of the Tobacco Merchants of Glasgow and Their Trading Activities, c. 1740–1790* (Edinburgh, 1975).

G.E. Dowd, *A Spirited Resistance: The North American Struggle for Indian Unity 1745–1815* (Baltimore, 1992).

R. Drayton, *Nature's Government. Science, Imperial Britain, and the 'Improvement' of the World* (New Haven, 2000).

S. Drescher, *Econocide: British Slavery in the Era of Abolition* (Pittsburg, 1977).

W. Eccles, *The Canadian Frontier, 1534–1760* (Albuquerque, 1984).

——, *France in America* (2nd edn, East Lansing, 1990).

P. Edwards, *The Story of the Voyage: Sea Narratives in Eighteenth Century England* (Cambridge, 1994).

D. Eltis, *The Rise of African Slavery in the Americas* (Cambridge, 2000).

F. Fernández-Armesto (ed.), *The Times Atlas of World Exploration* (London, 1991).

C. Fick, *The Making of Haiti: The Saint-Domingue Revolution from Below* (Knoxville, 1991).

J.R. Fisher, *Government and Society in Colonial Peru: The Intendant System, 1789–1814* (London, 1970).

J.R. Fisher, A.J. Kuethe and A. McFarlane (eds), *Reform and Insurrection in Bourbon New Granada and Peru* (Baton Rouge, 1990).

M.M. Fraginals, *The Sugarmill: The Socioeconomic Complex of Sugar in Cuba, 1760–1860* (New York, 1976).

A. Frost and J. Samson (eds), *Pacific Empires: Essays in Honour of Glyndwr Williams* (Carlton South, 1999).

J. Gascoigne, *Joseph Banks and the English Enlightenment: Useful Knowledge and Polite Culture* (Cambridge, 1994).

M. Giraud, *A History of French Louisiana* (5 vols., Baton Rouge, 1974–91).

W.H. Goetzmann and G. Williams, *The Atlas of North American Exploration* (New York, 1992).

J.P. Greene, *Peripheries and Center: Constitutional Development in the Extended Polities of the British Empire and the United States 1607–1788* (Athens, Ga., 1986).

A. Greer, *The People of New France* (Toronto, 1997).

G.M. Hall, *Africans in Colonial Louisiana: The Development of Afro-Creole Culture in the Eighteenth Century* (Baton Rouge, 1992).

D. Hancock, *Citizens of the World: London Merchants and the Integration of the British Atlantic Community, 1735–1785* (Cambridge, 1995).

T. Hatley, *The Dividing Paths: Cherokees and South Carolinians through the Era of Revolution* (New York, 1993).

S. Haycox, J. Barnett and C. Liburd (eds), *Enlightenment and Exploration in the North Pacific, 1741–1805* (Seattle, 1997).

D. Howse (ed.), *Background to Discovery: Pacific Exploration from Dampier to Cook* (Berkeley, 1990).

P. Hulme and N.L. Whitehead (eds), *Wild Majesty: Encounters with the Caribs from Columbus to the Present Day. An Anthology* (Oxford, 1992).

C.L.R. James, *The Black Jacobins: Toussaint l'Ouverture and the San Domingo Revolution* (London, 1980).

O.U. Janzen (ed.), *Merchant Organization and Maritime Trade in the North Atlantic, 1660–1815* (St John's, Newfoundland, 1998).

E.A.H. John, *Storms Brewed in Other Men's Worlds: The Confrontation of Indians, Spanish and French in the Southwest, 1540–1795* (College Station, Tex., 1975).

K.O. Kupperman (ed.), *American in European Consciousness 1493–1750* (Chapel Hill, 1995).

L.D. Langley, *The Americas in the Age of Revolution 1750–1850* (New Haven, 1996).

P. Lawson, *The East India Company. A History* (London, 1993).

B. Lenman, *Britain's Colonial Wars 1688–1783* (London, 2001).

G.M. Lewis (ed.), *Cartographic Encounters. Perspectives on Native American Mapmaking and Map Use* (Chicago, 1998).

J. Lynch (ed.), *Latin American Revolutions, 1808–1826: Old and New World Origins* (Norman, Okla., 1994).

J.J. McCusker and K. Morgan (eds), *The Early Modern Atlantic Economy* (Cambridge, 2000).

D.M. Mackay, *In the Wake of Cook: Exploration, Science and Empire, 1780–1801* (Wellington, 1985).

J.R. McNeill, *Atlantic Empires of France and Spain: Havana and Louisbourg, 1700–1763* (Chapel Hill, 1985).

C. Manning, *Fortunes à faire. The French in Asian Trade, 1719–48* (Aldershot, 1996).

P.J. Marshall (ed.), *The Oxford History of the British Empire, II: The Eighteenth Century* (Oxford, 1998).

P.J. Marshall and G. Williams, *The Great Map of Mankind: British Perceptions of the World in the Age of Enlightenment* (London, 1982).

D.W. Meinig, *The Shaping of America: A Geographical Perspective on 500 Years of History, I: Atlantic America, 1492–1800* (New Haven, 1986).

K. Morgan, *Slavery, Atlantic Trade and the British Economy, 1660–1800* (Cambridge, 2000).

J.R. Oldfield, *Popular Politics and British Anti-slavery* (Manchester, 1995).

A.J. O'Shaughnessy, *An Empire Divided. The American Revolution and the British Caribbean* (Philadelphia, 2000).

A. Pagden, *European Encounters with the New World, from Renaissance to Romanticism* (New Haven, 1993).

——, *Lords of All the World. Ideologies of Empire in Spain, Britain and France, c. 1500–c.1800* (New Haven, 1995).

R.L. Paquette and S.L. Engerman (eds), *The Lesser Antilles in the Age of European Expansion* (Gainesville, 1996).

G. Parker, *The Military Revolution. Military Innovation and the Rise of the West 1500–1800* (2nd edn, Cambridge, 1996).

J.H. Parry, *Trade and Dominion. The European Overseas Empires in the Eighteenth Century* (London, 1971).

T. Porterfield, *The Allure of Empire. Art in the Service of French Imperialism 1798–1836* (Princeton, 1998).

O. Prakash, *European Commercial Enterprise in Pre-colonial India* (Cambridge, 1998).

J.M. Price, *Tobacco in Atlantic Trade: The Chesapeake, London and Glasgow* (Aldershot, 1995).

R. Price, *Maroon Societies: Rebel Slave Communities in the Americas* (New York, 1973).

M.C. Ricklefs, *A History of Modern Indonesia since c.1300* (2nd edn, London, 1993).

A.J.R. Russell-Wood, *From Colony to Nation: Essays on the Independence of Brazil* (Baltimore, 1975).

R.B. Sheridan, *Sugar and Slavery: An Economic History of the British West Indies 1623–1775* (Baltimore, 1973).

B.L. Solow (ed.), *Slavery and the Rise of the Atlantic System* (Cambridge, 1991).

O.H.K. Spate, *The Pacific since Magellan, II: Monopolists and Freebooters* (London, 1983).

——, *Paradise Found and Lost* (Minneapolis, 1988).

I.K. Steele, *The English Atlantic 1675–1740. An Exploration of Communication and Community* (Oxford, 1986).

——, *Warpaths. Invasions of North America* (Oxford, 1994).

R.L. Stein, *The French Slave Trade in the Eighteenth Century: An Old Regime Business* (Madison, Wis., 1979).

J. Thornton, *Africa and Africans in the Making of the Atlantic World, 1400–1800* (2nd edn, Cambridge, 1998).

J.D. Tracy (ed.), *The Rise of Merchant Empires: Long-distance Trade in the Early Modern World 1350–1750* (Cambridge, 1990).

D. Turley, *The Culture of English Antislavery, 1780–1860* (London, 1991).

J. Walvin, *Fruits of Empire: Exotic Produce and British Taste, 1660–1800* (London, 1997).

D.J. Weber, *The Spanish Frontier in North America* (New Haven, 1992).

G. Williams, *The British Search for the Northwest Passage in the Eighteenth Century* (London, 1962).

—— *The Great South Sea: English Voyages and Encounters, 1570–1750* (New Haven, 1997).

INDEX

DATE DUE

APR 2002			

The World: European Possessio

ARCTIC

Treaty line of 1826

Greenland

to Den.

Godthaab

Icel
to D

Julianehaab
Founded 1775

ALASKA

Sitka
Founded 1799

NORTH-WESTERN TERRITORIES

NEWFOUNDLAND
Br. Crown Colony

UNITED
KINGDOM
United from 180

Kodiak I.1784
First Russian settlement

Aluetian Is.

OREGON COUNTRY
Jointly occupied by
U.S. and Gt. Britain 1816–46

1818

RUPERT LAND
• Ottawa

St. Pierre and
Miquelon

FRI

1818

CANADA

PORTUGAL

1803

Treaty Line of 1819

UNITED STATES

Azores

Gibralt

San Francisco, Founded 1776 •
Los Angeles, Founded 1781 •
San Diego •

1783

•New York

Madeira

•El Paso

Bermuda Is.

Canary Is.

Tropic of Cancer

MEXICO

Florida

Bahama Is.

Hawaiian Is.   Hawaii

Cuba

HAITI Puerto Rico

Mexico

Jamaica

St. Thomas

C. Verde Is.

SENE

BR. HONDURAS

St. Croix Guadeloupe

PACIFIC

UNITED PROVS. OF
CENTRAL AMERICA
1823–38

Mosquito
Coast

St. Lucia Barbados
1815 Tobago, 1815
Trinidad, 1797/1802
Brit. Dutch GUIANA
French

Bathurst, 1816

SIERRA LEONE 1787/1809

LIBERIA

Santa Fé de Bogota

REPUBLIC OF
GREATER COLUMBIA

Equator

Galapagos Is.

Quito • 1819–30

OCEAN

PERU

EMPIRE OF
BRAZIL

Asce
18

Lima

• La Paz

• Bahia
(Salvador)

BOLIVIA

Tropic of Capricorn

PARAGUAY Rio de Janeiro

Si

Pitcairn I.
1808/93

• Asuncion

ARGENTINE
CONFED.

CHILE

URUGUAY

Tristan de

Santiago •

• Buenos Aires

Montevideo

1815

Chatham Is.
1793

Patagonia

G

Islas Malvinas
(Falkland Is.)
1820–33 to Arg.

SOUTHERN

Spanish
possessions

Portuguese
possessions

British
possessions

French
possessio